THE GLOBAL
ECONOMIC SYSTEM
SINCE 1945

CONTEMPORARY WORLDS explores the present and recent past.
Books in the series take a distinctive theme, geo-political entity
or cultural group and explore their developments over a period
ranging usually over the last fifty years. The impact of current
events and developments are accounted for by rapid but clear
interpretation in order to unveil the cultural, political, religious
and technological forces that are reshaping today's worlds.

SERIES EDITOR
Jeremy Black

In the same series

Sky Wars: A History of Military Aerospace Power
David Gates

Britain since the Seventies
Jeremy Black

War since 1945
Jeremy Black

South Asian Conflicts since 1947
Robert Johnson

THE GLOBAL ECONOMIC SYSTEM SINCE 1945

LARRY ALLEN

REAKTION BOOKS

Dedicated to my children
Jeff, Laurie, Kris and Ryan

Published by Reaktion Books Ltd
79 Farringdon Road
London EC1M 3JU, UK

www.reaktionbooks.co.uk

First published 2005

Printed and bound in Great Britain
by Biddles Ltd, King's Lynn.

British Library Cataloguing in Publication Data
Allen, Larry, 1949–
      The global economic sytem since 1945. – (Contemporary worlds)
      1. Economic history – 20th century
      I. Title
      330.9'045

ISBN 1 86189 242 X

Contents

Preface   7

1   Introduction   9
2   A Global Postwar Economy Takes Shape   15
3   Prosperity Born of Depression   37
4   The Thesis and Antithesis of Capitalism   59
5   The Ebbtide of Postwar Prosperity   80
6   A Tug of War between Inflation and
    Economic Controls   101
7   The Political Pendulum Suddenly Swings   122
8   The Floodtide of the Capitalist Revolution   143
9   The Force of Speculation Enrolled in the
    Cause of Globalization   166
10 Global Confidence and Global Panic   186

References   207
Selected Further Reading   213
Index   216

Preface

This book aims to show how economic history opens the door to humanizing economic knowledge, to transforming the dry bones of economics statistics into the flesh and blood of living, usable and accessible truth. Those mental athletes who thrill at scaling the cold peaks of economic theory may be startled to discover the unsuspected wisdom that leaps to the eye from a study of economic history. Francis Bacon wrote that the study of history teaches wisdom, and the study of mathematics prolonged and unbroken concentration. Bacon overlooked the countless practical applications of mathematics. It must be conceded that the purest and clearest reasoning in all economic theory owes a large debt to mathematics. The debt is so large that economic theory is safely now enshrined in the temple of mathematics and economic history too often furnishes neglected addenda to post mortems on past economic crises.

A sobering foundation in economic history is what keeps airy castles of mathematical reasoning from going awry, from dressing in the garb of a mathematical edifice the beloved prejudices of our hearts or the political ideology of our uncles, from letting our economic theory lie where our treasure lies. Mathematical and statistical models invariably fill in gaps in verifiable and scientific knowledge with unprovable assumptions, permitting each model to conflict with other models. The final result can be zero. At worst mathematics only furnishes systems of economic thought that imprison an economic system, which in the eyes of economic history has a wily knack for escaping all formulas.

This book shuns the misclues (i.e., balanced budget multipliers) born of the infallibilities and potentialities inherent in mathematics, but it in no way shuns economic theory. The scaffolding of economic theory is never far from sight. Economic theory is what keeps the sideshows from swallowing up the circus in economic history. Interpretations drawn in a work of economic history should be subpoenaed to the bar of economic theory for cross-examination. As an added bonus economic history allows that uphill attention to exceptions that disturb every generalization. It is these exceptions that invariably hold the key to minting new coins of economic theory.

A special word of appreciation is due to two outstanding economists, Professor James K. Galbraith of the University of Texas at Austin, and Professor David Colander of Middlebury College. Professor Colander gave timely and robust encouragement that helped see this book to completion. The preparation of this book benefited from the intelligent and fruitful attention of Professor Galbraith. His help was ideal and his patient encouragement much appreciated. My son Kristopher Allen spared no pains illuminating the manuscript from a student's perspective. The librarians at the Mary and John Grey Library on the Lamar University Campus kindly and patiently shared their wide knowledge of electronic databases and research techniques. Responsibility and blame for remaining errors are mine.

Chapter 1

Introduction

Two central forces remoulded and redirected the study of the global economy over the last 50 years. First, inflation came to rival and even top unemployment as public enemy number one in the realm of economics. The fresh memory of galloping inflation in the 1970s wielded a major influence, usurping the more distant memory and psychosis of an unemployment epidemic during the 1930s. Towards the end of the last century Japan broke ranks with the inflationary world and became deflationary. Japanese deflation threatened to fan out, to give the global economy a deflationary turn, but it has not yet challenged the concerns of economic theory, and is a worry rather than a reality in most economies. Second, the world's largest trading partners installed a floating exchange rate regime, and governments around the world liberalized foreign trade and capital flows between sovereign countries. This new global exchange rate and trade regime enlarged the place of the money supply in macroeconomic theory because the exchange rate between currencies graduated into a key variable. The upshot of these dual forces refocused economics to stress inflation rather than unemployment, expected inflation rather than expected profits, monetary policy rather than fiscal policy, dynamics of hyperinflation rather than the dynamics of output instability, and predictable policies that an economy can easily assimilate

9

rather than unforeseen and extemporaneous counter cyclical policies.

Inflation plays pranks on political processes. During inflation the wages of government employees, including scholars and soldiers, lag behind inflation. The military may grow disgruntled and mutinous over substandard pay and capsize the government. Other government employees may welcome bribes to keep remuneration abreast of living costs. Once government employees become corrupt, an atmosphere of cynical corruption envelops the culture. More generally inflation makes wise behaviour unwise, and unwise behaviour wise, rearranging income distribution in ways that displease a wide segment of the population. Ordinarily, shouldering a crushing debt burden, and mortgaging one's property to speculate in real estate, precious metals, etc. is dimwitted behaviour, at least for anyone who does not wish to lie awake at night worrying. In a hyperinflationary environment such behaviour becomes highly intelligent. Saving money ordinarily passes as wise behaviour, but in a hyperinflationary environment it becomes irresponsible. Inflation decimates the purchasing power of savings.

Deflation represents an opposite polarity, rewarding opposite types of behaviour. In the case of inflation and deflation, people sharing extreme patterns of behaviour survive, prosper, and in time carry disproportionate weight in political processes. Inflation or deflation agitates and churns economic currents and spawns a shifting playing field in which old habits, instincts, customs and practices may become unsuitable and counterproductive. Deflation nurtures populist political movements and government policies that gum up price flexibility. Inflation redistributes income in favour of debtors and speculators, which tips the balance of political forces to the side of policies friendly to capitalism, breeding conservative political movements and government policies that favour free markets and price flexibility. In the last two decades of the twentieth century fear of inflation overrode and sedated fear of depression, and economic regulation and control lost out to free-market capitalism. Capitalism found itself re-established in the confidence of electorates and governments.

This book charts the postwar trajectory of the global economic system, which took shape from the broad economic disarray and ruin of World War II. It is organized chronologically, opening with the Bretton Woods conference of 1944, the Marshall Plan for rebuilding Europe and the Korean War. (The latter unleashed a bullish economic development in Japan.) After World War II new factories and infrastructure had to be built, new institutions for an international monetary order had to be negotiated and organized, and new ground rules established to govern trade between nations. The dark legacy of the Depression cast a long and menacing shadow into the postwar years, nudging government policies along lines aimed at combating a relapse into wholesale unemployment and deflation. The Depression dulled the lustre and credibility of capitalism, leaving governments in Europe and elsewhere friendlier to socialist ways and means, including the nationalization of industries.

For the first two decades following World War II the Depression ordeal weighed heavily in the evolution of economic institutions and laws. Surplus goods appeared a likelier problem than shortages, unemployment a larger hazard than inflation, and price wars a higher worry than scarce raw materials. In the United States a Republican administration left intact the anti-Depression measures of the Roosevelt administration, and went on increasing government spending. Following the Korean War the global economy entered a quieter economic phase of low-priced raw materials, and soon thrived within the settled framework of an economic system that mistrusted and curbed price flexibility and competition. The Bretton Woods system shackled exchange rates between currencies. In 1947 the global trading partners began easing trade restrictions, spurring growth in foreign trade. The US dollar promised a stable world currency. In the past colonies stood in high esteem as the trappings, perhaps the secret, of economic success. In this new economic order Germany and Japan, shorn of colonies, swiftly blossomed into two exuberant economic miracles.

Foreign trade grew at a hurried pace, and multinational enterprises headquartered in the United States, Europe and Japan threw economic nets around the globe, weaving an infinite web of economic currents and forces. In the United States a small number of vast corporations accounted for nearly half the gross national product, and in Europe many industrial firms underwent nationalization. In large corporations, whether public or private, decision-making processes sank into the hidden depths of bureaucracies. Corporate bureaucracies forged decisions by committees of experts representing numerous fields and managers largely ratified these decisions. These companies shunned price competition out of fear of price wars and cut-throat competition, and homed in on non-price competition. They perfected the use of the media to manage the demand for products.

While in the United States, Europe and Japan the legacy of the Depression left the feeling that price wars represented the dark side of market capitalism, the developing parts of the world pointed the finger of suspicion at foreign owned capital and imperialism. Until the 1970s governments and giant corporations schemed and experimented to remove the delicate processes of industry from the hand of economic law, and replace supply and demand with economic planning. The socialist and communist countries turned more clearly and overtly to economic planning for guiding production and consumption decisions. US direct foreign investment favoured countries that shared borders with socialist economies and faced threats from the Eastern Bloc.

The 1970s stand as an economic turning point, a change of economic phase, a zenith of forces that had been gathering strength since 1945. In 1971 the Bretton Woods system of fixed exchange rates fell apart, and the world shredded the last vestiges of the once reverenced gold standard. The price of gold and exchange rates between currencies of the world became matters of unfettered market forces. The value of the US dollar was no longer defined in terms of gold, and exchange rates obeyed free market forces rather than official government policies. Jolting spikes in prices of crude oil and staple commodities sorely strained a global economic system in which businesses formulated plans and made decisions based upon projected prices. Inflation also ate away at fear of deflation and competitive price-cutting, and fear of inflation began to supplant fear of unemployment and deflation.

To defend and underpin economies against escalating energy and staple prices, governments at first imposed price controls, a culmination of economic policies born of the Depression. These policies disdained and sidetracked markets, regarding them as the happy hunting grounds of price-gouging middlemen, as fertile soil for cut-throat price-cutting. Voices favouring markets arose from industries enjoying strident acceleration in prices, fearing government price controls might cheat them of their due. Shortages stirred electorates and governments to lose patience with meddling and overgrown government policies that hampered production. Large tax bites came under fire for undercutting economic incentives. Governments began lowering taxes and holding down government spending for the sake of boosting private sector incentives and thus productivity. As scarcities outnumbered surpluses, government spending turned into a redundant and obsolete force for maintaining high levels of demand.

As inflation ripened into a generalized phenomenon, a new fount of income arose from speculative profits afforded by inflation. Millions of small entrepreneurs, as well as many family homeowners and landlords, stood to earn handsome capital gains from real estate property. As the voice of this new income and wealth was heard in the corridors of governments, market-oriented economic polices grew in favour. This new money saw a friend in the market. The swing in the political pendulum toward free market policies partly stemmed from the redistribution of income in favour of debtors and speculators, a redistribution directly owed to inflation. The winners in this reshuffling of wealth credited the market system for breeding the speculative opportunities that exalted them to wealth and prestige. On the tide of this political upheaval Margaret Thatcher, François Mitterand, Felipe González, Helmut Kohl and Ronald Reagan rode to power and launched a global capitalist revolution showcasing free markets and privatization. Conservative governments assaulted inflation with hard-nosed monetary restraint, and ignored pleadings for the cruel plight of the unemployed.

By 1990 a worldwide capitalism revolution was under way. Inflation was tamed and monetary authorities developed a fervour for corralling inflation rather than pegging unemployment rates at low levels. Fears of new inflation outweighed fears of another Depression. Governments everywhere had a passion for denationalization, privatization and market deregulation. Developing countries began dismantling controls and restrictions that hampered capital flows. Many developing countries discouraged and narrowed foreign investment out of dread of the cultural and political derivatives of foreign-owned companies. Entrepreneurship flourished and the global economy underwent a resilient surge of growth on the back of innovations in computer networking and telecommunications. With the added impetus of global financial liberation the last decade of the twentieth century saw a burst of foreign investment activity: direct foreign investment reached levels that had not been seen since the end of the nineteenth century. Strong growth led to speculative manias in stock markets.

Before the century was out a financial crisis in East Asia rocked the global economic system, and laid bare the vulnerabilities in global market capitalism. East Asian countries discovered that inflowing capital can fuel a robust growth rate, but a sudden outflow brings in its wake stock market crashes, currency depreciation and economic depression. The global economy still reeled from the East Asian financial crisis when financial euphoria infected the US stock market. The NASDAQ speculative bubble burst in 2000, heralding a period of economic deceleration with worldwide repercussions. Yet, even with economic weakness, the pledge to market-oriented capitalism has remained secure in the developed world.

Chapter 2

A Global Postwar Economy
Takes Shape

In economics the power of expectations is very directly felt on economic behaviour and diagnosis of economic ills, and adds its own twist to economic policy. These expectations rarely stray far from experiences fresh in the social psyche. World War II and the preceding Great Depression left a murky and conflicting legacy for the formation of expectations. It was natural and unavoidable to look to the years following World War I for clues about what the future held in store following World War II, but the post World War I experience in Europe held out small reason to be cheerful. The lingering discordant notes of World War I gave the world the spectacle of harassed governments (Germany, Austria, Hungary) cancelling weighty internal government debts with riots of hyperinflation. France dodged hyperinflation, but suffered muffled inflation over a longer time span. An elementary principle in economics says that inflation befriends debtors at the expense of creditors, and an observer in 1945 could hardly miss the inference that governments weighted down in debt from wartime expenditures may ally with other debtors and play the inflation card. The United States came out of World War II economically erect with victory, the sovereign economic power, but shouldering a public debt swollen by wartime expenditures. The public debt of the US federal government measured a breathtaking 107 per

15

cent of US GDP in 1945, roughly three times the peak reached during World War I.[1] With the US dollar capping the arch of the international monetary system, worldwide fear of inflation could not be blotted out.

A polar opposite and conflicting expectation of Depression also lay on the economic horizon. Following World War I the United Kingdom embarked on an uphill and frantic effort to re-establish the gold standard with the pound sterling fixed at its prewar value. As economic events swiftly proved, the pound sterling at its prewar value was overvalued, and maintaining an overvalued currency equates to a deflationary policy. During World War I prices doubled in Britain, and continued climbing until 1920. Then prices fell, at first wildly and then quietly, until 1933. The UK patiently endured a decade of sorry economic performance and elevated unemployment before the Great Depression tumbled the global economic system into an economic bog. The Great Depression struck singularly hard in the United States and seared the collective consciousness there more deeply than World War I, so inflation seemed unimportant after World War II, the compelling issue was avoidance of another shattering Great Depression. The US lived with the fear that the production of World War II was only a passing reprieve from a monstrous economic Depression ready to reassert itself with a return to peacetime conditions. A return to the prewar economy meant a return to the darkest and bitterest of economic outlooks. The UK's unhappy experience following World War I underlined this fear. In a nutshell, the combined economic history of post World War I Europe and the Great Depression darkened the economic horizon in 1946, even in the United States. There may have been a suspicion that world war could have been avoided if world Depression had not intervened, even in the United States.

THE INFLATION EPIDEMIC

Events stirred inflation jitters. Over the years Switzerland came to enjoy a reputation for financial probity. The Swiss franc became a shining star in the ranks of national currencies, a legendary symbol of monetary strength and reliability. Amid the financial worries of World War II it was largely unshaken, though not as immovable as in World War I, when it had gained ground against the currencies of the belligerents, including the US dollar. After World War I, Switzerland reinstated the Swiss franc on the gold standard at its prewar parity, and obstinately clung to this until 1936, when it fell in with the last of the countries during the 1930s to undertake currency devaluation. By July 1945 the Swiss franc had held its own but not shown unusual strength, trading at a 3 per cent premium against the US dollar.

In July 1945 hyperinflation burst out in Hungary, and lasted until August 1946. On 1 August Hungary phased out its depreciated pengo, replacing it with the florint, at a rate of one florint to 400 octillion pengo. The Soviet army slyly lent a helping hand in Hungary's inflation, printing its own Hungarian notes, and issuing the highest denomination bank note ever known to fly off the printing press – a 100,000,000,000,000,000 pengo note.[2] In Germany cautious occupation forces carried on with German wartime price controls until 1948. German Reichsmarks passed as worthless, cigarettes, coal and other commodities substituted for money, and barter was widespread.

To sidestep the inflationary fallout of World War II, the government of Finland seized upon an extreme innovation. Rather than recklessly print money and levy an inflation tax to finance government outlays, the Finnish government bisected notes in denominations of 500, 1000 and 5,000 markkaa. The left halves of the notes remained in circulation at half face value, without any type of government overstamp. The government took possession of the right halves as a forced loan.

Inflationary worries and threats loomed worldwide. Free China saw prices soar 10,000 per cent between December 1941 and December 1945. Japan held sway over 90 per cent of China's tax revenue base, and blocked imports into China. Inflation quieted, however, at the war's close. Prices even declined briefly before rocketing upwards when peace negotiations with the communists folded. Under China's archaic tax system, revenue rose only as transactions multiplied, not just with higher prices. The beleaguered government rolled the printing presses to finance colossal military outlays. Shanghai saw prices soaring 179,400 per cent between January 1946 and July 1948.[3] The government issued a new currency in replacement of the old at a rate of 1 unit of the new to 3,000,000 of the old. Inflation raged on, lifting prices in Shanghai 112,390 per cent between August 1948 and April 1949. Free China was no isolated stronghold of inflation in Asia. In Japan consumer prices surged 1,000 per cent between 1946 and 1949.

Latin America chronicled milder bouts of inflation. Chile began charting its long and unbroken graph of inflation in 1879. In 1931, when many countries reeled from deflation, Chile logged a lukewarm 8.5 per cent inflation, which perked up to 15.1 per cent by 1940, and reached a crescendo of 47.8 per cent in 1952 before skidding to rates between 20 and 40 per cent during the 1950s and 1960s. Brazil's inflation rates fluttered at around 2 per cent per month between 1948 and 1965.

The United States and Britain enjoyed no immunity from inflation. After lifting price controls Britain saw a wild surge in prices between 1945 and 1948. With minor breaks, inflation bewildered and pestered Britain at varying rates until 1975. Two thirds of the world's monetary gold backed the US dollar.[4] Nevertheless the United States watched heated consumer prices advance 23 per cent between 1946 and 1948. US consumer prices lay flat from 1948 until 1950, and leaped up 7.9 per cent in 1951 before levelling to modest ranges for the remainder of the decade.

In the United States and Britain, however, dread of another nightmare of high unemployment and deflation overrode worries of inflation. Britain had had its fill of laissez-faire capitalism. After driving itself to utter exhaustion reinstating the gold standard, and weathering the worldwide Depression, Britain had reason to be pleased with the performance of its highly regimented war economy. In 1945 the British electorate turned the Conservative Party out, and turned its back on Winston Churchill, in favour of a Labour Party committed to remoulding British society along the contours of socialism. Less bluntly France lined up industries for nationalization. The United States had reason to be more buoyant and cheerful. It owned two thirds of the world's monetary gold, and the US dollar was the sovereign of currencies. Britain laboured under too heavy a debt for the pound sterling to hold its position as a leading international currency. The United States owned the atomic bomb and the best in transcontinental aircraft, and held up a friendly beacon to European scientific talent dislocated by war and civil strife. US industry stood upright, untouched by wartime destruction, and ready to assimilate the rapid technological advance spurred by world rivalry.

FIRST POLICY INITIATIVES

People change from within to meet change from without. The United States took hearty steps to pre-empt another Depression, but contented itself with tackling inflation issues on an ad hoc basis, counting inflation a passing annoyance and depression an enduring menace. Britain's World War I inflation had remained alive until 1920 before lapsing into over a decade of deflation. Congress passed the Employment Act of 1946, which read, in part:

> The Congress hereby declares that it is the continuing policy and responsibility of the federal government to use all practical means consistent with its needs and obligations and other essential considerations of national policy, with assistance and cooperation of industry, agriculture, labor, and State and local governments, to coordinate and utilize all its plans, functions, and resources, for the purpose of creating and maintaining, in a manner calculated to foster and promote free competitive enterprise and the general welfare, conditions under which there will be afforded useful employment opportunities, including self-employment, for those able, willing, and seeking to work and to promote maximum employment, production, and purchasing power.

For the United States inflation worries merited no parallel legislation action. Combating inflation required high interest rates. Nerves were racked at the unwelcome reminder that higher interest rates had a flip side – brutal losses to government bondholders, of whom many were commercial banks. As interest rates rise, bonds issued earlier at lower interest rates can only be sold at discounted prices to stay competitive with bonds issued later at higher interest rates. The freshly empowered

Labour Party in Britain immediately nationalized the Bank of England, making British monetary policy subservient to elected officials, widely applauded as the enemy of tight money policies. The Bank of France fell before the nationalization guillotine in December 1945.

West Germany remained the only country haunted by long past inflation. In 1957 West Germany restructured the central banking system set up by the Allied occupation authorities. The statute organizing the Bundesbank sheltered its independence from political authorities, myopically narrowed its mission to maintenance of price stability, and shunned any mention of full employment or economic growth. In the words of the statute:

> The Bundesbank, making use of the powers in the field of monetary policy conferred upon it under this Law, shall regulate the money circulation and supply of credit to the economy with the aim of safeguarding the currency and shall ensure the execution by banks of payments within the country as well as to and from foreign countries.[5]

In the same year the British government appointed an official committee to study Britain's monetary and credit system, and recommend an overhaul in light of the newest and best thinking in monetary policy. The Radcliffe Report disavowed the money stock as the controlling agent at the bottom of inflation or the economy, saying 'the Government's function in issuing [bank]notes is simply the passive one of ensuing that sufficient notes are available for the practical convenience of the public.' The report, more a plaintiff's brief than a dispassionate scientific analysis, declared money innocent of causing inflation until proven guilty.

The atmospherics of the postwar period guaranteed that the reaction to every turn of economic events embodied the latent and subterranean fear of another Depression. Many governments would have laughed at the mere hint that inflation was likelier than depression. The caution born of the Depression may have kept economic downdrafts in check and propped up postwar prosperity. Households toughened and disciplined by the Depression and war took to savings with penny-pinching zeal. They kept a ready supply of liquid assets to fall back upon should the economy sail through foul weather, or to spend if a sunny reprieve briefly eased fears of another economic calamity. Any reprieve was brief since every increase in the unemployment rate roused fear that another ugly Depression was around the corner.

And the economic climate following World War II sank deeper into the fabric of the economic system than mere atmospherics. Just as individuals change within to meet change from without, economic institutions evolve and compensate internally to assimilate external changes. There is a saying in financial circles that the four most dangerous words among stock market investors is 'this time is different'. The same foresighted principle applies in economics. The reactions of economic institutions to broad and unstoppable deflation mirror a pattern that can be traced back hundreds of years. The overlapping ground in these reactions lies in policies that gum up price flexibility, particularly downward price flexibility. In deflation people develop a sobering fear of markets, happy hunting grounds that invite middlemen buying cheap and selling dear, with cut-throat competition and price wars. In 1551, England's pound sterling started bounding upwards in foreign exchange markets after the English crown halted a policy of currency debasement. English exports of 'cotton' (cheap woollens), now more costly to foreigners, sank to 50 per cent of 1550 levels, and stayed there until the next century. Parliament enacted legislation to limit production and in 1563 enacted the Statute of Artificers. This devolved upon justices of the peace the micromanaging power to fix ceilings and floors on wages for every skill and species of employment in their jurisdiction, and to levy fines for employers dismissing workers without just cause.

After a financial crisis in 1873, Europe, and to a lesser extent the United States, tasted a diet of broad but thin deflation until the 1890s. Over this time frame Germany, where deflation cut deepest, pioneered the development of cartels, agreements between members of an industry to fix industry prices, pare back production and apportion market territory. During the 1880s Germany also broke new ground developing social, unemployment, medical and old age insurance. The Third

Reich also favoured the formation of cartels, which remained legal in Germany until Allied occupation. Finance capitalism also blossomed in Germany during the late nineteenth century. Under finance capitalism banks owning vast blocks of stock in competing corporations rationed the supply of credit to these corporations, using the power of the purse strings to quiet competition between corporations, safeguard bank investments and protect borrowing customers from bankruptcy.

Cartels were illegal in the United States and Britain, but finance capitalism did take hold. In the United States the banking house of J. P. Morgan held sway over a sprawling financial kingdom by securing representation on interlocking systems of corporate boards of directors. Having the same individuals sitting on the boards of directors of competing corporations muted competition. Trusts were also a weapon for guaranteeing cooperation between natural competitors. During this era the US Congress began outlawing anti-competitive practices with the passage of the Sherman Antitrust Act of 1890, but Britain began turning a blind eye to monopolistic practices (price-fixing) after the decision in the Mogul Steamship case of 1891, which significantly eroded British common law doctrines forbidding restraints of trade. Only after World War II would Britain pass legislation clamping down on monopolistic practices.

Not until the 1930s did the United States undergo a wave of deflation that stamped an unmistakable signature on laws governing the economic playing field. The US warmed to programmes of social insurance that Germany had embraced during an earlier period of deflation. Aside from social security, the US enacted unemployment insurance, hammered out programmes to limit production and support prices in agriculture, and erected governmental machinery for regulating prices in certain industries such as trucking. The US Congress enacted its first minimum wage law during the 1930s. The Miller-Tydings Act of 1937 gave legal sanction to manufacturers' right to enforce resale price agreements with retail distributors, forcing all retailers to freeze the price of a product at identical levels. These despotic price agreements shackled retailers selling brand-named and trademarked products to the prices chosen by manufacturers. A year earlier Congress had enacted the Robinson-Patman Act, which forbade manufacturers from handing deep discounts to large chain stores and not small businesses. Discounts had to be justified as quantity discounts with proportionate cost savings.

In the 1930s Germany graduated several notches above the United States in fettering price flexibility, going as far as wage and price controls in 1936.

THE BRETTON WOODS SYSTEM

The laying of the groundwork for the postwar global economy betrayed glaring traces of worries inspired by the Depression. The Depression of the 1930s marked the first time a finger of blame pointed to a breakdown of international trade and foreign capital flows. The two culprits that shared the highest guilt were the US stock market crash and sudden arteriosclerosis in the international trade and financial system. In July of 1944 the United States hosted a conference to finish negotiations establishing an orderly postwar international monetary and financial system. The conference, officially billed as the United Nations Monetary and Financial Conference, took its popular name from Bretton Woods, a vacation resort in New Hampshire where it was held. Forty-four nations sent delegations to the conference, but the central proposals came from the United States and Britain. The brilliant and persuasive John Maynard Keynes led the British delegation, but the United States had the largest say in the end. Early in the talks, Keynes advised the formation of an institution that might evolve into a world central bank, but the United States was in favour of a simpler and smaller plan.

The keystone of the Bretton Woods system lay in a structure of fixed exchange rates between currencies, setting official fixed ratios at which currencies such as pounds sterling and US dollars could be exchanged. The rate at which pounds sterling and US dollars can be exchanged holds a high place in setting the price of British goods in US markets and the price of US goods in British markets. During the 1930s many countries unilaterally depreciated domestic currency, automatically making home goods cheaper in world markets. Competitive currency devaluations equate to price wars on a grand scale, a means of exporting unemployment to neighbouring countries and trading partners whose industry and workers are suddenly pitted against bargain foreign imports. This is another case where the 1930s sowed misgivings toward price competition. Under the Bretton Woods agreement 32 countries by 1946 had declared par values of home currencies in terms of gold or the US dollar. The dollar was set at $35 per ounce of gold. Member countries were expected to keep their spot exchange rate within 1 per cent above or below the officially declared par value, and could not make an official change in their exchange rate of more than 10 per cent without the approval of the International Monetary Fund. It was intelligently argued that a system of fixed exchange rates spared importers and exporters the risks of fluttering exchange rates, providing a cosier environment to nurse a rebirth of foreign trade after depression and war.

The Bretton Woods agreement fathered the International Monetary Fund (IMF), the cornerstone institution in this new international monetary and financial order, to put the vertebrae and lubricated grooves in the fixed exchange rate regime. It required that each country be able and willing to redeem its own currency in gold or in another currency appraised as good as gold, such as the US dollar. Currency that might need redemption was currency flowing out of the country from the importation of foreign goods, or investment in foreign countries. Currency outflows were nullified by the currency inflows attending exports to foreign countries and foreign investment at home. As long as currency inflows remained neck and neck with or ahead of currency outflows, a country faced no need to empty out foreign currency reserves redeeming redundant supplies of its currency in the hands of foreigners with no further use for it. The foreigners had no further use for it only when they neither wanted to use the currency to pay for goods from the currency's home country nor to invest in the currency's home country. Foreigners holding a currency quickly convertible into gold or hard currency were more apt to hold the currency in expectation that one day it would be needed. A weak point in the fixed exchange arrangement lay in the likelihood that all countries would undergo times of balance of payments deficit, where the outflow of home currency exceeded inflow, unleashing a trend that, left unchecked, bled dry officially held reserves of gold and key foreign currencies. Situations were bound to develop in which governments needed loans of foreign exchange reserves to beef up confidence in home currency.

This is where the International Monetary Fund (IMF) entered the picture. It was set up to lend foreign exchange reserves to countries running low of reserves, allowing them to buy time until more lasting and structurally fundamental solutions to domestic economic problems paid off. The IMF steered governments away from devaluations of home currency to meet passing economic ailments such as cyclical downturns. If a country's balance of payments deficit warned of more deep-seated economic woes, a slipped cog keeping underlying economic forces permanently out of whack, then the IMF gave the nod for devaluation. A devaluation made imported goods costlier in home markets and home goods cheaper in export markets. A glut of currency outflow over inflow evaporated as more competitive exports advanced and costlier imports receded.

The IMF owed its capital endowment to subscriptions of member countries. Each country paid an assigned subscription or quota proportional to its national income and the volume of its international trade. Member countries paid 25 per cent of their assigned quota in gold and the balance in home currency. A member country borrowing foreign currency from the IMF put up a matching amount of home currency for collateral. The IMF earned its income from loans to member countries and investment in US government bonds. Headquartered in Washington DC, the IMF's policies and operations fell under a Board of Governors that had the last word in the affairs of both the IMF and the World Bank, an institution also born of the Bretton Woods agreement. Each member country chose one governor, and an alternate to attend an annual meeting of both institutions. The work of the IMF depended on a group of sixteen executive directors, five of whom were chosen directly by their governments. Others were elected by groups of countries to be their representatives. The number of votes each director cast varied with the amount of subscriptions paid by the country the director represented. The United States, the largest contributor, enjoyed the undivided representation of its own director who controlled above 20 per cent of the votes.

On 25 June 1946 the World Bank opened its headquarters in Washington DC. The World Bank was the briefer, unofficial name given to an institution generously titled the International Bank of Reconstruction and Development. According to the articles of agreement, its central aim was 'to assist in the reconstruction and development by facilitating the investment of capital for productive purposes, including the restoration of economies destroyed or disrupted by war, the reconversion of productive facilities to peacetime needs and the encouragement of the development of productive facilities and resources in less developed countries'. At its organizational apex this bank was bound together with the IMF, sharing the Board of Governors. The managerial upper hand for general bank operations lay with twenty executive directors. At the outset five of these directors served as direct appointees of the five largest shareholders of the bank, the United States, France, West Germany, the United Kingdom and India. The same formula for fixing the quotas of member countries of the IMF set the subscription quota of capital stock for each World Bank member. The World Bank marshalled lending capital, selling bonds and notes to private investors in member countries, chiefly in the US, Canada and Western Europe. As a sweetener, governments of member countries underwrote World Bank bonds, scaling back interest rates paid to raise capital from private sources.

The Articles of Agreement authorized the World Bank to grant loans to governments, governmental agencies, and to private enterprises residing within a member country's territory if the member country's government or governmental agency guaranteed the loan. In 1955 the International Finance Corporation, an affiliate of the World Bank, was set up to advance loans directly to private enterprise without government guarantees. In 1960 the World Bank organized another division, the International Development Association, as a separate centre of initiative within the bank to furnish soft and interest-free loans to the poorest countries, those ineligible for loans under the gently tight-fisted lending policy of the World Bank.

The Bretton Woods system, the IMF, the World Bank, and the nationalization of the Bank of England and the Bank of France signalled a perception that private banking had mishandled the monetary and financial affairs of the world. In the past banking dynasties such as the Morgans, Rothschilds and Barings held court over the financial world, brokering loans for businesses, kings and governments. Baring Brothers, who had handled financing for the United States' purchase of Louisiana, regrouped as a limited liability corporation after the Baring Crisis of 1890. By 1890 Argentina had soaked up nearly half of Britain's foreign investment through the financial conduit of the Baring Brothers. A political revolution in Argentina left Baring Brothers holding a large volume of unmarketable financial assets, threatening to suck Britain into a full-blown financial crisis. It took the cooperative initiatives of the Bank of England and other London bankers and merchant bankers to save Baring Brothers and ward off financial crisis. The Rothschilds helped Britain to finance the Napoleonic Wars, France to finance a war indemnity paid to Germany after the Franco-Prussian War of 1870–71, and raised the £4 million sterling the British government needed to become the principal stockholder of the Suez Canal Company. European governments dangled access to capital as a means of beguiling foreign governments into subservience without sabre rattling.[6] The late nineteenth century saw a Mississippian flow of European private foreign investment around the globe, but world wars and world depression stopped all but a trickle of foreign investment in the first half of the twentieth century. From 1931 to 1933 debtor countries saw capital outflows as capital retreated into safe harbours such as the United States.[7]

THE ASCENDANCY OF FREE TRADE PRINCIPLES

Paralleling the belief that the world economy needed a new monetary and financial framework lay an innovative perception that the world owed part of its economic debacles and woes to trade barriers between nations. This shift in attitude toward trade barriers marked a sharper break with the past than the Bretton Woods system. The fixed exchange rate system was custom tailored to replace the gold exchange standard that evolved in the 1920s. Until the 1930s trade barriers held out a ray of hope to depression stricken economies. Russia, France and the United States had raised tariff walls in the 1890s as immunization against economic depression. Against a rising tide of trade liberalization Germany in 1879 swung around to tariffs as a rich vein of government revenue. Tariff defenders came to see Germany's robust economic development in the decades before World War I as the fruit of intelligent and judicious tariff policy. The United States touched off a wicked trade war with the enactment of the Smoot-Hawley Act of 1930, setting the highest tariffs ever for the United States. Britain, always the stronghold of free trade, turned aside pressures to raise trade barriers in the 1890s, but in the 1930s tumbled into the orbit of high tariff countries. In 1932 Britain's u-turn on trade policy closed nearly a century of free trade, enacting the Import Duties Act of 1932. The world threw itself wholeheartedly into trade barriers, but was soon bedevilled with retaliation. World trade crumbled to one third of 1929 levels, adding no small spiralling downdraft to the depression forces already in motion.

To tackle the thorny maze of trade barriers, 23 countries, including the United States, Britain and France, signed an agreement in 1947 to hold multilateral negotiations for scaling back trade barriers and import quotas – the General Agreement on Tariffs and Trade (GATT). The first round of trade negotiations was held in Geneva in 1947, as part of negotiations to draft a charter for the International Trade Organization, and won wide applause for hammering out mutually acceptable reductions in trade barriers, touching 45,000 tariff rates. GATT began as a loose cluster of contracting parties rather than an organization, but graduated into dignity as a de facto organization with annual meetings after the US Congress turned down ratification of the treaty forming the International Trade Organization in 1950. GATT began chipping away at trade barriers on 1 January 1948 when eight of the contracting countries put into effect the tariff concessions negotiated at Geneva.

GATT set down principles that lent a guiding hand to negotiations: (1) nondiscrimination in trade relations between participating countries, (2) commitments to observe the negotiated tariff concessions, (3) prohibitions against the use of quantitative restrictions on exports (quotas) on exports and imports, and (4) special provisions to promote the trade of developing countries. As a forum for negotiation of trade barriers, GATT at first disappointed the hopes inspired by the first round of negotiations at Geneva. In 1949 a second round of negotiations held in Annecy, France met with less success. Torquay, England hosted a third round of negotiations in 1951, and Geneva a fourth round in 1956, in each case chilling hopes of a quick dismantling of trade barriers. Trade barriers were doomed to fall but with unenthusiastic leisureliness.

THE MARSHALL PLAN

Conferences and negotiations touting a fresh start for global capitalism afforded small hope to starving populations in Europe. Agricultural production in war-ravaged Europe barely eked out enough to feed the countryside, and coal production for warming homes and stoking industrial furnaces stood still. Much of the tangled wheels of European industry lay motionless and silent. Amid this dreary picture, one of the winning powers proudly preached a new gospel, one that not only blasted capitalism for the Depression and the economic difficulties of the interwar years but cited it as the guilty party for war itself. In a world with no more fresh and innocent lands for colonization, parasitic capitalistic countries were given to violently reshuffling the ownership of existing colonies in hopes of coming out better. Colonization had become a zero sum game that invited everlasting war. In the populations of Europe lurked the festering suspicion that equality of votes was a sham substitute for equality of wealth, a mere sleight of hand diversion from the real issues. Communist parties stood decent chances of winning legitimate power through the ballot box. Little thought was given to war reparations such as the Allies levied against Germany after World War I. Soft whispers that Germany and Japan should be demoted to agricultural societies fell silent. The communist menace was singularly persuasive in saving Japan. Circumstances and past experience coaxed the allies into doing something akin to war reparations in reverse. The war-crushed countries of Europe became favoured heirs to foreign aid from the United States.

The Allies contented themselves with punishing the leaders of Germany and Japan as war criminals. The heavy war reparations levied against post World War I Germany had taught them a hard and bitter lesson. Exacting revenge against an entire people might only fan smouldering embers, perhaps igniting another conflagration. Besides, populations overtaken by poverty become fertile ground for the gospel of communism to sink roots, a gospel now fortified with victory over Hitler, and basking in the sun of newly won credibility.

The famous US foreign aid programme that befriended war-savaged Europe was officially titled the European Recovery Program, but came to be labelled the Marshall Plan after US Secretary of State George Catlett Marshall. At a Harvard commencement speech on 5 June 1947, Marshall announced that the United States welcomed a proposal to financially underwrite a cooperative and coordinated European plan for economic recovery. Congress passed the Economic Recovery Act in April 1948, enabling the United States to funnel over $13 billion into Western European countries over the years to June 1952.[8] The Soviet Union shunned the idea of cooperation with Western Europeans, and withdrew the Eastern Bloc from participation. With the Eastern Bloc countries out of the picture, Western European countries organized the Committee for European Economic Cooperation (later the OEEC). This group wrote up the original proposal for submission to the United States, and afterwards shouldered responsibility for handling the Marshall Plan in Europe. Congress approved an aid programme for seventeen European countries, including Greece and Turkey. Greek communists emboldened with material support from neighbouring communist countries revolted against the Greek government in 1946, and Turkey felt communist pressure from within and without. The largest recipient was Britain, followed by France, Italy and West Germany in that order. Sweden unexpectedly discovered that it met the qualifications for US aid despite an officially neutral stance during the war. Spain, not so fortunate, was turned away, perhaps explaining the short-winded dynamics of Spain's economy in the first decades after the war.

In the Bretton Woods system, the GATT decisions on trade and the Marshall Plan lay the chief multilateral negotiations and actions that redirected and remoulded the world's war economy into a strident and buoyant peacetime economy. Underlying the talks and actions was the growing intelligent recognition that individual economies suffocated when walled in, and that each economy had high stakes in the prosperity of other economies. There remained issues crying for the individual attention of the allied powers. The stress and storms of wartime finance debauched two currencies that later graduated into linchpins of the global monetary system. In the days after World War II redundant Reichsmarks counted for hardly more than ghost money, leaving Germany without a useful medium of exchange. Beginning in 1936 Germany regimented prices in a straitjacket of wage and price controls while food and other goods grew ever more scarce. Since wages and other incomes and payments held up at the same rate, consumers earned the same buying power but met with fewer and fewer goods to buy. Shopping became a messy business of rationing cards and coupons plus the money to pay the selling prices. Shopkeepers demanded an added sweetener, such as cigarettes or coal, to consummate a transaction. A barter economy usurped the monetary economy. Anxious city residents walked to the countryside carrying whatever goods they had and humbly bartered face to face with farmers for food.

The road to German monetary reform lay in finding a fair and equitable way for whittling down the stock of money held in bank accounts and circulating as currency. By May 1946 the Allies had settled on a plan, the brainchild of two American economists, Raymond Goldsmith and Gerhard Colm, and an American banker, Joseph M. Dodge. Its execution hit a snag after an agreement between France, the Soviet Union, the United Kingdom and the United States to treat Germany as a single economic unit fell apart, setting back monetary reform from May 1946 until June 1948. A question mark for France, the United Kingdom and the United States was entrusting the Soviet Union with plates for printing up a new currency to replace the Reichsmarks. The only printing presses in Germany suitable for printing new notes were in the Soviet zone of occupation. Access to the printing plates would invite the Soviet Union to print up extra currency for its own use, imposing a rapacious inflation tax on Germany rather than restoring monetary integrity. As the rift between the Western Occupation powers and the Soviet Union widened, the Western powers opted to print the new notes in London.

The new currency was christened the Deutsche Mark, and the plan to swap it for the Reichsmark was enveloped in a cloak of the highest military secrecy, under the code name 'Operation Birddog'. The Allied authorities quietly guarded against encouraging shopkeepers to withhold goods in anticipation of the new currency. Operation Birddog began on 20 June 1948. In the three Western zones, every inhabitant received 40 Deutsche Marks in exchange for 40 Reichsmarks. Two months later every inhabitant received 20 Deutsche Marks in exchange for 20 Reichsmarks. This per capita distribution put an egalitarian slant into the currency reform, favouring those owning smaller amounts of Reichsmarks while shutting out speculators owning large quantities. This sheltered low income individuals, often financially unsophisticated and therefore the likeliest losers in currency reform. Beyond the one to one distribution, Deutsche Marks were exchanged for the Reichsmarks at a rate of 1 Deutsche Mark per 10 Reichsmarks. All debts including government debt, mortgages, bank loans, and insurance policies underwent deflation on a ten to one basis, meaning 1 Deutsche Mark was owed for every 10 Reichsmarks formerly owed. The same factorial adjustment scaled back bank deposits. Both the asset side and the liability side of business balance sheets were written down by a factor of one-tenth of original values. The reform mandated that all future debts be contracted in Deutsche Marks. Atop this new currency system the authorities erected a new central bank to manage monetary affairs. The Bank of the Deutscher Lander (Bank of German States), formed out of the branch banks of the Reichsbank, lasted until 1957 when West Germany restructured it as the Deutsche Bundesbank. On 24 June 1948 the authorities dissolved all price controls. Goods flew onto store shelves that had been bare for years, indicating shopkeepers had been holding back goods, slyly betting on currency reform.

Innumerable transactions that had sunk into the underground economy bubbled up to the surface.

Currency issues widened the political fissure that later split apart East and West Germany. Reichsmarks unusable in the Western zones threatened to rain down on the Soviet zone. Soviet authorities saw no choice but to enact their own currency reform. They issued the Deutsche Mark East, equal in value to the Deutsche Mark West. Briefly the Deutsche Mark East circulated alongside the Deutsche Mark West at a one to one exchange rate. The end of July 1948, however, saw the Deutsche Mark East tumble to roughly half the value of the Deutsche Mark West, driving the wedge deeper between West and East Germany.

Japan's monetary affairs were in a mess as well, but not one electric with potential for bickering Allies to gum up decision making processes. Black market prices jumped 30 per cent between September and December 1945, and doubled by February 1946.[9] Bank of Japan bank notes in circulation doubled within six months. In February 1946 the stern Emergency Monetary Measures Ordinance was promulgated. It froze bank deposits, allowing only limited withdrawals for monthly living expenses and necessary business transactions. A head of household could withdraw 300 yen per month, and each additional member of a household 100 yen. Cheques for some transactions such as tax payments could be drawn on frozen accounts. From 2 March the authorities nullified the legal tender status of all Bank of Japan notes circulating in denominations of 5 yen or less. Up to 100 of the old yen could be traded in for new yen. These subtracting measures whittled down the Everest of circulating bank notes from 61,824 million yen to 15,200 million yen.[10] Inflation took a brief holiday, but deflation policies held no magical and quick cure for Japan's difficulties. Japan's inflation problem lay elsewhere than excess demand at full employment. Factories stood idle and workers unemployed while famine and panic sent prices through the stratosphere. The government had to spend money and allow business enterprises to spend money before passage to a peacetime economy was possible. Deficit spending, partly for subsidies to businesses, remained vital, and restrictions on frozen accounts were frequently eased. By January 1947, Bank of Japan bank notes in circulation topped 100,040 million yen, well above the pre-monetary emergency measure levels. By March 1949, bank notes in circulation had multiplied by twenty times the number immediately after the March 1946 emergency measures. Prices took flight to the sound of soaring money stocks. In April 1946 the wholesale price index had perched at fifteen times a base 1934–6 level. By March 1949 it was at 197 times this base level.[11] Foreign trade remained subservient to the sovereign upper hand of the Supreme Command of the Allied Powers, and exchange rates between the yen and the dollar ranged from 100 to 900 yen per dollar.[12]

In February 1949, the United States government dispatched Joseph Dodge as ambassador to Japan with authority to inflict deflationary policies and break the back of Japanese inflation. In consultation with the US State Department, Dodge, who had shared in designing West Germany's currency reform, took a hard line against inflation in Japan. In a news conference with Japanese reporters on first arriving in Japan, he painted a colourful analogy between the Japanese economy and a man walking on stilts. One stilt symbolized US foreign aid, and the other hidden subsidies from Japanese financial institutions, such as the Reconstruction Finance Corporation.[13] Dodge warned that the stilts had been allowed to get dangerously high, and that the Japanese economy at any time could topple over and crash. His plan, coldly dubbed the Dodge Line by unfriendly Japanese observers, was a draconian fiscal policy that called for a balanced budget. In practice the plan chalked up tidy budget surpluses. Subsidies to producers from the government's general or special accounts and lending from the Reconstruction Finance Corporation screeched to a near halt. These funds still irrigated key industries needing plant and equipment, and exporting and importing industries needing foreign capital. The plan also called for a fixed exchange rate between the yen and the dollar. On 25 April 1949 the authorities set the Japan's official exchange rate under the Bretton Woods system at 360 yen per 1 dollar.

As an antidote against inflation the Dodge plan deserved a standing ovation. The wave of swelling consumer prices crested and prices retreated until mid 1950, but the penalty for choking inflation on the economic front was paid in wholesale derailment of Japan's economic recovery. Bankruptcies and unemployment mounted and Japanese newspapers reported presidents (sometimes the whole family) of small and medium size companies committing suicide.[14] Japanese authorities sent diplomats scurrying to Washington in hopes of negotiating a relaxation of the stiff-necked anti-inflation policies. Dodge's iron resolve remained undaunted. Not a ray of hope lit a bleak horizon when a turn of events changed everything. The Korean War broke out on 25 June 1950, and Japan's economic outlook brightened as US government spending in the region increased.

The stabilization of currencies and the adoption of the Bretton Woods system pinned down a secure structural and mechanical matrix within which the global economic and financial system could unfold in its drive to maturity. Developed countries thrust aside Depression era systems of multiple exchange rates and exchange controls in favour of one exchange rate for all uses. Foreign exchange use became unfettered. The World Bank eased the flow of capital from capital rich to capital poor countries. The GATT talks opened up new avenues and opportunities for international trade. The Marshall Plan spurred and fuelled a spirited renewal of postwar Western Europe. Within a decade hardly a soul would concede that World War II held back European economic development.

The unfolding of economic growth and development over time reflects interaction between varied structural, mechanical and routine rigidities and parameters on the one hand, and unexpected shocks on the other. The outbreak of the Korean War belongs in the class of unexpected shocks. The economic system assimilates these shocks and may rechannel and orchestrate its own development in order to transmute them into fuel for growth. The secret to diagnosing the graph that an economic system charts over time rests in seeing clear to the bottom the dynamic reactions and feedbacks of the economic system to these random shocks. No one could have foreseen in 1948 how the pound sterling and French franc would slip from the front seat to the back seat as world currencies, and how far the Deutsche Mark would outdistance other hard currencies, becoming second only to the US dollar as major world currencies. Economic history had always oscillated between prosperity and depression, and prosperity had always been a nomad, moving around geographically. The question still dangling in the air was what species of prosperity might ripen on the back of reforms born of stock market crashes, Depression, trade wars and devastating military conflict.

Chapter 3

Prosperity Born of Depression

A NEW JAPAN

Tensions in divided Germany, the Korean War (1950-53), and tug-of-war stalemates in these areas, lifted the sullen spectre of communism to a towering menace, diluting fears of Germany and Japan into distant and faded memories. Instead of worrying about a monstrous Japan springing to life from ashes, the US warmed to the inviting prospect of Japan developing as a checkmate against Asian communism, particularly after Japan wholeheartedly cooperated with the United States during the Korean War. The occupational authorities had broadened and deepened westernization in Japan with an anti-monopoly law, land reform and worker empowerment to unionize. As a highly industrialized country neighbouring the Korean War zone, Japan enjoyed a kingly share of the swelling war procurement spending necessary to prosecute the war. Japanese industry supplied sandbags, army blankets, cloth, trucks, gas tanks for planes, ammunition and barbed wire.[1] When peace talks opened, Japan took to supplying materials for the reconstruction of Korea. Besides procurement spending for the Korean War, extra defence spending worldwide led to a roaring boom in the global economy, and Japanese exports shared in a flowering of world trade. Japan recaptured its standing as the worldwide leader in textile exports. Steel exports, at 30,000 tons per month in the first half of 1950, grew to 100,000 tons per month by December 1950.[2] Economic growth in Japan accelerated to a stampeding 12 per cent annual rate from 1950 until 1952.

This juncture in Japan's economic history furnishes an illustration of how the development of one country only becomes totally intelligible after examination of the trends and development in the wider world economy. As plausible as it is to trace Japan's economic troubles solely to the jolts and wastes of war, it is no less revealing to see how Japan's economy marched in step with worldwide economic trends. Japan's economic recovery rode the crest of worldwide expansion, but that expansion bred strangling imbalances and shortages that threatened to cruelly abort Japan's hopeful beginnings. Japan counted on imported raw materials, and China indignantly shut the resource door on Japan. At the Korean War's peak a worldwide scramble for raw materials sent prices steeply and quickly spiralling upwards. Once again events fell out in Japan's favour. The boom in raw material prices suddenly petered out, and the world economy entered into a calmer phase of cheaper raw materials.

The large place of long-term economic trends when placed beside recent shocks of war looms into clearer view when seen through the eyes of economic historians who have studied trends and long swings in prices dating back to the eighteenth century.[3] Since 1790 the world economy has undergone phases lasting from 15 to 25 years in which prices in general rose and agricultural and raw material prices climbed faster than others. Faster rising agricultural and raw material prices quicken the inflationary thrust. A ballpark dating of phases fitting this pattern is: 1790–1815; 1848–73; 1896–1920; 1935–51; 1972–83. Intervening between these phases are deflationary phases in which prices in general weaken, and prices of agricultural and raw materials fall against prices in general. Sagging agricultural and raw material prices soften prices overall. In these phase prices are also depressed by newer, cutting edge industries that briskly expand output on the strength of cheap raw materials and new technology. Intervening time spans that exhibit these characteristics are: 1815–48; 1873–96; 1920–35 and 1951–72. The latter period saw thin inflation rather than the deflation linked with earlier periods, which can be explained by structural changes in the economy and conscious use of government spending and money stock growth to underpin and bolster prosperity. Each phase has its own individual physiognomy yet shares contours with other phases. For the 1920–35 period, Britain hit a long and acute pocket of deflation, finishing the war short of gold reserves. Sixty per cent of the decline in British prices transpired between 1920 and 1922, but prices continued skidding downward before reaching a trough in 1933. The United States saw its gold holdings swell during the war and deflation lay dormant until 1929. The United States also shared disproportionately in hot leading sectors compared to Europe. European governments administrated bitter doses of deflationary monetary policies in a bid to reinstate the gold standard, infusing deflationary downdrafts in Europe.

The time span from 1935 until 1951 is vital for understanding the turning point that Japan and the global economy experienced at the close of the Korean War. Large stocks of basic commodities that overhung markets in the 1920s and early '30s melted away with the helping hand of government policies. Agricultural and raw material prices outclimbed prices in general. War in Europe and later in Japan and China further pinched agricultural production. The panicky food shortage in postwar Japan mirrored a worldwide drift that had been gathering strength since 1935. General price levels worldwide turned upwards in the second half of the 1930s. In England prices jumped 8 per cent between 1935 and 1937. In the United States wholesale prices stood 19 per cent higher in 1940 than in 1933, but still fell shy of 1929 levels.[4] In China, where war with Japan stretched resources drum tight, consumer prices rocketed upwards 200 per cent between December 1937 and December 1939. We have already seen how Free China, locked in civil war, shared in the world inflation and monetary disorder of the late 1940s, lifting prices 179,400 per cent in Shanghai between January 1946 and July 1948 in a burst of hyperinflation that accelerated until the communists consolidated control.

Upward trends in overall prices and relative prices of basic commodities eased in 1951. Agricultural productivity grew with wider and wiser use of fertilizers and chemicals. Worldwide trade, which nearly folded in the 1930s, expanded under a new international trade and monetary order, widening access to agricultural products from less developed countries. Agricultural production also rebounded from the dislocations and ruin of war. According to an index of world export prices, the prices of food and raw materials sank 10 per cent between 1951 and 1971. Prices of manufactured goods went up 25.7 per cent during the same time frame. Fuel prices fell from 1951 until 1967, but returned to 1951 levels by 1970.[5] In most countries a tame general price inflation flickered in positive territory between 1951 and 1972, rarely rising to the stormy levels reached in the years directly following World War II or in the 1970s after supplies of food and raw material prices tightened. Chile is a useful gauge of disinflation trends since it has logged continuous inflation since 1879. Chilean inflation stood at a mere 8.5 per cent in 1931, climbed to 15.1 per cent by 1940, and peaked at 47.8 per cent in 1952. It then fluttered between 20 and 40 per cent before raging to 178 per cent in 1972.

The bitter deflation odyssey of the 1920s and '30s may have hardened governments and electorates to patience toward some inflation during the 1950s and 60s. They had learned that deflationary policies dull the edge of growth and increase unemployment. Whatever the case, in 1952 the world economy stood poised to favour industrialization for countries able to exploit the golden opportunity, and Japan and West Germany squarely met the distinct needs of the times. In the decades ahead, the economies of two countries with no colonies outshone competitors who enjoyed the trappings and markets of colonial empires.

THE GLOBAL ECONOMY STANDS READY FOR GROWTH

While inflation remained an obdurate annoyance, economic growth numbers belie any hint of stagflation. In fact, the world economy was in for a burst of unforeseen and unsuspected growth and prosperity in 1952. A composite index of industrial production measuring the pooled output of eight countries (Belgium, Canada, France, West Germany, Italy, Japan, the Netherlands and the United Kingdom) posted an unbroken string of positive growth rates for the years 1953 through 1972.[6] Industrial production growth in peak years reached levels of from 8 to over 10 per cent. Only in one recession year did growth dip to 0.4 per cent. The combined real GNP numbers for these eight countries tracked a parallel trajectory to industrial production. For one year the combined GNP growth for these countries sank to 2.4 per cent, but in every other year between 1953 and 1972 it stood above 4 per cent, and for seven of these years above 6 per cent. The United States outgrew by a handsome figure most countries during World War II, but lapsed into slackened growth in the postwar era. Growth in US industrial production and real GNP tumbled into the negative column for the years 1954, 1958 and 1970. Real GNP growth measured a healthy 4.5 per cent between 1955 and 1972, smartly above a long-term trend rate of 3.3 per cent. The other eight countries chalked up even healthier numbers, averaging a stirring 5.1 per cent real GDP growth between 1955 and 1972. Over these years business cycles pulsated as accelerations and decelerations in positive growth rates rather than shifts between positive and negative growth.

The world expansion got going on the back of the petrochemical, electronics and aerospace industries. In the United States and Great Britain the steel industry faded out as a key economic growth propellant in the 1920s. The high place of steel in the reconstruction of Europe kept the steel industry a spur to growth in France and Germany into the 1950s and it remained an economic driver in Japan throughout the period.

In the United States the motor vehicle industry finished the 1950s as a leading, growth-spurring industry. In Great Britain it marched on into the 1960s, and continued to play a singular role in the French, German and, above all, Japanese economies.

LAISSEZ-FAIRE CAPITALISM WINS NEW CONVERTS

A passing observer might credit the triumph of laissez-faire capitalism for the unbroken stretch of dazzling growth after the war. As mentioned earlier, Germany favoured cartels. A cartel lets member firms monopolize an industry, fixing prices, splitting up markets and setting production quotas. In 1933 the Nazi government enacted a statute that empowered the federal minister of economics to compel cartelization from above. After the invasion of France, the Nazi government handed down a parallel mandate for French industry. Japan brewed its own model of monopoly capitalism under the zaibatsu, the gargantuan family-controlled financial combines that held sway over the newer and industrialized sector of Japan's economy. In the 1930s four large zaibatsu often held the upper hand in every key Japanese industry. Against the German and Japanese models of monopoly capitalism, the United States pioneered and pressed ahead with anti-trust legislation against monopolistic practices. Ancient English common law held restraints of trade unlawful. Great Britain grew more indifferent to monopolistic practices after the Mogul Steamship case in 1891, but both the United States and Great Britain belonged to the laissez-faire sect of capitalism. Given the human inclination to applaud and emulate the traits and behaviours of winners, not just cynics would expect the capitalist world to be enamoured of laissez-faire after World War II. The world economy enjoyed a burst of growth as self-respecting competition edged out monopolistic practices around the world. Nevertheless conquering countries often exhibit a penchant for usurping customs and practices from conquered nations. It will pay to take a hard and thoughtful look at how national economies evolved under the prestigious influence of the United States and Great Britain.

The United States emerged from World War II a towering influence among capitalist countries. It doggedly dismembered monopolies and disarmed monopolistic practices at home. In 1945 the United States government broke up Alcoa Aluminum in a landmark anti-trust case. Before the anti-trust action Alcoa turned out 100 per cent of the primary aluminium in the United States, and commanded 90 per cent of the home market. Its monopoly lay tightly anchored in the exclusive ownership of critical patents and irreplaceable raw materials. Alcoa vertically integrated and fused aluminium production from top to bottom, weaving together all stages of production from bauxite ore to aluminium ingots, to fabricated aluminium. No evidence surfaced that Alcoa had acted aggressively or in an exclusionary way against competitors, or engaged in unreasonable actions to outflank and quell competition. The courts ruled in the Alcoa case that monopoly violated the Sherman Antitrust Act unless the monopoly market share was thrust upon a company and virtually unavoidable. The opinion in the case came from the pen of Judge Hand of the New York Court of Appeals: 'Many people believe that possession of unchallenged economic power deadens initiative, discourages thrift and depresses energy; and rivalry is a stimulant to industrial progress. . .'[7]

In 1947 the United States Justice Department zeroed in on the United Shoe Machinery Corporation for monopolistic business practices. The case went before the Supreme Court in 1954. The court broadened and stiffened its stand against monopoly in this case. United Shoe owned a legal patent on a machine needed to manufacture shoes, which entitled them to a monopoly on the manufacture and sale of this machine. Its profits were normal and machinery costs accounted for a mere 2 per cent of the wholesale cost of shoes. The Supreme Court ruled against United Shoe Machinery Corporation for usurping monopolistic privileges. Rather than selling its patented machinery outright, United Shoe sucked its customers into lease agreements. These agreements required lessees to: (1) sign a 'tying agreement' guaranteeing to lease all machinery, patented and unpatented, from United Shoe, (2) sign leases for a minimum of ten years, (3) fork out a hefty financial penalty for returning machines before the lease was out. When the Justice Department first sued United Shoe in 1917, the courts sensed nothing odorous in United Shoe's marketing practices. By the 1950s their thinking had turned against monopolistic practices.

The United States assailed monopolistic practices in the occupied countries. In November 1945 the Japanese government, at the direction of the General Headquarters of the Allied Forces, froze the assets of the fifteen largest zaibatsu, and commenced action to dissolve them. In 1946 the government organized the Holding Companies Liquidation Commission and charged it with overseeing the break-up of the zaibatsu. In 1947 the General Headquarters of the Allied Forces prodded the Japanese government to enact the Anti-Monopoly Law of 1947, patterned after US anti-trust law. The Japanese government also enacted the Law for the Elimination of Excessive Economic Concentration. Under this law 325 firms were liable for dismemberment. The net of anti-trust action enmeshed highflying companies such as Mitsubishi, Mitsui, Sumitomo and Yasuda. The policy of liquidation dethroned family control of the zaibatsu, but failed to erase large industrial combines from the economic landscape of Japan. After the peace treaty was signed in 1951, the policies of the occupation authorities touching anti-trust were largely rewritten. Mitsui and Mitsubishi quietly won consent to reorganize themselves and resumed their prewar names. Concentration of economic power still bedevilled Japan with banks controlling large blocks of corporate stock. Nevertheless, as family ties held a smaller place, a managerial class arose, signalling a divorce between capital and management more characteristic of the modern corporation.

The German cartels met with an unfriendly reception from occupying authorities looking upon dissolution of cartels as a weapon against Germany's revival as a military power. Little had been done when the military governments of the United States and Great Britain in May 1949 began to agree on decartelization and sold off one of the 70 companies combined in the I. G. Farben chemical trust. Other businesses were reeled in for decartelization, the Robert Bosch electrical combine and the Ufa film trust among them. The new Bonn government pleaded with the Allies to halt a plan for dismantling industries linked to military power, such as synthetic oils, steel and rubber. To win concessions the new state vowed among other things to enact legislation against cartels. In 1957 West Germany enacted legislation banning domestic cartels, but not cartels formed out of a need for cooperation in international trade. Exemptions for international trade often modulate anti-trust legislation.

Great Britain also firmed up its soft stand toward monopolistic practices. This turnabout sprang from Parliament's passage of the Monopoly and Restrictive Practices (Inquiry and Control) Act of 1948. This act had no teeth for stopping monopolistic and restrictive practices, but gave the government the power of inquiry into them, allowing it to unmask the presence of monopoly and its repercussions. Later, the government awarded itself the power to dissolve price fixing, collusive and restrictive agreements with the passage of the Restrictive Trade Practices Act of 1956. The act compelled collusive parties to register all agreements that touched on price fixing, production quotas and agreements and narrowed freedom to sell and buy on terms mutually agreeable to the parties of a transaction. The act provided for the establishment of a Restrictive Practices Court to evaluate these agreements and nullify them if they were deemed against the public interest. This Court could uphold collusive agreements for assorted reasons, including neutralization of monopoly power in related spheres.[8]

THE ECONOMICS OF OLIGOPOLIES

By no means did fresh anti-trust legislation and prosecutions herald the certain annihilation of concentrated economic power. It was not enough if anti-trust policy worldwide bore the stamp of US policy and favoured the laissez-faire model of capitalism above monopoly capitalism. In 1969, 5 of the largest corporations owned 11 per cent of all United States manufacturing assets, 50 owned 38 per cent, and 500 owned 74 per cent.[9] Corporations holding assets above $1 billion accounted for 46 per cent of all manufacturing assets. About four fifths of all US manufacturing assets belonged to corporations with assets above $100 million. Concentration of economic power had hardly mushroomed as a new postwar scourge. An eye-opening study for 1933 estimated that 57 per cent of assets of non-financial corporations belonged to the 200 largest firms and their subsidiaries.[10] A sobering study by the Federal Trade Commission for 1947 measured that 46 per cent of all manufacturing property, plant and equipment belonged to the 113 largest manufacturing corporations.[11]

Digging into employment numbers unearths a reciprocal parade of concentration. The top 5 manufacturing firms of 1969 ranked by workforce size employed 11 per cent of all manufacturing workers, and the top 17 firms engaged 20 per cent of manufacturing workers. In each of the sectors, manufacturing, mining, retailing and wholesaling, the top 11 corporations engaged 10 per cent of the workers employed. In 1969 the three largest United States industrial corporations, General Motors, Standard Oil of New Jersey and Ford, reported income above the income of all farmers even with government subsidies included. In

1968 the five largest industrial corporations scored 64 per cent of all industrial sales in the United States. A handful of firms lorded over production in most industrial markets. In the early 1970s, John Kenneth Galbraith thought that 1,000 of the largest manufacturing, merchandising, transportation, power and financial corporations produced roughly half of all United States goods and services supplied after subtracting what was produced by the state.[12]

In highly competitive markets firms are powerless to sway the selling prices of their products and their pioneering energies zero in on cost reductions as the only sure road to survival. When a market is an oligopoly, that is, a tiny handful of firms produce most of the industry output, firms stand dictator over the their own prices. When these firms go toe-to-toe, they may at one extreme opt for an emaciating and self-cancelling price war, or at another huddle into friendly collusion, coalescing into one smiling seller setting monopoly prices. Behemoth firms must engage in planning stretching over years to maintain, update and enlarge vast facilities. To be sure they can profit from costly equipment purchased at today's prices, they count on future prices of their output remaining sound, without risk of a wrenching free fall. Given the high place of secure and predictable prices, these colossal enterprises shun a price war as pure folly, a rock of danger. In agriculture, where unfettered prices haphazardly fluctuate beyond the control of individual sellers, governments propped up farm incomes with price supports and subsidies as farmers embraced more costly capital goods. The gnawing fear of another unnerving Depression meant the beating drums of a price war never hushed, however muffled. Many firms warmed to the fatherly price leadership of a celebrated firm as a signal that they wanted no part of a retaliatory price war.

One corollary of this horror of price competition is that firms found playing fields with lower stakes. The automobile companies battled every year to whet the consumer's appetite, unveiling fresh designs with longer lengths and bolder fins. Television commercials popped up four to five times per hour. Financing became a non-issue. Writing about the German cartels of the 1930s W. F. Bruck cited the tendency of large-scale operations to free themselves from the hand of economic law, and replace supply and demand with foresight and planning.

According to Bruck:

> From the theoretical point of view, the large undertaking has the novel feature of organizing demand as well as supply. It is no longer a mere competitor with other undertakings of production on the supply side. It is the mark of a modern industrial state that the big undertakings of production have to create their own markets, with all the corollaries such as the financing of the producer and consumer.[13]

Once these stately enterprises gained a measure of market independence, decision-making sank into a bureaucracy of countless technocrats and managerial elites. This bureaucracy prized its own security, growth and autonomy above everything, even profits and dividends. It outflanked the prying eyes of nosy bankers by retaining and saving earnings internally and raising capital from myriads of guileless stockholders. It set aside funds to finance the development of new products when it could not get government funds to underwrite these things. The relative growth of government spending during the 1930s and 40s widened the public sector, leaving it an unprecedented and irreplaceable force in the overall demand for goods and services. Corporations learned that whenever total demand for the economy's output slackened, government could be counted on to trim the economic sails, filling the spending vacuum with fatter government spending and slimmer tax rates. Shunning price competition and counting on government to maintain full employment, the managerial and technological bureaucracies of corporations commanded a fortified autonomy for long-term planning. Even in the United States, the country with the longest and most bare-knuckled commitment to anti-trust legislation and enforcement, the industrial structure took on many of the characteristics that Bruck wrote about in a German economy ruled by lawful cartels.

The hunger for economic security surfaced in other areas as well. In the 1930s the US Congress enacted programmes of unemployment and old age insurance, and minimum wages to ease the alienation and impoverishment of workers. Congress also hampered the freedom of employers to hound workers making a bid for unionization. We have already cited price supports and subsidies for farmers. In a few industries, trucking, airlines, railroads and telecommunications, the government clutched the sceptre of price tsar, dictating prices and sparing firms any thought of price competition. This drift toward softening economic insecurity touched most advanced capitalistic societies but was nowhere clearer than in Britain, which enacted the National Insurance Act in 1946, furnishing beefier benefits for recipients of old age and unemployment insurance, and pulled ahead of the United States with socialized medicine and the National Health Service. Revenue for these programmes poured in from an ambitious tax structure that took high and steeply graduated bites out of income. If cushioning economic insecurity sapped incentives, the effect was muted by everlasting worries about depression. Productivity and economic growth took wing in the 1950s and 60s, even with nationalization of industries in Europe, and a 90 per cent tax bracket in the very heart of capitalism, the United States.

THE RISE OF ECONOMIC PLANNING

In a nutshell it might be said that the US economy, despite spirited enforcement of anti-trust laws, evolved on a trajectory favouring decentralized and tacit planning free from government prying. Giant corporations enjoyed the broadest security and power to plan their own future on the strength of a price structure that remained stable, a freedom to finance research and development out of profits, and a government that could be counted on to nullify downdrafts in demand for private goods and services. Between the government's control of total demand, and mass media for advertising, corporations acquired a keen watchdog instinct over the demand for their own products. Vertical integration bridged and cleared the paths to raw material supplies.

In advanced capitalist countries the postwar tendency for economic planning to displace supply and demand reached a zenith in France. That was where the government's hand weighed heavier in the planning process, and the hammer of anti-trust enforcement fell lighter on industry. In December 1945 the French government nationalized the Bank of France. That was not an unusual step. In many countries nationalization measures swallowed central banks. The Bank of England underwent nationalization in March 1946, and the Netherlands Bank in 1948. Developing countries gladly flocked to the banner of government-owned central banks. The law nationalizing the Bank of France also nationalized the four largest deposit banks in France. In 1946 the National Constituent Assembly of France decreed the nationalization of the 45 largest insurance companies. It also harnessed up to government controls and steerage all private investment banks with assets above 500 million francs. Control over credit flows could be no dull and hollow instrument in the hands of government planners. There was a conviction that private capital lacked the bullishness to make up for years of feeble growth. The French government in 1946 snatched up for nationalization the electrical power and gas industry and the coal industry, and some individual firms, like the Renault automobile manufacturer. Governing boards of nationalized industries gave over day-to-day management of companies to a managerial elite, letting managerial bureaucracies in nationalized companies usurp the same autonomy as the corporate bureaucracies in the United States. In talks and discussions with industry representatives, French government planners brokered and charted a viable rate of overall expansion, and plotted a matrix showing the expansion that was both needed and possible in individual sectors. Each sector had a goal. The plan afforded individual enterprises the confident expectation of meeting with the necessary suppliers and customers at the forecasted growth rate. The government orchestrated taxes, subsidies and access to credit to rechannel efforts toward goal achievement. By 1962 French planning drew applause worldwide. President Kennedy dispatched a team of experts to study French economic planning at first hand.

Britain threw itself less heartily into planning. Within the grand sweep of British nationalization fell the coal industry (1947), the railway, road haulage and canal and coach industries (1948), the electrical industry (1949), and iron and steel industry (1951). In 1951 the iron and steel industry reincarnated into the private sphere as part of a Conservative Party programme of denationalization. Oversight responsibility of nationalized industries fell to public boards, such as the National Coal Board and the British Transport Commission. These boards invariably acted to strengthen managerial elites and bureaucracies at the expense of market forces.

Britain kept tight economic controls locked in place through the late 1940s to early 50s before slanting toward more laissez-faire economic policies. Selective rationing of goods lasted until 1954. The immediate postwar controls entailed some economic planning, but only to tackle shortages and financial stringency. In 1961 Britain swung a gentle turn about and launched a new government-sponsored economic planning initiative in light of the trumpeted success of planning worldwide.

More than France, the United Kingdom or Japan, West Germany remoulded itself in the likeness of the United States. It warmed to anti-trust policies and exalted market forces above economic planning. The concept of the 'social market economy' underpinned and shaped the reconfiguration of the West German economy after price controls were lifted in 1948. It evolved from the thinking of Walter Euchen, whose role as an architect of German economic policy rivals Keynes's role in Britain. The secret to a humane economic system, according to Euchen, lay in an economic coordination naturally arising from the hidden processes and enmeshing dynamics of a competitive order. The government humbly served as an economic midwife, lighting and paving the path for development of this competitive order, including the useful assurance of a monetary policy underscoring price stability. A seesawing circuit between inflation and deflation loomed an ever-lasting enemy to the competitive order. The concept of the social market economy belonged in a species of socialized policies since it made room for minimum wage laws, child labour laws, environmental protection laws and even progressive income taxation. It was a market concept as far as the government banned restrictive and quasi-monopolistic practices and shunned protective tariffs. The foundation of a safe and sound environment for business planning and investing lay in government economic policy that remained as constant as possible. Healthy competition equated with neither large numbers of sellers, nor price wars between a few firms, but with a parallel race for improvement.

In addition to siding internationally with policies of multilateral trade liberalization, West Germany acting on these principles became one of the rare countries in the 1950s to unilaterally reduce tariffs. West Germany also pressed ahead of Europe in tearing down hurdles dampening inflows of foreign capital and outflows of German capital to other countries by the close of the 1950s. The West German government first drafted anti-trust legislation in 1952. Its enactment in compromised form came in 1957 after hard and bitter political debate. It was generally softer and narrower than American anti-trust law, among other things giving the government no legal power to stop mergers. With exceptions it banned cartels and restrictive agreements of either the horizontal or vertical species. Like the US anti-trust laws, resale price agreements enjoyed an exemption. In one corner of the battle against monopolies and cartels, the West German government launched policies and earmarked funds with an eye to encouraging small businesses. It underwrote financial aid for the establishment of small and medium size businesses, and for backing research and development helpful to these firms, which also received privileged standing in bids for government contracts. Denationalization buttressed and widened the promotion of a competitive order. In 1959 the Prussian Mining and Smelting Company somersaulted into the private sector. Only individuals with taxable incomes below 16,000 marks per year could buy stock, and the amount was capped. The year 1961 saw the denationalization of Volkswagen with a sale of 60 per cent of capital stock. This sale unfolded with an eye toward diffusing ownership and aiding lower income individuals. The same principle governed the transfiguration of United Electricity and Mining Company. In 1965 this giant state-owned holding company was left bestriding the public and private sectors under a programme of partial denationalization.

The glorification of competition afforded West Germany, like the United States, no inoculation against currents and forces favourable to planning. Unlike the United States, banks in West Germany remained free to invest in corporate stock. In 1960 West German banks owned a 25 per cent share or greater in 138 companies. In 58 of those companies, the banks owned shares above 50 per cent.[14] Two thirds of the bank-owned shares belonged to the three largest banks, which had bought hefty blocks of shares outside the exchanges. Banks also wielded an unsubtle sway over corporate governance through proxy votes cast of behalf of bank customers, a practice abolished in 1965. Until then, bank customers kindly deposited stocks and shares in banks with blanket authorizations to cast shareholder votes by proxy. A study of 425 incorporated companies quoted on stock exchanges, representing 75 per cent of the capital of all quoted companies, unmasked bank ownership or control of a tidy 70 per cent of the voting power. Representatives of industry and trade also sat on boards of the three largest banks, but no one shareholder boasted the upper hand. German banks openly wooed companies into mergers, a practice shared with British banks. Both banks and individual investors reached for shares of large companies as safer bets, and state planners in France smiled on large firms. An oligopoly of German banks, wielding stockholder voting muscle and holding the credit purse strings, may have orchestrated an unseen planning influence akin to overt French state planning. German banks nurtured planning out of fear for their own investments.

West Germany never organized anything like the state planning initiative in France. The Marshall Plan gave birth to the European Recovery Program Fund, kept alive in West Germany with home funding. This troubleshooting programme irrigated sectors in need of individual attention with grants and credits. It stood in the outer wings of German economic policy making, used more to tinker with and ease tensions in the market economy rather than directing the economic picture. In 1963, the West German government enacted legislation requiring establishment of an expert committee aimed at dissecting and appraising overall economic development. Composed of five experts drawn from universities and other economic and social institutes, this committee faced the knotty task of plotting an economic course uniting high employment, price stability and external equilibrium without breaching the principles of the market economy. The committee could not endorse individual economic policies. It could spotlight raw tensions between demand and supply and other hazardous and festering trends, and unveil a list of options for handling them. It was West Germany's puny nod to the rising sun of state planning in the 1950s and 60s.

Japan also marched in the parade of post Depression, postwar economic systems assimilating a tide of economic planning at the cost of flexible market prices and competition. Japan aped Germany in letting its banks become coordinating and initiating centres in industry, but soon relaxed anti-monopoly laws after signing the peace treaty. A burst of bankruptcies following the Korean War boom stirred the Ministry of International Trade and Industry (MITI) to action. It applauded agreements to restrict output and threaten to withhold foreign exchange to reluctant firms. First the government peeled away anti-monopoly restrictions on small and medium size firms. In 1959 it further diluted anti-monopoly legislation and MITI gave the nod for large firms to huddle into cartels, sometimes openly counselling firms to broker restrictive agreements, and injecting its own whips and scorns to command cooperation. MITI befriended mergers of firms, believing larger firms would be more competitive with American and European rivals. By 1963 cartels in Japan numbered above 1,000, about 100 of which were composed of large firms.

The easing of anti-trust law in the early 1950s also cleared the way for the firms of prewar zaibatsu to regroup. The wholesale dissolution of family-owned and controlled zaibatsu lasted, but the zaibatsu banks, aside from the Mitsui Bank, which had shorn itself of the Dai Ichi Bank, survived the dissolution process. Banks now became a financial nucleus for a regrouping of firms linked to the same bank and financial institutions (trust banks, insurance companies). There were six chief groups. As of 1971 the Mitsubishi consisted of 86 firms, the Sumitomo of 80, Mitsui of 70, Fuji of 71, Dai Ichi of 27 and Sanwa of 52.[15] The core banks bought stocks in member companies as strings for knitting the group together. Group companies borrowed from both the group bank and outside banks, and group banks advanced loans to outside companies. The presidents of firms in the same group habitually held face-to-face talks to air out mutual problems, share information and plot strategies. The magnetic cohesion of these groups reached beyond the shared financial dependence and linkages with a few financial institutions and perhaps belonged to species of social phenomenon unique to Japanese culture. By the late 1960s Japanese corporations pyramided a towering degree of vertical integration. The 100 leading firms ranked by paid-up capital owned a controlling interest in 4,270 dependent firms. Controlling interest meant the parent company owned 30 per cent or more of stock, or as little as 10 per cent of stock combined with interlocking management.[16]

Another coordinating element in Japan stems from businessmen's associations, such as the Federation of Economic Organizations, the Japanese Federation of Employers Associations, the Japanese Chamber of Commerce and Industry and the Japanese Committee for Economic Development. These groups hammer out plans and proposals, and lobby the government. Lastly, the Japanese government kept the Economic Planning Agency throughout the postwar period. This agency kept the pulse of Japan's economy on the radar screen, and wrote reports diagnosing and sketching what current developments held in store for the future of the economy. MITI shouldered the key responsibility for government planning. In a little less than four decades following World War II, a string of Japanese governments kicked off no less than eleven successive economic plans. By the 1960s these plans tackled matters such as development of human resources, wage differences between large and small enterprises and between agriculture and manufacturing, and social overhead requirements. Like West Germany, Japan set out measures to shield and rouse small and medium size businesses, in 1963 enacting the Medium and Small Enterprises' Basic Law to spur the modernization and rationalization of smaller firms. Japan's approach to planning from several angles may be symptomatic of a dualistic economy bestriding a modern sector and a traditional sector of small family businesses founded in ancient customs of labour relations.

In the first decades after World War II, developing countries emulated the standard of economic planning, exhibiting far more fervour and boldness than the developed countries. In areas of the world where poverty and despair obstinately festered, a ubiquitous malady, governments unveiled economic plans as hopeful stairways to economic development. The United States forced developing countries to hammer out economic plans before receiving foreign aid. Government sponsored economic plans can be merely glorified wishful thinking, suggestive as in the case of Western developed countries, or concrete blueprints of government initiatives and entrepreneurship. The latter bore a marked resemblance to planning in the Eastern Bloc countries where the power to enforce planning lay almost solely with government.

THE BEGINNINGS OF THE EUROPEAN UNION

Governments worldwide in the 1950s and 60s were in no hurry to apply anti-trust laws against large business enterprises, but they had another tactic for checking and taming the power of titanic corporations. Oligopolistic corporations had often monopolized national markets, walled in by high tariffs, unharassed by the discipline of foreign competition. Japan's resolute insistence that large-scale enterprises were better equipped to meet foreign competition may betray the impetus lurking beneath government toleration of large businesses. Anti-trust agitators in the United States fell silent about breaking up General Motors after Japanese automobiles invaded US markets. The Japanese automobile manufacturers accomplished what the anti-trust division of the Justice Department could not. European governments were lukewarm on anti-trust issues, but ready to open talks for reductions of trade barriers across Europe. The key signpost on the road to European economic integration appeared with the establishment of the European Economic Community, unofficially the European Common Market. A common market is a higher step on the ladder to economic integration than either a free trade area or a customs union. A free trade area clears the field of tariffs and trade restrictions between area members. A customs union unifies member countries behind the shield of a common tariff wall, sheltering the goods of member countries from competition with goods from non-member countries. A common market allows the free flow of capital and labour between member countries.

The European Common Market emerged on 1 January 1958. Six countries, Belgium, France, West Germany, Italy, Luxembourg and the Netherlands had met in 1957 in Rome for negotiations and signed a treaty that led to its formation. The treaty forming the European

Atomic Energy Commission was an offspring of this same meeting. This commission undertook the inter-country synchronization of research and management in atomic energy development. The treaties grew out of an earlier pact in 1951, when the same six signatories concluded a treaty in Paris creating the European Coal and Steel Community, charging it with meshing the production and distribution of coal and steel among the six countries. The three treaties advanced the founding principles for the Constitution of the European Economic Community (EEC). The avowed purpose of the new organization lay in the development 'of an integrated market for the free movement of goods, services, capital, and people . . .'. The treaty establishing the European Common Market called for the gradual dismantling of tariffs, quotas and other trade restrictions over a twelve to fifteen year period. The target date was moved up, and the EEC blossomed into a mature customs union in July 1968 when all internal trade restrictions became null and void and a common tariff wall went up against imports from non-members. The members even brokered a way out of the thorny matter of agricultural price supports. EEC agricultural policy barred all production quotas, but ratified a common policy of price supports for all farmers in the common market. Agricultural imports from non-members faced restrictions. At first other countries balked at joining, but in 1973 Denmark, Ireland and United Kingdom cast in their lot. Greece joined in 1981 and Portugal and Spain in 1986. The 1960s saw trade between EEC countries lurch forward, and overall economic growth rates for member economies outshone average performers.

THE BROAD PICTURE OF ATMOSPHERICS AND TRENDS BEHIND
A VIBRANT GROWTH

The overtones of the aforementioned economic characteristics and trends reverberated from 1951 until 1971. Food and raw material prices sagged against prices in general, keeping the muffled drums of depression always resonating. Weak food and raw material prices had overshadowed the decade before the Great Depression, and many economic polices and practices of the 1950s and 60s aimed at exorcising and outflanking signs of economic lassitude. In the United States corporations vertically and horizontally integrated production to leverage power for secure planning. Short-term profit maximization took a backseat to economic security friendly to foresighted planning. Out of fear of price wars, corporations displaced price competition with rivalry in product development, styling and advertising. The enactment and enforcement of US style anti-trust laws did little to splinter the concentration of economic power in the aggregate. In the face of aggressive anti-trust enforcement, the US economy remained overgrown with clusters of oligopolistic firms. In Germany and Japan banks aided economic planning and coordination, and in France nationalized banks underpinned government economic planning. Among developed countries the government's involvement sank deepest into the planning process in France and Japan. The drift toward government planning grew out of the same tarnished credibility of market economies that redirected economic evolution in the United States away from price competition. In Britain and France the nationalization of strategic industries subtracted from market competition and the trauma of the Great Depression still fermented in the social psyche. The United States shied away from official economic planning, but shared in the drift toward big government and the welfare state. Government spending had to be large to act as a balance wheel against oscillations in private sector spending. Only big government could make the glacial shifts in taxes or government spending vital to generating a large impact in the overall economy.

Some misalignments cried out for tweaking under the Bretton Woods system of fixed exchange rates. In 1949 several European countries devalued home currencies by 30 per cent. Britain slashed the pound from $4.03 to $2.80. France ratcheted down the franc in 1957 and 1958. In 1967 Britain devalued again, this time from $2.80 to $2.40 per pound. France devalued again in 1969. Germany and the Netherlands alone revalued domestic currencies upward, in 1961, and Germany again in 1969. Japan held its exchange rate flat at 360 yen per dollar. The Deutsche Mark and the yen owed their muscle to the competitiveness of German and Japanese exports. By 1971 West

Germany ranked the second largest trading nation in the world, accounting for 10 per cent of the world's trade.[17]

The use of government spending and money stock management to keep economies inflated beyond fear of depression may be at the bottom of the mild but unstoppable inflation from 1951 to 1971. Unemployment ranked higher on the roster of public enemies than inflation. Accordingly eyes remained glued to the unemployment rates while inflation rates remained in the hazy peripheral vision. Businesses were aware of the tie between the unemployment rate and the market for their product.

Despite big government, high taxes, tacit oligopolistic planning and obtrusive government economic planning, the economies of the world posted above average growth rates. Brazil, with inflation averaging an ominous 57 per cent between 1945 and 1959, logged a reputable 3.9 per cent economic growth during the same time span.[18] Foreign trade swelled and fanned out as governments dismantled trade barriers. Innovations in petrochemicals, electronics, aerospace and synthetic fibres propelled a bullish expansion aided by an abundance of low cost raw materials.

Chapter 4

The Thesis and Antithesis of Capitalism

Capitalism breeds exploitative systems in outpost and satellite regions at the same time that central areas bow to humanitarian reforms. The first half of the nineteenth century saw slavery and serfdom thrive in the United States and Russia while England and France eradicated slavery and embraced child labour laws. The French and American revolutionaries drew inspiration from the same ideals. The French Revolution, for all its revolutionary and bloody madness, outlawed slavery and the slave trade. The gentlemanly and philosophic revolutionaries in America shunned disorderly and messy extremes but left slavery unscathed. The United States and Russia crushed slavery and serfdom in the early 1860s, but the US had hardly wiped out slavery in the east when it resuscitated indentured servitude in the western United States with the Act to Encourage Immigration of 1864. Indentured servitude thrived in the British West Indies after the British government outlawed slavery in the 1830s. The United States cast aside indentured servitude in 1885, but the Caribbean and Latin America clung to it until 1917.

On a brighter note, the menace of colonial exploitation softened as the remaining colonial empires fell to pieces after World War II. At the end of the war, the British Empire either formally or informally still ruled one fourth of the world's population, well outpacing the French and Dutch empires, which still held vast colonial possessions. The richest European colony in resources, the Belgian Congo, remained the lone colonial possession of Belgium. Two sizeable holdings, Angola and Mozambique, still orbited in the circuit of the ageing and inert Portuguese empire. Germany and Japan emerged from World War II shorn of colonial possessions.

Britain brokered a friendly dissolution of its empire, transfiguring a centralized empire into a free association of nations drawn together by commercial ties and loyalty to the British crown. The British Empire reinvented itself as the British Commonwealth of Nations. India and Pakistan, together the largest of Britain's colonies, gained independence in 1947. Britain's larger colonial holdings in the Far East and Africa also graduated into independent nations. Britain kept a few small holdings, including Hong Kong under a long-term lease with China that expired in 1997. Hong Kong is now part of the People's Republic of China.

France took up arms to save its colonial empire, but met with poor success. After weathering military losses, France ditched Indo-China. France had 400,000 troops on the ground in Algeria when it signed a peace treaty that handed over independence to that country.

After the withdrawal of Japanese occupation forces, Holland tried to uphold its claim over the Dutch East Indies, part of the Dutch Empire since the seventeenth century when the Dutch monopolized the spice trade. Nationalist forces defied and embattled Holland's small military resources, and in 1949 the Indonesian islands budded into the independent nation of Indonesia. The Dutch clung to West New Guinea until 1962 when it joined Indonesia.

The Portuguese, whose imperial and maritime sway predated the empires of the British, Dutch and French, held their empire until the mid 1970s. In 1974 a military coup brought a junta to power espousing democracy at home and peace in colonies where liberation armies were putting up a resistance. In 1974 and 1975 Portugal ceded independence to Guinea-Bissau, Mozambique, the Cape Verde Islands, Sao Tome and Principe, and Angola, and withdrew from what is now East Timor.

Disimperialism heralded no hearty prosperity for the developing quarters of the world. The demand for food and raw materials grew grudgingly as incomes in the 1950s and 60s raced ahead in Europe,

Japan and the United States. As people advance in wealth they do not automatically eat more food. Technological advance often displaced agricultural raw materials with synthetics. A glance at the ratio of export prices to import prices, that is the 'terms of trade', for the country with the largest of the colonial empires, yields a clue to the economic ailments and instability of developing countries during the postwar era. Britain, a country stressing manufactured exports, saw its terms of trade worsen during the later 1930s and 40s. Its terms of trade were 33 per cent less favourable in 1951 than in 1938, echoing an era of rising foodstuff and raw material prices. The downward drift in its terms of trade reversed in 1951, and by 1971 were 50 per cent more favourable than 1951. The upturn mirrored less costly foodstuffs and raw materials relative to manufactured goods. In 1972 Britain's terms of trade sharply shifted against Britain and in favour of countries producing foodstuffs and raw materials.[1]

North America (United States and Canada) saw its index of terms of trade advance from 86 in 1951 to 102 in 1971 on a scale fixed at 100 for 1963.[2] The EEC countries saw the terms of trade index climb from 85 in 1951 to 103 in 1971. The developing countries as a group saw the index sink from 118 in 1951 to 102 in 1971, after gaining ground from 1938 to 1951, lifting the index from 79 to 118. If petroleum is removed from the calculations, the index for developing countries recoiled from a high of 128 in 1951 to 101 in 1971. Even the Middle East, where petroleum holds a high place, saw terms of trade retreat from an index level of 116 in 1951 to 96 in 1971. The terms of trade for the Middle East veer deeper into negative territory when petroleum is subtracted from the picture. The developing countries of Africa saw terms of trade sag from an index level of 126 in 1951 to 103 in 1971. Latin America, even with petroleum in the mix, saw terms of trade worsen, from 124 in 1951 to 101 in 1971, after escalating from 70 to 124 between 1938 and 1951.

These statistics show that the developing regions of the world, that is the poorer countries, suffered while Western Europe, Japan and the United States saw unexpected and unforeseen acceleration in economic growth. More so than developed countries, developing countries were driven back to the economic policies of the 1930s, yielding the front seat to varied species of government controls, government planning and government initiative to stir and quicken economic growth and development. In the face of sinking terms of trade, many developing countries humbly welcomed intergovernmental aid and assistance from developed countries. One ray of hope, a budding of manufacturing exports, helped developing countries participate in the swift growth of world trade. Even with decolonization, Britain, France and Holland shared in the growth and prosperity of the 1950s and 60s. Portugal also came alive to the sound of European growth and prosperity while holding together its ancient empire.

Muted question marks overhung the developing countries. They wondered if the prosperity of the developed world would spread to them and invigorate their economies, or if they were slaves to backwash effects thrown off by the robust economies and were fated to endure everlasting poverty. It was hard to tell if the gap between the wealthiest countries and poorest countries grew wider or narrower. A Marxian wrath often tinted the worldview of the developing countries as they strained to see to the bottom of economic troubles. Developing countries shared in the growth of international trade, but not on as grand a scale. In 1953 developing countries accounted for 27 per cent of world exports. By 1970 exports from developing countries had multiplied by 164 per cent in absolute terms, but had shrunk to a 17.7 per cent share of world exports.[3] The share of world exports from centrally planned economies remained flat over the same time frame, while the share originating from developed market economies grew from 63 to 71.6 per cent.

THE MULTIPLICATION OF MULTINATIONALS

Around 1900 US multinational corporations took to erecting quiet outworks in Latin America. In the first half of the twentieth century progress in transportation and communications unfolded at a dizzy pace. The internal combustion engine and wireless transmission permitted businesses in the United States and Europe and Japan to extend parasitic tentacles and advance agents to every nook and cranny of the globe. Businesses pyramided skywards as they exploited the minerals, oil and ore deposits of a wider area. Multinational corporations headquartered in the developed countries outgrew in size and economic power many governments in the poorer regions.

In 1974 the United States was home to 24 of the 50 largest corporations in the world, and Europe claimed another 20 of the largest corporations. The other six headquartered either in Japan, Brazil or Iran. The largest of the multinational corporations, Exxon, boasted sales of $42.1 billion, above the GNP of Belgium, Denmark or most South American countries. IBM ranked thirteenth in size, putting its total sales on a level with the GNP of Austria. Foreign companies belonged to the class of large property owners in host countries. In 1957 the United Fruit Company owned 147,770 acres on the island nation of Cuba. Even the United States exempted from anti-trust laws domestic firms engaging in price fixing outside the country. The 1960s saw US foreign investments more than double. Banks such as Chase Manhattan backed multinational customers in international markets, often forming consortia with other banks.

THE EXPROPRIATION CURE

The United Fruit Company's involvement in Central America laid bare forces that put governments in developing countries on a collision course with multinational corporations. In the first half of the twentieth century, United Fruit carved out railroads, shipping and subsidiary interests, in addition to banana plantations in Central America. Displeased Central Americans christened United Fruit, the largest foreign corporation and largest employer in the area, the 'Octopus'. In 1951 tensions between United Fruit and locals grew ugly in Guatemala after costly hurricanes and worker strikes left the company impatient with government demands. Locals hotly zeroed in on payment of taxes on profits earned in Guatemala and operations of company-owned wharves. The company consented to stay and pay a 30 per cent chunk of profits as taxes to the Guatemalan government. In June 1952 the Guatemalan government cracked the whip again with a land reform law that proposed to confiscate idle agricultural land held by large landowners and redistribute it to landless farm workers. The programme swallowed 225,000 acres belonging to United Fruit and offered recompense well below United Fruit's expectations. For two more years United Fruit fumed at the hostility of a leftist government, but in 1954 the US government ran roughshod over the Guatemalan leftists, overturning the government in a coup that put the country in the hands of military rule. The CIA blared radio broadcasts and dropped leaflets to cow the population, magnifying and embroidering the legion of invaders. The invading brigade consisted of CIA trained Guatemalan exiles and military officers.

An analogous drama occurred in Honduras between late 1954 and 1955. Conservatism had kept Honduras free from labour law and social and agrarian reform, the lone Latin American republic without these. Floods preceded by a three-month worker strike rasped nerves to the flashpoint. The government dispatched troops to coastal banana plantations to foil violence. Again United Fruit peeled away 30 per cent of its profits in taxes. A left-leaning party won the next election. In 1956 a squad of US-trained army officers snatched power in a coup, and labour leaders mediating a contract dispute with United Fruit were jailed.

While the developed world engineered economic polices to act as sterilizers against infectious economic depression and the consequences of cut-throat competition, the developing world sifted for cures to an ongoing state of economic depression. Economic policies in the developing countries descended in a direct line from policies initiated in the 1930s, and echoed a deeper scepticism and antagonism toward capitalism as the 1950s and 60s wore on. The government of Mexico kicked off the expropriation movement between 1936 and 1938 with the confiscation of spacious plantations and ranches belonging to foreigners, including the property of the Sinclair Oil Group and Standard Oil of New Jersey. The seizure of humbler American-owned farms and ranches was underway in 1915, but multinational corporations had largely gone untouched. In 1937 Bolivia took the holdings of Standard Oil of New Jersey. Between 1959 and 1960 the Cuban expropriation routinely took property owned by US interests.

Between 1959 and 1962 Brazil's government expropriated the properties of the American Foreign Power Company and International

Telephone and Telegraph (ITT), while in receipt of aid under the US Alliance for Progress Program. A miffed US Congress passed legislation requiring foreign governments to either repay owners of expropriated property or receive no aid. As compensation, however, foreign companies received payment in fifteen-year government bonds affixed with a requirement that proceeds be reinvested in Brazil. Many countries adopted this formula for compensating owners of expropriated property, which allowed expropriating governments to opt for an annulment of debt by generating inflation. ITT complained that the bonds came without insurance against inflation.

In 1963 Standard Oil of New Jersey and ten other oil companies saw Argentine holdings slide into the jaws of expropriation, and between 1969 and 1971 the Peruvian government took large estates, mining interests and smelters and made payment with twenty-year bonds earning 5 per cent interest. The selling prices corresponded with the last five years' production.

Countries outside Latin America could hardly insulate themselves from expropriation. Iran, Iraq, Egypt and Indonesia are among Middle Eastern countries who practised expropriation. In 1951 the Iranian government commandeered the properties of the Anglo-Iranian Oil Company, in which the government of the United Kingdom owned a majority interest. Iraq moved more leisurely but nationalized its oil industry by 1975.

Indonesia unfurled the banner of expropriation on a wide scale. In July 1953 the Indonesian government expropriated the Bank of Java, the only Java note-issuing bank in 150 years. Indonesia recast it as a government-owned central bank, the Bank of Indonesia. The government pursued sporadic expropriation of Dutch owned enterprises, a disorderly process that lasted into the mid 1960s. In 1965 the last of the foreign-owned businesses, including oil interests, underwent expropriation.

The Suez Canal was appetizing prey in an era given to expropriation. An audacious Egyptian government claimed it in 1956, President Nasser of Egypt suggesting that canal revenue would underwrite construction of the Aswan High Dam, after the United States and the United Kingdom shelved offers to finance the construction. Soon after expropriation war broke out between Israel and Egypt, and British and

French military forces advanced upon Egypt vowing to keep the canal open for free passage. Egyptian forces sank 40 ships in the canal, sealing it off with an impenetrable and bulletproof blockade. Before the year was out the United Nations, with the United States playing a key role, hammered out a truce, and British, French and Israeli troops pulled out. The canal reopened as a nationalized company of the Egyptian government. By 1962 the Egyptian government had sweetened the deal by handing the original shareholders full payment in a negotiated financial settlement.

The expropriation wave reached its zenith in Chile between 1971 and 1973. On 11 July 1971, Chile's Congress unanimously ratified a constitutional amendment permitting the nationalization of mining interests, conferring upon the state unimpeachable dominion over all mines and mineral deposits. Three US companies, Anaconda, Kennecott and Cerro Corporation owned large copper mines that passed into the hands of the Chilean government. The Andino mine was newest, and its owner, Cerro, quickly settled with the Chilean government. It was unclear that Anaconda and Kennecott would collect compensation after subtractions for 'excess profits' earned in prior years. The Chilean government also became a buyer of stocks in foreign banks, by July 1971 making agreements to purchase three of the four foreign banks operating in Chile. In addition to holdings of US copper companies and a subsidiary of International Telephone and Telegraph, between 1971 and 1973 the Chilean government cast its expropriating net across sectors, intervening in, purchasing or confiscating the Bethlehem Steel Corporation subsidiary coal mine complex; Editorial Zig-Zag (one of the largest Chilean publishers); US-owned Anglo-Lautaro Nitrate Company; RCA of Chile; the Chilean petrochemical complex of Dow Chemical; and a closed Santiago Ford Motor plant.

After 1973 fears of future expropriations chilled and envenomed the foreign investment atmospherics in poorer countries. Expropriation graduated into an insurable risk, and insurance premiums upped the costs of doing business. In 1977 Liberia ousted two American firms, Sun Company, Inc. and Dynalectron Corporation, from part ownership in the Liberia Refinery Company. Bickering over the price of refined petroleum products preceded the expropriation. Before that year was out Angola also expropriated a Portuguese-owned oil company.

Expropriation equated to more than a weapon in the arsenals of prickly and impatient governments friendly to socialist ideas. Plausible economic thinking underpinned expropriation moves. Foreign-owned companies such as subsidiaries of ITT in Chile earned profits measured in the currency of the host country. To be sent home to US investors, these profits had to be converted into dollars. ITT counted on the Chilean government upholding the convertibility of its currency into dollars. Seen from the angle of the Chilean government, Chile earned dollars by selling goods to the United States, and ideally these dollars could be earmarked to purchase capital goods, tractors, factory equipment, and so forth, that aided Chilean economic development. Dollars sent back to the United States as profits of ITT subsidiaries subtracted from the dollars to purchase badly needed modern equipment. US-owned Chilean companies were also more likely to employ US citizens in higher paying jobs, robbing Chilean citizens of opportunities to acquire useful skills and experience. Expropriation empowered the Chilean government to force the employment of more Chilean citizens. Perhaps the temper of the times encouraged scholars to zero in theoretically on economic circumstances that favoured expropriation as a tool of economic development. According to Martin Bronfenbrenner, expropriation quickened the pace of economic growth 'in societies whose income distributions include high property shares not ploughed back into economic development'.[4] The clear-eyed cases for expropriation assumed that original investors received compensation without loss, perhaps through a foreign aid programme. In practice original investors were cheated of fair compensation and expropriation policies pushed countries into an isolationist corner that was only bearable because of heated and myopic competition between Eastern and Western blocs. Another drawback of expropriation lay in the difficulties that expropriated companies faced recruiting the crucial technical and managerial skills in local labour markets.

Exchange rate controls belong to another policy area in developing countries where the economics of depression stayed alive and flourished well into postwar years of prosperity. They also underscore the scepticism towards free markets that marked the 1950s and 60s. Early in the 1930s Germany unfurled a highly structured system of exchange rate controls, which dictated varying exchange rates across commodities and countries, and across different imports and exports. Soon most countries in Eastern Europe, as well as Denmark and Iceland, bowed to exchange rate controls. Japan also put together a detailed system of exchange rate controls equipped with a scale of varied exchange rates for imports and exports and types of goods. Various Latin American countries installed exchange rate controls in the 1930s. During World War II most countries turned to official or unofficial exchange rate controls. The Bretton Woods agreement pledged members of the International Monetary Fund to dismantle and bar exchange controls and systems of multiple exchange rates, and the United States threw itself into the forefront of the movement, but it was not until 1958 that ten Western European countries dissolved exchange rate restrictions on imports and exports, while keeping some exchange rate controls governing flows of capital. Until 1958 only eleven countries, all in the Western hemisphere, had eradicated exchange rate restrictions.[5]

Exchange rate controls thrived among developing countries long after developed countries had ceased to feel their lure. Just as Germany by elaborate exchange controls sidestepped devaluation in the early 1930s, developing countries in the 1950s and 60s harnessed a wider scale of exchange rate controls to rechannel devaluation pressures that arose from expansionary and pro-growth monetary policies. One popular species of exchange rate controls for developing countries was a discriminating system of multiple exchange rates. In a bid to enliven economic development countries enforced higher exchange rates for imports of capital goods than for imports of luxuries. The higher the exchange rate, the less imported goods cost homebuyers. Exchange rates varied for assorted imported goods depending upon how vital the goods were for economic development. Countries also extended help-ing hands to some export industries over others in the furtherance of economic development. In 1975 Colombia plied an exchange rate regime in which one US dollar equalled a mere 26.7 pesos if the dollar went to purchase coffee, a Colombian export with a wide and fortified market. Other Colombian exports enjoyed a kinder exchange rate of one US dollar per 35.2 pesos, so a dollar did not stretch as far buying Colombian coffee as other Colombian exports.[6] Countries custom-tailored multiple exchange rate regimes to snatch revenue from export industries that wielded monopoly or extra economic power, and boost newly fledged industries angling for foreign markets. Later, the 1990s saw a backlash to this kind of thinking. In 1975 the IMF listed the following countries in the column under multiple exchange rate regimes: Afghanistan, Argentina, Bahamas, Brazil, Chile, Colombia, Dominican Republic, Ecuador, Egypt, Ethiopia, Ghana, Guinea, Laos, Nepal, Paraguay, Peru, Somalia, Sudan, Turkey, Uruguay, Venezuela, Vietnam and Yemen.[7] No major industrialized countries were on the list.

INFLATION AND GROWTH IN DEVELOPING COUNTRIES

A glance at inflation rates highlights how developing countries coarsely slanted economic policies to the side of anti-depression policies. Inflation signals a 180 degree u-turn from the deflation of depression. The seductive logic of inflationary finance invited devel-oping countries to pay for land reform, social overhead capital, hydroelectric generating plants, and expropriation with the printing press. In theory, printing up money to pay for a hydroelectric generat-ing plant laid an open path for faster industrialization, putting a down payment on lasting economic development at the cost of passing infla-tion. The extra money had the welcome side effect of keeping up demand pressure on productive capacity, riveting production to the maximum level. A study of inflation rates and growth rates for the developing world between 1960 and 1970 reveals no transparent correlation between inflation and economic growth.[8] As inflation accelerated and economic growth decelerated worldwide in the 1970s, economists set to partially pinning the blame for stagflation on the accruing effects of long-term inflation. In Brazil prices were over 38 times higher in 1970 than in 1960, and Brazil's per capita GNP growth rate averaged between 2.5 and 3 per cent. In Chile prices in 1970 outdistanced prices in 1960 by a factor of 10, and Chile's per capita GNP growth rate averaged roughly 2.5 per cent. With a growth rate analogous to Brazil's, Argentina's prices multiplied 7 times between 1960 and 1970. Prices crept up less than threefold in Paraguay, which posted modestly weaker economic growth than Chile. In Uruguay the price level in 1970 was over 38 times the price level of 1960, but Uruguay muddled through roughly zero economic growth for the decade. Nearly stable prices becalmed Mexico, which luxuriated in a roughly 3.5 per cent growth rate. Venezuela registered even less inflation than Mexico but also fainter growth. Haiti enjoyed a bittersweet decade unsoiled with inflation but racked with negative growth in per capita GNP.

Data from the 1950s also cast up a kaleidoscope of results.[9] Cuba and Haiti boasted stable currencies, but idled economically. Brazil saw a riot of hyperinflation in the 1950s and galloping growth in real per capita income. Mexico had much less inflation than Brazil but also quieter economic growth. Between 1945 and 1959 economic lassitude in Chile and Bolivia lingered in the slipstream of hyperinflation. Venezuela and Nicaragua thrilled to boisterous growth with stable prices during the same time frame. Argentina, which purred to decent growth in the 1960s, languished between 1945 and 1959 amid monstrous hyperinflation.

In the 1960s inflation as a rule was less in Asia than Latin America. Only in South Korea did prices climb more than 60 to 70 per cent for the decade. In 1970 South Korean prices were nearly 3.5 times their 1960 level, and only Japan outpaced South Korean annual economic growth of over 7 per cent. Taiwan roughly matched South Korean growth but its prices rose a calmer 40 per cent for the decade. Iran reported lower inflation and growth than Taiwan. Malaysia bore the least inflation for the period but its growth rate barely topped 1 per cent.

Africa also dodged the raging inflation rates that beset Latin America in the 1960s. Prices doubled in Ghana while per capita GNP remained flat.

Prices were stable in Morocco, but economic growth a mere 1 per cent. South Africa witnessed inflation on a par with Morocco, but growth of nearly 5 per cent. Nigeria endured faster inflation than Morocco, but enjoyed a 1 percentage point higher growth rate.

These mixed inflation and growth numbers may indicate that inflation can be a symptom of weakness or strength. Inflation can be the normal measles and chicken-pox of economic growth. In a swiftly growing economy some sectors get ahead of others, shortages and bottlenecks sprout up, and prices shoot up in selected areas. On the weak side, inflation may rank among the deadly offspring of chaotic governments unable and unwilling to marshal tax revenue or borrow funds to pay for economic development.

ECONOMIC INEQUALITY AND LAND REFORM IN DEVELOPING COUNTRIES

The Depression of the 1930s unmasked in developed and developing countries the thorny issue of income inequality. The developed countries had reached a burgeoning and good-natured affluence that afforded a peaceable and modest redistribution of income thanks to graduated income taxes, higher minimum wages, protection of unions, support of education and social security programmes. In the 1950s and 60s economic growth in developed countries diffused and softened the income inequality issue. All boats rose with the tide of rising prosperity. Living standards in the United States took a breathtaking leap forward from the 1930s to the 50s, and the wealthy learned to be discreet. Talking about income inequality betrayed dullwitted ill-breeding.

Matters were different in the developing countries where income inequality festered in the postwar years, a gnawing issue unwilling to go away. Data on income inequality in developing countries is imprecise. A sample of data for 66 countries gathered through the Bank for Reconstruction and Development, available in the early 1970s, showed that countries with per capita income levels between $201 and $300 funnelled 67.9 per cent of all income earned to the top 20 per cent of income earners. For countries with per capita income levels between $101 and $200, and between $301 and $400, the top 20 per cent of income earners swept up a tidy 57 per cent of all income earned. Only the poorest countries, that is, countries with per capita incomes at or below $100, saw the income share of the top 20 per cent dip to 46.1 per cent. In countries where the per capita income stood above $1,000, the top 20 per cent of the income earners settled for a 44.9 per cent share of total income. In the United States the top 20 per cent of income earners reaped a 38.8 per cent share of total income, and in the United Kingdom a 39 per cent share of total income belonged to the top 20 per cent of income earners. In Ecuador a 73.5 per cent share of the income fell to the top 20 per cent. In Kenya, Sierra Leone, Iraq, Tanzania, Madagascar, Senegal, Rhodesia, Honduras, Turkey, Colombia, Brazil, Peru, Gabon, Jamaica, Mexico and Venezuela, the top 20 per cent income earners earned between 60 per cent and 69 per cent of total income. Not all developed countries exhibited a glaring disparity in income distribution. The share of income earned by the top 20 per cent fell within the 40 per cent to 45 per cent band for Chad, Niger, Korea and Taiwan.[10]

Delving into shares of total income going to the lowest 40 per cent of income earners bears out the severe income inequality. In the United States in the early 1970s the lowest 40 per cent of income earners collected 19.7 per cent of the total income and in the United Kingdom 18.8 per cent. In Mexico the lowest 40 per cent of income earners gained a scanty 10.5 per cent of total income. In Panama, South Africa, Jamaica, Gabon, Peru, Brazil, Colombia, Turkey, Ecuador, Honduras, Rhodesia, Iraq, Sierra Leone and Kenya, the lowest 40 per cent settled for no more than 10 per cent.

Per capita income between countries also exhibited glaring disparity. In 1971 annual GNP per capita stood at $5,160 in the United States, and $2,430 in the United Kingdom. In Mexico it was a measly $700. Taking Latin America as a whole, excepting Puerto Rico, annual per capita GNP ranged from a low of $120 in Nicaragua to a high of $1,230 in Argentina. Only three Latin American countries outside Puerto Rico (Argentina, Venezuela, Trinidad and Tobago) reported annual per capita GNP above $1,000. The populations of Malaysia, Pakistan, India,

Iran, Burma, Afghanistan, Philippines, Thailand, Turkey, Indonesia, Iraq, Jordan and Syria lived on per capita GNPs ranging from $80 to $450 per year.

Wide income inequality can favour economic development. Human wants for goods and services know no limits. Even in the wealthiest societies the supply of goods and services equates to a tiny cake against an endless and gargantuan appetite. If everyone received an equal slice of cake, it would soon be gone, with hunger still raging. It would leave society denuded of savings to finance capital investment. Handing a few individuals large slices of cake exalts them into an enviable position. They can save some cake without enjoying less than humbler members of society. Lifting a few lucky souls above average consumption levels puts pressure on them to consume. They can save and still outstrut the Joneses. Even in the face of unquenchable wants, society can marshal savings to finance the production and acquisition of capital goods. Otherwise production withers away since capital goods do nothing to directly slake the thirst of human wants.

Therefore income inequality can be a friend to economic development unless extra income goes into heavier consumption in place of higher savings. In the 1950s and 60s this resulted from high affluence in the developed world. When the wealthiest members of society in developing countries strove to stay neck and neck with consumption levels in developed countries, wider income inequality in developing countries yielded no savings benefits. Furthermore, the high consumption of wealthier members of society rubbed raw the divisions between rich and poor, resulting in a distempered and unbalanced state of political affairs.

In agricultural societies large ranches and plantations invited a head-on assault against income inequality. Farmers in the United States would have met with an outcry proposals to break apart ancient and spacious land holdings into smaller ones, but the US government often gave the nod to such schemes in Latin America. In many cases governments yielded to the intoxication of land reform without the spur of outside pressure. Like other policy initiatives of developing countries, land reform got going in the Depression. Mexico undertook land reform after the enactment of its revolutionary constitution in 1917, but not until

1938 did it grant land titles to peons receiving redistributed land. Before 1938 confiscated land remained in communal ownership. The postwar era saw a parade of land reform activity fanning out worldwide, touching virtually every developing country at some point.

In Bolivia a revolutionary regime began a programme of land reform in 1953. After broadening the voting franchise to all adults, it enacted a land reform law, confiscated the estates of large landlords, split them into small plots, and devolved ownership of small plots on native farmers. In 1960 Venezuela hailed a long-awaited land reform programme. Between March and the end of June the government handed over 500,000 acres to some 6,606 peasant families. An Agrarian Bank and Ministry of Agriculture buttressed the programme, advancing credit and technical assistance.

After hard and bitter debate Peru turned the corner on land reform in 1964. It had already taken baby-steps toward land redistribution. A new agrarian reform law sanctified the confiscation of all holdings of irrigated land above 150 hectares and all plantations of irrigable cultivated land above 300 hectares. Haciendas above 450 hectares of unirrigated land and all grazing ranches above 1,500 hectares also fell within the legal sweep of confiscation. Commercially held coastal plantations producing sugar, wheat and wool were spared. Owners received cash compensation up to 100,000 soles, and 20-year government bonds at 5 per cent interest for the remainder. Landless peasants bought land with long-term financing. To strengthen productivity the government applauded the establishment of cooperatives, and made available technical assistance and credit.

In 1964 Brazil created the bureaucratic machinery to back a land redistribution and colonization programme, and supply technical assistance. It signalled a new forward urgency to land reform in the north and northeast in 1971 with a new agency, Proterra. Funds were set aside for the purchase of land and reimbursement of land already expropriated. The new agency infused credit and technical assistance from below, and set price floors for exported products from above. Ecuador saw a round of land reform in 1966, launched by a military junta symbolically clothed in civilian dress, and at least outwardly wearing the guise of liberal reformers. The junta organized agricultural cooperatives carved out of idle lands from large estates. The cooperatives were populated with small farmers owning their own land. The reform drew idle lands into fruitful production and freed Indian peons from feudal shackles.

The US-sponsored Alliance for Progress, a foreign aid programme commenced in 1961 and ending in the early 1970s, cheered land reform in Latin America. It sent financial assistance to help achieve development goals. Aside from promoting industrialization and lifting agricultural productivity, this programme coaxed countries towards fairer income distribution.

Countries outside Latin America also courted land reform. One of the more successful land reform programmes surfaced in Taiwan. By 1955, 75 per cent of Taiwanese farmers proudly worked their own farms under this programme. The Taiwan government rained down funds to back projects for irrigation and control of insects and animal diseases. Six years of agrarian reform enriched rice yield per hectare 48 per cent.

A passion for land reform seized Egypt in 1952. For over a hundred years large cotton and sugar growers luxuriated in the upper strata of Egyptian society. Twenty per cent of agricultural land belonged to about 2,000 landowners, the king ranking among them. Another 13 per cent of the land belonged to smaller holders numbering above 2 million, while hordes of landless peasants eked out a bleak living on farms. In 1952 the Egyptian government put an upper ceiling on the size of individual and family holdings, and scaled back the upper ceiling in 1961 and again in 1962. These measures laid about 260,000 hectares at the feet of peasant families. Egypt dodged the disorderly and crippling pitfalls of land reform, and Egyptian agricultural output rose.

Early in the 1950s Burma made forays down a path to develop agriculture and enrich productivity. A phalanx of Burmese measures included redistribution of land, and ceilings on rent farmers paid for land, easing their debt burdens.

In 1958 a coup brought to power in Iraq a government loyal to land reform. The target of reform was large private estates farmed by peasants, but the government laid plans to distribute some state land. The confiscation of estates went in small and timid steps, and by 1961 a mere 880,000 acres had been redistributed, far shy of the proposed 9,300,000 acres the government set forth as a goal. As often happened with land reform, the transition was disrupting and at first production remained flat.

Soon after achieving independence in 1947, the national government of India undertook measures to split apart large estates, and redistribute the land. The landlords rallied to defend themselves in the supreme courts of several states, and effectively checkmated and stalled the land reform initiative. A history of land reform in India brings to light a fissure between rhetoric and action, between ideals and achievement. Half-hearted measures to consolidate holdings into cooperatives centred around villages. The imposition of ceilings on land holding has been tried on a piecemeal basis. Anything that might send critical food production into chaos was too risky for India's highly democratic government to tackle with resolute purpose. India's experimentation with a panorama of agrarian reform measures left observers debating whether it had conducted land reform, but land reform measures did unshackle peasants from a number of bitter rental relationships. Responsibility for passage and execution of land reform laws belonged to state legislatures. Many feebly rooted laws cracked through the legislative shell, probably more than in any other country, but their significance was diluted by timid enforcement.

From its inception in 1947 Pakistan fitted the archetype of countries bedevilled with a suffocating monopolization of arable land by colossal estates and absentee landlords. Tenant farmers tilled the land. The first crack at land reform in 1959 left large estates intact and only provided security of tenure for tenants. In the 1970s the Bhutto government enacted laws that curbed the size of land holdings, and compelled landlords to surrender excess holdings without recompense. Landlords aided and abetted by a sleepy government bureaucracy largely sidestepped the land reform aims. By the end of the twentieth century a tiny minority of wealthy landowners still held about half of Pakistan's arable land. Some corollaries of land reform boosted agricultural productivity, however, lifting Pakistan to self-sufficiency in wheat production by the late 1970s.

Land reform became the darling of the Philippine government in 1956, but angry landlords slowed land reform progress to a crawling speed. The concentration of land ownership may have even narrowed.

The government passed another land reform measure in 1963, but results remained disappointing. In the 1970s land reform in which farmers owned land they tilled remained out of reach.

In Algeria years of rhetoric about land reform ripened into action in 1973. The initiative belonged to a government trying to build a new political base. Within a few months the government distributed 618,000 hectares of land among 44,000 families. The programme subsidized new owners until harvest time, and set aside money to build 1,000 new villages.

The Iranian government decreed land reform in 1963, and no country outshone it in the originality of land reform initiatives. The government's plan called for buying villages from former landlords, and restructuring them as village cooperatives. Some 40,000 villages fell within the scope of the plan. It turned its back on land ownership for peasants, but entitled them to shares of revenue cooperatively earned by a village. Further proposals were made for large holdings that lay outside the first land reform initiative, affording large landlords several choices. One let them divide their land with sharecroppers according to the traditional shares by which the output of the land had been split between owners and sharecroppers. At first land reform inched forward to avoid rattling an already shaky business confidence, but by 1971 the Iranian government reported striking progress.

Developing countries in the 1950s and 60s were in a hurry to modernize their economies. In their eyes the highest hurdles to modernization lay in tradition and foreign influences. They cast aside ancient land tenure systems and rushed to expropriation of foreign investment. They ignited inflation striving to do too much with too few resources. Every developing country showcased an economic plan. The United States required Latin American countries to have an economic plan to meet a qualification for aid under the Alliance for Progress. Economic planning cast a spell over these countries anyway because planning and socialism belonged to newer thinking than laissez-faire capitalism, and the socialist sun appeared in the ascendant. Two world wars proved that unshackled capitalism bred internecine wars by parcelling up and reshuffling the developing world for exploitation by the developed world.

One of the more illuminating clues to the postwar global economic system can be spied in flows of foreign investment. As a country drives to its maturity developing natural resources, its income and savings multiply. Once resources become fully developed future investment decelerates unless fed by a burst of technological advance. Therefore it is normal for wealthy societies to save more than is needed for domestic investment. Investment opportunities in countries owning virgin and redundant natural resources woo these leftover savings. Following this logic, wealthy countries should tally up a net capital outflow against developing countries. The United Kingdom in the nineteenth century, the leading economic and technological power of the day, was the chief financier of foreign investment around the globe, backing the construction of canals, railroads and infrastructure in the United States. The United States soaked up a net inflow of capital until 1900.[11] By the mid-twentieth century, the United States had entered a lofty and dazzling level of affluence and infrastructure development. Expectations formed on the development trajectory of the United Kingdom foresaw the United States turning into a leading fount of foreign investment in developing countries. In the first decades after the war the United States exported foreign investment, but on a small scale when put side by side with the nineteenth century United Kingdom. As a share of per capita income the United States' foreign aid and direct foreign investment in the 1950s was one tenth the United Kingdom's foreign investment in the nineteenth century.[12] When foreign aid is measured as a proportion of GNP the United States' foreign aid during the 1960s and 70s was in the same league as the aid of Western Europe, Canada, Australia and Japan. The same set of countries outdistanced the United States in private capital flows as a proportion of GNP. The latter part of the twentieth century saw the United States slide over to the net debtor column vis-à-vis the rest of the world.

The United Kingdom of the nineteenth century and the United States of the twentieth century may owe changing historical conditions for the dissimilar ways in which they looked upon developing countries. In the nineteenth century the developing areas had yet to celebrate political independence, and technically superior countries were ready to dictate political stability and friendly government. The United Kingdom's military muscle gave confidence among investors that foreign holdings could be policed. International investors counted on gunboats to enforce international business contracts when necessary.

The first half of the twentieth century saw wars, depression and conflict between capitalism and socialism embitter and muddle the atmospherics for foreign investment. Amid high default rates and depression worldwide, cowed creditors shied away from riskier and unfamiliar investments. War remained a fresh and jarring memory. Developing countries stood torn between capitalism and socialism, seeking last-ditch answers to stubborn problems, and often living under the dark threat of civil war between conflicting factions armed by two superpowers. Acts of expropriation scared away foreign investment. Foreign investors fumed when developing countries favoured domestic firms over foreign firms in matters of taxation and regulation, or domestic labour over foreign firms when disputes flared up. Developing countries also shrank back from foreign investment. In the gospel of socialism foreign investment bore the stench of capitalist exploitation. The conspicuous and unprecedented rise of foreign aid and official development assistance in the 1950s and 60s can be diagnosed as another symptom of capitalism's dulled prestige and its corollary, the displacement of private enterprise with government action. When investor jitters and chilly host governments crippled private underwriting of investment needs in developing countries, public initiative filled the vacuum. The United States cleverly counterbalanced domestic savings with government budget deficits, safeguarding prosperity at home. Its stimulus to the world economy lay in open markets to products from all countries, making the United States market the locomotive of the world economy. Countries with high savings rates profited handsomely from this policy.

Chapter 5

The Ebbtide of Postwar Prosperity

The onset of the 1970s saw the global economics system moving quietly into bumpy air, an economic turning point analogous to that witnessed in the late 1940s and early 50s. Recall that foodstuffs and raw material prices from the mid 1930s through the 40s exhibited strength over prices in general. An economic expansion grew out of the black soil of depression, lasted during a wartime boom, and exhausted itself in a burst of postwar inflation. Rising food and fuel prices against prices of manufactured goods put pressure on real wages, and clashes between labour and management erupted. In 1947 the United States Congress, over a presidential veto, enacted the Taft-Hartley Act in answer to a rash of ugly strikes and work stoppages. This legislation sought to weaken unions after legislation of the 1930s had befriended and revitalized them. But scarcities of food, energy and raw material supplies eased at the end of the Korean War. The 1950s and 60s saw a hurried pace of economic growth lift Western capitalist countries to a dizzy height of affluence and vigour. Economists talked as if the unsolved problems and riddles in macroeconomics had only to do with fine-tuning. Economics textbooks triumphantly celebrated the Depression as a bogeyman that had been securely shackled. Economists recalling the economic policies that beat the Depression resembled generals proudly outlining unimpeachable strategies. The food shortages and soaring inflation of the late 1940s and early 50s faded into a discordant remembrance. Those outside the corridors of power voiced worries over budget deficits, inflation and the power of unions, but no Cassandra stepped forward to precisely envision and articulate the perilous corner the economy was about to turn. No one guessed that a replay of the late 1940s was a likelier scenario than a replay of 1929. The coming turn of economic events in the 1970s echoed the economics of the period between 1946 and 1951, but radiated wider and profounder repercussions. The inflation and shortages right after World War II did little to quiet the psychosis rooted in the Depression. Until the 1970s unemployment was public enemy number one, overshadowing inflation, and the cure for tangled economic troubles lay in more rather than less government regulation.

The 1970s exhibit a familiar pattern. Rising food, energy and raw materials prices outdistanced prices of finished goods, paring down real incomes of workers. A wave of inflation lifted all prices as workers pressed for wage hikes to recover lost purchasing power. Governments angrily scurried for ways to dilute union power. The late 1940s to early 50s had the same overtones. Perhaps the seeds for the 1970s turning point lay in uneven growth between the developed countries, including economic 'miracles' such as West Germany and Japan, and the developing countries. In the latter economic growth laboured against the headwinds of hesitant and dispirited foreign investment, though they held the likeliest prospects for latent potentialities in food and energy production.

Tension in markets for key foodstuffs and raw materials oozed to the surface in the period between 1965 and 1971.[1] Latin America switched from a net exporter of world grain to a net importer, and the USSR and Eastern Europe multiplied grain imports nearly sixfold. Asia enlarged grain imports. The United States quickened the tempo of grain exports and scaled back the amount of idle cropland.

Rising demand in the United States was directly felt in the energy field. In 1950 the United States exported energy, but demand outgrew domestic supplies, and by 1960 it imported 7 per cent of its energy.[2] Each upsurge in economic growth commanded a larger surge in energy consumption. In the United States crude oil imports grew from

10 per cent of domestic consumption in 1960 to 28 per cent in 1968, while the nominal world price of oil remained roughly even at $3 per barrel. Gently rising inflation rates in the US in the late 1960s chipped away at the inflation-adjusted price of crude oil until 1970. In March 1971 the Texas Railroad Commission unleashed 100 per cent recovery rates, innocently yielding supremacy over crude oil prices to the Organization of Petroleum Exporting Countries (OPEC). The United States no longer dictated a price ceiling by wielding the upper hand over production. Burgeoning environmental anxieties gummed up and convoluted the processes for opening new oil fields, holding up exploitation of new oil fields in Alaska and the outer continental shelf. The 1960s also saw US demand for natural gas sprint ahead of supply. Government regulation mishandled pricing, pegging the price of natural gas below profitable levels for drilling.

Supplies of another key commodity quietly tightened up in the late 1960s. In 1948 the United States held $25 billion gold reserves, roughly 71 per cent of the world's monetary gold reserves. US net gold reserves, that is, gold reserves minus US official and bankers' short-term liabilities to foreigners, stood at $18.6 billion. Subtracting these short-term liabilities still left a well-heeled United States 54 per cent of the world's monetary gold. The US incessantly ran balance of payments deficits, pushing the outflow of dollars above the inflow. The rest of the world, hungry for monetary reserves under the Bretton Woods system, welcomed the US deficits, revering dollars second only to gold as the preferred monetary reserve.

Gold production worldwide sagged amid rising private demand for gold. The United States outlawed the private ownership of gold as a monetary asset and forbade US citizens to purchase gold at the US Treasury or official agencies of foreign governments. Citizens of other countries faced no sanctions against owning gold, and foreign central banks sold gold to private individuals as world demand for gold mounted. Ordinarily rising demand for a commodity walks hand in hand with a higher price, enriching the rewards and profits of suppliers and rousing wider initiatives to enlarge supply. The price climbs, boosting the reward for producing and the penalty for consuming the commodity until the gap between supply and demand closes. In the case of gold, however, the United States decreed a fixed price of $35 per ounce, the price at which the US Treasury handled gold sales to official foreign agencies. Moving up the price of gold equated to devaluing the dollar. Since prices of everything but gold inched up, profits from gold production melted away. Only the dogged pursuit of a deflation policy in the United States could have created an enticement to unearth more gold.

In 1960 the United States still owned 44 per cent of the world's monetary gold reserves, but its net gold position ebbed away to $1 billion. In 1961 its net gold reserves flipped over to the negative position. Yearly the deficits grew wider, and more US gold reserves migrated to the rest of the world. The other advanced countries, Belgium, Luxembourg, France, West Germany, Italy, Netherlands, Norway, Sweden, Switzerland, the United Kingdom, Canada and Japan, beefed up their gold positions. By 1963 these countries possessed 46 per cent of the world's gold while US holdings shrank to 38 per cent.[3] At the annual meeting of the IMF in 1967 participants unveiled the Standard Drawing Rights, sometimes called paper gold, to gloss over the international shortage of gold reserves. In time US gold holdings evaporated to roughly $12 billion.

EXPERIMENTS WITH WAGE AND PRICES CONTROLS

With shortages brewing in food and energy, the US government eased up on jawboning, the policy of wielding government pressure to hold wage and prices hikes within a span of recommended guidelines. The new Nixon administration turned its back on jawboning as heavy-handed government meddling with private enterprise. The Consumer Price Index in the United States inched up, registering 2.9 per cent in 1967, 4.1 per cent in 1968, 5.4 per cent in 1969 and 5.9 per cent in 1970. Price indices around the world shared a kindred trajectory of quickening inflation. In the United Kingdom consumer prices registered growth of 2.5 per cent in 1967, 4.7 per cent in 1968, 5.4 per cent in 1969 and 6.4 per cent in 1970. In West Germany, consumer price inflation rose from 1.1 per cent in 1967 to 1.5 per cent in 1968, 2.6 per cent in

1969 and 3.7 per cent in 1970. In Japan consumer prices climbed 4.0 per cent in 1967, 5.4 per cent in 1968, 5.2 per cent in 1969 and 7.6 per cent in 1970. Consumer prices in France barely veered from the pattern, climbing 2.6 per cent in 1967, 4.7 per cent in 1968, 6.5 per cent in 1969 and 5.3 per cent in 1970.[4] France enforced a price freeze in the mid 1960s, which was replaced by a plan that counted on government leverage to hold prices down. The government owed its leverage to a far-flung system of national planning, which accounts for the variance in the French pattern.

The pick up of inflation touched off decisive policy somersaults in the United States and United Kingdom. After shunning voluntary wage and price guidelines, President Nixon in August 1971 decreed mandatory wage and price controls, marking the first time the US observed wage and price controls in peacetime. This policy u-turn was sudden and unforeseen. A year earlier an impatient and noisy Congress devolved upon the President statutory authority to impose wage and price controls, flinging down a challenge no one thought an avowedly conservative President would accept.

Step one, officially named Phase I, of the new controls froze wages and prices throughout most of the economy for 90 days. After 90 days Phase II replaced Phase I, lasting from November 1971 until January 1973. Phase II shoehorned a pliable margin of flexibility into a system of wage and price controls. It permitted wages to rise 5.5 per cent yearly, but afforded flexibility for gross inequities and low-paid workers. It let businesses pass on higher costs in the form of higher prices. Phase II let small firms and agricultural and imported commodities off the hook. It was billed as a system of wage and price guideposts in which observance of mandatory rules or standards was backed up by law. The responsibility for handling and executing Phase II lay in a dual administrative arrangement. The Pay Board set forth general policies on maximum pay increases, settling on the 5.5 per cent standard rate for labour contracts. The Price Commission administered price increases, setting its sights on keeping within an average of 2.5 per cent. It was estimated that labour productivity rose about 2.5 per cent yearly. Price increases in the order of 2–3 per cent annually could underwrite 5.5 per cent annual wage increases without squeezing profit margins.[5]

Phase III replaced Phase II on 11 January 1973. It came in the guise of a quasi-voluntary system. The government vowed to be hard nosed when needed, but packaged Phase III as a transition phase heralding a return to free markets for wages and prices. In 1973 supplies for foodstuffs and energy stretched drum tight. A poor harvest in 1972 sent food prices into a steep upward spiral of 20 per cent annual growth. In 1972 food prices went up 5 per cent for the year.[6] In 1973 prices of oil and other energy resources ignited, pushing up retail prices of gasoline and motor oil 39 per cent between September 1973 and May 1974.[7]

On 13 June 1973 President Nixon handed down a wage and price freeze for 60 days. Phase IV commenced on 11 August 1973 and lasted through April 1974, lifting controls on some industries while tightening the grip on others. Rising oil prices fuelled a skyrocketing inflationary surge in the first four months of 1974, propelling the annual inflation rate to the 15 per cent range. After 32 months Congressional approval expired and the programme of wage and price controls died. A chastened Congress made no offers to renew authorization for controls and the administration asked for none.

In the United Kingdom another conservative government under fire made an about face on economic policy. In the summer of 1970 the Conservative Party captured power after mouthing the gospel of competition, economic incentives and less government intervention in the economy, including collective bargaining. Instead this government resurrected programmes for handing out subsidies to ailing industries and firms. It enacted a hotly contested Industrial Relations Act that set out rules to regulate wage bargaining and strikes. Amid a tide of rising unemployment the inflation rate lifted to 9.4 per cent for 1971, although normally rising unemployment helps restrict inflation. The unemployment rate edged up from 2.6 in 1970 to 3.4 in 1971.[8] Early in 1972 resolute miners audaciously demanded a 25 per cent wage hike from the government. Recall that the coal industry underwent nationalization in 1947. The miners struck, disrupted power supplies and bent the government to their wishes after seven weeks. The miners' success stirred other unions to press harder for handsome wage settlements, and inflation took on galloping dimensions.

In the autumn of 1972 the Conservative government abbreviated a wave of inflation by freezing wages and prices. The freeze was scheduled to last from 90 to 150 days. The inflation rate finished at 7.1 per cent in 1972, down a bit from 1971, but weekly wage rates of manual workers grew 13.8 per cent, up from the 12.9 per cent the year before. Wages and salaries per unit of output rose 7.6 per cent, down from 9 per cent in 1971. Wage inflation nudged the government to embrace a statutory wage policy following the freeze. The freeze and controlled pay policy tranquillized inflation until oil prices exploded in the last quarter of 1973. Prices finished up 9.2 per cent in 1973, betraying an unmistakable acceleration over 1972. The growth rate of weekly wages for manual workers remained flat at 13.8 per cent. The winter of 1973–4 again saw miners daring to strike for higher pay. The government put the country on a three-day week to meet the crisis, and carried the issue into an election, which the Labour party won. The Labour party ratified and fortified the wage policy with a Price Commission with the power to veto price increases. Inflation still gathered momentum, measuring 16.1 per cent in 1974, and peaking at 24.3 per cent in 1975. When annualized inflation registered 35 per cent in August 1975, an anxious and dispirited Labour government unveiled a more explicit four-phase programme with specific guidelines for wage and price increases. Inflation grudgingly retreated to tamer rates of 16.5 per cent in 1976, 15.8 per cent in 1977 and 8.3 per cent in 1978. In 1978 Phase IV's 5 per cent inflation guideposts had been met when the flow of North Sea oil stoked the furnace of the British economy. The government despaired of enforcing the guideposts, and the loyalty of public sector unions toward the Labour government tapered off into a rash of strikes in the winter of 1978–9.

Every circumstance ensnared conservative governments in the United States and the United Kingdom into liberal policies to escape blame for an inevitable economic slowdown. A period of economic sluggishness and inflation was foreordained once skyrocketing energy and food costs crippled the fast-growing industrial sectors that had led postwar prosperity. West Germany shied away from wage and price controls, relying chiefly on disciplined money stock growth to curb inflation. This policy abbreviated inflation with equal but more lasting success. In 1973 inflation in West Germany stood at 6.9 per cent, at 6.2 per cent in the United States and 9.2 per cent in the United Kingdom.

DRAWING THE CURTAIN ON THE GOLD STANDARD

Far wider implications for the future lurked in another announcement President Nixon made in the televised speech of August 1971 announcing a freeze on wages and prices. In 1971 foreign governments and central banks held above $50 billion dollars. The United States Treasury owed these foreign governments ready redemption of dollars for gold. At a redemption rate of $35 per ounce of gold, the United States had handed over half of its gold stock since 1948. President Nixon shut the gold window at the Treasury, suspending the convertibility of dollars into gold and removing the keystone from the Bretton Woods system. The shrewdest financial experts from around the globe convened over the next two years to save a cherished but dying patient. No longer moored in the gold standard, the Bretton Woods system faced certain extinction.

Cracks in the foundation had come to light in the late 1960s. In November 1967, the British government devalued the pound from $2.80 to $2.40, a 14.3 per cent devaluation against the US dollar. The crisis brewed over years of balance of payments deficits and quick fixes. In 1968 confidence in the dollar reached a crisis stage. Speculators bought gold in the European gold market anticipating a devaluation of the US dollar, lifting the market price of gold above the official price of $35 per ounce. Outstanding dollars the United States owed to foreign governments and central banks and shrinking US gold stocks combined to feed worries of a devaluation. In the past the United States and other governments had sold gold out of their own stocks when necessary, pegging the market price at the official price. This time the United States and major European governments agreed to keep the price of gold at $35 per ounce for official transactions between governments, but let the market price of gold rise. It rose to $45 per ounce before the speculators blinked and the market price settled back to $35. A monetary crisis of international dimensions triggered further currency tweaking in 1969. Speculators bet heavily that West Germany was on the road to currency revaluation and appreciation. They sold French francs and bought German Deutsche Marks. The crisis only cooled after West Germany raised the value of the Deutsche Mark and France devalued the franc against the US dollar. In 1971 speculation against the dollar heated up in expectation that an official devaluation of the dollar lurked around the corner. Speculators sold dollars and purchased Deutsche Marks. In May 1971 West Germany let the Deutsche Mark float upwards against the dollar, and Switzerland, the Netherlands and Austria revalued domestic currencies upwards against the dollar to calm and defuse the crisis.

It is worth noting how often Germany marched in the forefront regarding matters of economic policy. In the 1880s Germany broke fresh ground with development of social insurance programmes, insuring workers against accident, sickness and old age. In the 1930s German thinker W. F. Bruck sketched the modern industrial enterprise as one that manages demand as well as supply, creating its own markets and financing producers and consumers, an idea later elaborated in the United States by J. K. Galbraith. In the 1970s West Germany became the first industrialized country swayed by the transparent logic that rising prices were merely a matter of money losing its value because there was too much of it. In other words, prices on average could never outgrow the money stock, an axiom West Germany welcomed as the key to combating inflation. History reminded West Germany better than other countries that keeping inflation at bay meant cracking the money stock whip. Thanks to post World War I hyperinflation and a post World War II currency debacle, Germany was the one country where inflation fears spawned more nightmares than depression fears. Recall that the Bundesbank was distinguished by sovereign independence and insulation from political authorities, and its lone mission lay in sustaining the integrity of the currency. Aside from booming West German exports to the United States, sound and disciplined monetary policies supported the rising value of the Mark. A boost in the value of domestic currency cools inflation since it scales back the costs of foreign produced goods against domestic produced goods, favouring foreign goods at home and abroad, and undercutting prices of goods produced at home.

In May 1971 West Germany navigated a watershed in economic policy when it suspended convertibility of the Deutsche Mark into dollars, and let the Deutsche Mark float unfettered. The Bundesbank turned up its nose at the mainstream policy of faster growth rate for West Germany's domestic money stock and dogged purchases of dollars with Deutsche Marks. Such a policy whetted rather than eased inflationary forces, and hoisted a white flag of surrender to a tide of global inflation. Neither did the West German government opt for capital controls, crimping the inflow of foreign capital and therefore foreign demand for Deutsche Marks. These policies would have kept the value of the Deutsche Mark down against the dollar and propped up the Bretton Woods system of fixed exchange rates, but at the cost of more inflation and/or more controls at home.

At first West German officials saw the free-floating Deutsche Mark in a holding pattern that awaited realignment of the system of fixed exchange rates and US restoration of dollar convertibility into gold. The 1920s taught the Germans that suspension of gold convertibility signalled hyperinflation and a breakdown of world trade. West German officials clung to the worldwide gold standard as a shield against inflation and monetary chaos, and spared no diplomatic pains efforts to save the Bretton Woods system. In December 1971 the finance ministers and central bank officials from the leading industrialized nations (West Germany, France, Japan, the United Kingdom, the United States, Italy, Canada, Belgium, the Netherlands and Sweden) descended on the old Smithsonian building in Washington DC, intent on brokering a fix for Bretton Woods. The conferees hammered out a fresh system of fixed exchange rates that devalued the dollar from $35 to $38 per ounce of gold. Japan, Germany and Switzerland consented to revalue their currencies upward against the dollar, and Britain and France kept the exchange rates of the pound sterling and franc unchanged against the dollar. The agreement buried the convertibility of dollars into gold, but enlarged the dollar value of US gold reserves. It permitted currencies in foreign exchange markets to fluctuate within 2.25 per cent above or below the official parities set by the new agreement.

In March 1972 six members of the European Economic Community (France, West Germany, Italy, Belgium, the Netherlands and

Luxembourg) agreed to cooperate in closer-knit monetary integration, to buy and sell their own currencies in support of a fixed exchange rate system among themselves, and to hold exchange rates fixed within a band of 2.25 per cent. They agreed to buy and sell dollars as needed to jointly maintain parity between member currencies and the dollar. Currency markets dignified these currencies as 'the snake in the tunnel'. The tunnel equated to the band of 2.25 per cent parity with the dollar. Britain danced to the tune of the snake for a couple of months.

The so-called Smithsonian Agreement soon fell to pieces. In mid 1972 Britain pulled out of the snake, and Britain and Canada let their currencies float. In January 1973 the United States started loosening wage and price controls. Edgy speculators around the world, fearing inflation in the United States, hurriedly abandoned dollars for Deutsche Marks, Swiss francs, Japanese yen and Netherlands guilders, all unimpeachable currencies. In the space of a week, the Bundesbank bought $5 billion, keeping the Deutsche Mark from rising above official parity against the dollar for a time. In February the United States devalued the dollar again, by 10 per cent this time, in a last ditch effort to rescue the Smithsonian Agreement, but time had run out. West Germany and Switzerland set their currencies afloat against the dollar, and other European countries soon cast their lot with the float. European countries still modulated exchange rate discordance between their own currencies as a forerunner to full and broad monetary integration. The 'snake in the tunnel' reincarnated as the 'snake in the lake'.

THE BIRTH OF FLOATING EXCHANGE RATES

The system of floating exchange rates saw light in 1973, an unofficial system since the IMF's constitution barred floating exchange rates. In 1976 members of the IMF officially rewrote the constitution to square it with a floating exchange rate system. Historically suspensions of currency convertibility into gold and precious metals occurred during wars, as measures to aid and accommodate wartime finance. England suspended convertibility of the pound sterling during the Napoleonic Wars; all belligerents suspended the gold standard during World War I and in 1971 the United States suspended convertibility of the dollar into gold amid an arms race and the Vietnam War. This last suspension logically evoked memories of past suspensions.

Since the 1950s a new school of economics, monetarism, had risen to distinction in academic circles. It taught that the value of money belonged to the sphere of supply and demand, and that inflation and a depreciating exchange rate merely signalled a money stock carelessly outgrowing a money demand. Money lost value out of overly abundant supplies, and depreciating money secreted inflation. Since government owns a monopoly on the privilege to issue money, it wields power to keep money stocks in line with demand and pre-empt inflation or deflation. Monetarists argued that in a market economy all prices yield to the dictates of supply and demand.

Monetarist thinking drew a devout following among staff and officials in the Deutsche Bundesbank, and in 1973 the leadership of the bank slipped into the mantle of full-fledged monetarism.[9] The flow of dollars into West Germany had fuelled a rapid growth in the money stock, which kindled speculative fever in real estate and housing markets. Monetarism in its most fundamental and unalloyed form says that money stock growth should never be allowed to veer from a modest and steady rate. It frowned upon officials who tolerated meandering and unmethodical monetary growth while single-mindedly chasing a targeted exchange rate, interest rate or unemployment rate. A non-fluctuating money supply growth rate should only be geared to the long-term growth rate in real output. The only target worthy of self-respecting monetary policy lay in a chosen rate of money stock growth.

The Deutsche Bundesbank in March 1973 took to reining in money stock growth. Although it raced ahead in the first quarter, the yearly growth rate for 1973 paled against growth for 1972. The Bundesbank's main measure of the money stock, central bank money (CBM) grew 8 per cent in 1973 against 14 per cent in 1972. M2 growth measured 14 per cent in 1973 against 17 per cent growth in 1972. M1 grew a mere 2 per cent in 1973 against 14 per cent in 1972.[10] M1 is the narrowest measure of the money supply, excluding time deposits, savings accounts and money market accounts, which are included in the broader measure M2. In 1974 it became clear that inflationary expectations obstinately remained elevated in the face of biting monetary restraint. Unions pressed hard for pay rises as OPEC quadrupled oil prices and the Bonn government, helping the economy weather high interest rates and oil prices, eased a tight fiscal policy. In 1974 CBM grew only 6 per cent while workers' wages grew 13 per cent. It was no surprise that output grew only 0.5 per cent.[11]

Monetarists cling to the idea that economic cycles feed on gaps between actual and expected inflation rates. Sluggish output walks hand-in-hand with weakening actual inflation relative to expected inflation. A sound and resolute monetary authority can broadcast plans to slim down inflation rates, and expected inflation retreats accordingly, easing economic stress and dislocation. In December 1974 the Bundesbank began publicizing targets for monetary growth. It announced a target of 8 per cent growth in CBM for 1975, signalling some slackening in the monetary reins from 1974. By broadcasting plans and developing a hawkish reputation for sticking to them, monetarist central bankers aimed to defeat the entrenched expectations of interminable inflation. They could then ratchet down actual inflation without prying open a raw gap between actual and expected inflation and touching off a brutal recession. By announcing policies and shunning policy surprises, a central bank helped the private sector develop plans rooted in realistic expectations.

A DIGRESSION ON OIL AND FOOD PRICES

Economic pressures and tensions had been mounting for several years to drive a harassed government in the United States to ditch the gold standard and welcome wage and price controls, a Conservative government in the United Kingdom to ape US wage and price controls, and a West German government to pioneer a new monetary strategy for combating inflation. These pressures and tensions were gentle compared to the rocketing world oil prices that turned the name of an international cartel into a household word in 1973. No other sudden and unforeseen economic development or shift in the 1970s put government policies through a test like the tenfold multiplication of oil prices between 1973 and 1981. A brief detour is in order to illuminate the history of a revolution in crude oil prices that hobbled the global economic system until the decade was out.

OPEC burst upon the world in 1960, founded by Iran, Iraq, Kuwait, Saudi Arabia and Venezuela. Six other countries, Qatar, Indonesia, Libya, the United Arab Emirates, Algeria and Nigeria, joined them in 1971. On 5 October 1971 Egypt and Syria attacked Israel, opening the Yom Kippur War. Israel enjoyed wide support in the West, which Arab oil-producing countries revenged by an embargo on oil exported to the United States and other Western countries. The power to control crude oil prices had passed from the United States to OPEC, a passage underscored by this episode. From 1972 to the end of 1974 the price of crude oil climbed from $3 to $12 per barrel. (OPEC set crude oil prices in US dollars.) From 1974 until 1978 crude oil prices rose in line with inflation in the US, lifting the price of a barrel from $12 in 1974 to $14 in 1978. In 1979 crude oil prices exploded again when Iranian oil production lessened in late 1978 after that country became embroiled in the chaos of political revolution. In 1980 war broke out between Iran and Iraq, choking off oil production in Iran, and also cutting into Iraq's. Between 1978 and 1981 crude oil prices climbed from $14 to $35 per barrel. The US government may have nudged the oil shortage along, as after the 1973 embargo it imposed price controls on domestic crude oil in a bid to spare the economy the ugliest ravages of stratospheric oil prices. Suppressed domestic oil prices eroded profits and rewards for oil exploration in the United States.

The tortuous assimilation of exploding oil prices accounts for the visible writhing of the global economic system through most of the 1970s and part of the 80s. A crippling shortage of crude oil marked a glaring failure of economic planning, the very thing economic planning laboured to avoid. Wage and price controls in the United States and United Kingdom sounded the dying gasp of the tacit and at times overt system of industrial planning that blossomed and crystallized out of the Depression. Unleashing government power to save it betrayed the store set on economic planning. Large firms that outlasted the 1930s never again wanted to find themselves trembling at the mercy of an unthinking and aimless market, and amassed the economic power to guarantee their own well-being. France and most developing countries openly articulated and embraced planning, and in the US informal planning calmed economic anxieties. Regardless of the country, economic planning failed to keep energy supplies abreast of growing demand, a deadly and irreversible failure.

Soaring oil prices afforded the United States a small reprieve from forces dragging down the dollar in foreign exchange markets, as it was less in need of imported oil than many industrialized countries. Imports outgrew exports in countries living on imported oil because of higher prices paid for oil. Rivers of currency outflows for burgeoning imports welled up in foreign exchange markets and undercut currency values. Between January 1974 and June 1976 the dollar rallied against the pound sterling, the Japanese yen and the Italian lira, sank slightly against the French franc, and just under 10 per cent against the Deutsche Mark.[12] The Bundesbank's policy of targeting monetary growth rather than interest rates led to unprecedented interest rate hikes in West Germany, exalting Deutsche Marks to foreign investors and speculators as a path to tantalizing interest rate earnings. The dollar depreciated notably from 1977 through 1979 but in 1981 sharply rallied in the face of doubling oil prices.

A huge food price inflation was almost lost in the glare of the monstrous oil rise. In 1973 food prices in the United States showed annual growth rates of 12.3 per cent in the first quarter, 18.3 per cent in the second, 15.4 per cent in the third and 19.2 per cent in the fourth. In 1974 food prices leaped up 17.4 per cent in the first quarter, 11.5 per cent in the second, 7.1 per cent in the third and 13.7 per cent in the fourth. Food price inflation slackened in 1975, posting double-digit rates only in the third quarter. Poor harvests had touched off a food scarcity. Wheat production in the Soviet Union lost 13 per cent from 1971 to 1972.[13] Droughts and monsoons bedevilled developing countries. An odd turn of events, the disappearance of the fabled Peruvian anchovies, took away an important source of protein-rich animal feeds, sending the prices of alternative animal feeds spiralling upwards.[14] Despairing activists sighed at competition between livestock and humans for limited supplies of feed grains. High grain prices triggered a slaughter of livestock, delaying an acceleration of meat prices until 1975.

A ubiquitous trend of rising foodstuffs, raw material and energy prices hamstrung economic growth in the developed world. Exploding oil prices above all threw sand in the gears of the industrialized economies. The leading sectors in these economies turned out energy intensive goods such as automobiles and consumer durables. Statistics on economic growth and inflation-adjusted hourly compensation of workers sketch a snapshot view of what happened in leading industrialized countries. After reporting yearly real GDP growth averaging 4.0 per cent between 1963 and 1972, the United States saw real GDP growth dip to -0.06 per cent in 1974, and -1.2 per cent in 1975.[15] West Germany averaged 4.5 per cent yearly real GDP growth between 1963 and 1972, but muddled through 0.5 per cent growth in 1974 and -1.6 per cent in 1975. Japan, scoring an eye-catching 10.5 per cent average yearly real GDP growth between 1963 and 1972, surrendered to a plummet of -1.2 per cent growth in 1974 and a faintly positive 2.4 per cent growth in 1975. The United Kingdom, averaging a weak 2.8 per cent yearly real GDP growth between 1963 and 1972, saw bloodier carnage, registering -1.8 per cent growth in 1974 and -1.1 per cent in 1975. France weathered and processed the economic jolt better than most. Its average yearly real GDP growth tapered off to 3.2 per cent in 1974 and 0.5 per cent in 1975 against an average of 5.5 per cent between 1963 and 1972.

The growth rates in all these countries rebounded to positive territory from 1976 through 1979, aided by a quieter oil market. Exploding oil prices in 1979 again rocked the major industrialized countries. By 1979 these countries had largely bounced back to full employment, but decent growth in real GDP had a hollow ring, masking longer-term dislocations to industrialized economies. Statistics on growth rates of real (inflation-adjusted) hourly compensation uncover the subterranean agitation that fanned out as these economies swallowed and digested unprecedented oil prices. Between 1962 and 1969 real hourly compensation for individuals with jobs advanced on average 3.4 per cent annually in the United States. This statistic retreated slightly to an average 2.7 per cent annual growth between 1970 and 1973, but sank to -0.3 per cent average annual growth between 1973 and 1975, and averaged a mere 1.9 per cent annual growth between 1975 and 1978. Between 1962 and 1969 Japan's annual real hourly compensation growth was in the order of 8 per cent. Between 1969 and 1973 this jumped to

11.6 per cent, but it fell back to 5.3 per cent between 1973 and 1975, and 2.2 per cent between 1975 and 1978. West Germany's growth in real hourly compensation averaged 5.4 per cent per year between 1962 and 1969, 8.2 per cent between 1969 and 1973, 5.7 per cent between 1973 and 1975, and 3.3 per cent between 1975 and 1978. France's real hourly compensation grew yearly in the 5 per cent range for all time periods from 1962 through 1978, but dropped off between 1975 and 1978. The United Kingdom's real hourly compensation steadily grew through 1975, averaging 2.9 per cent yearly growth between 1962 and 1969, 4.6 per cent between 1969 and 1973, 6.3 per cent between 1973 and 1975. Between 1975 and 1978 average yearly growth in real hourly compensation screeched to –1.3 per cent.[16] Negative growth rates in real hourly compensation of workers cruelly crushed the cheerful expectations of the postwar era. The confident hope that each generation would jauntily stride up the stairway of economic progress could no longer be counted on. Negative growth cleared the field for other economic philosophies to come forward and hold out the pleasing prospect of a return to the days of rising living standards for rank and file workers.

Rising prices of foodstuffs, raw materials and crude oil spawned golden opportunities to invest in developing countries, gaining it a dignity not seen since the 1920s. Oil-rich Middle Eastern countries, awash in dollars, acted to rechannel global capital toward developing countries. Some of the best opportunities for expanding production of foodstuffs, raw materials and crude oil lay in the developing world. From 1975 to 1979 debt to foreign banks multiplied 4 times in Argentina, 2.49 times in Brazil, 5.6 times in Chile, 2.27 times in Mexico, 3.12 times in South Korea, and 2.5 times in Thailand. International financial markets waxed more international, widening their scope for easier and friendlier entrées to developing countries.

The rising cost of imported oil also weighed on developing countries. Costly oil imports soaked up scarce dollars, subtracting from dollars left over to pay for the industrial products that economic growth requires. Not all the credit for these capital flows belonged to exploding oil prices. Mexico was a net exporter of oil and still multiplied its indebtedness to foreign banks by a handsome factor. Mexico averaged 6.8 per cent yearly growth in real GDP between 1970 and 1974.

A global economic deceleration dragged down its growth to a low of 3.4 per cent in 1977, but between 1978 and 1981 it had yearly growth rates above 8 per cent for four straight years.[17] During those years doubling oil prices threw the developed countries once again into confusion and recession. In 1980 European countries collectively, and United States and the United Kingdom in particular, slid to negative growth. In 1981 both West Germany and the United Kingdom posted negative growth, and France posted a scanty 0.4 per cent growth.[18]

Some developing countries besides Mexico exhibited a healthy immunity from the economic turmoil and strain wrought by rising foodstuff, raw material and energy costs. Between 1977 and 1981 average real GDP growth per year stampeded above 10 per cent in Paraguay. Between 1977 and 1981 Chile luxuriated in yearly growth rates averaging above 8 per cent. In 1980, when the United States and Europe slipped into negative growth territory, Latin America as whole averaged an upbeat 5.1 per cent growth. In 1981 Latin American growth paled to 1.7 per cent as the global economy sickened with a recession that broke out in industrialized countries.[19]

One might guess that brisk growth in oil exporting countries brought up the average growth overall for developing countries. If developing countries are split into two groups, net oil exporters, and net oil importers, net oil exporters boast loftier growth rates than net oil importers. Between 1978 and 1981 net oil exporters among developing countries logged average yearly real GDP growth of 6.8 per cent. For the same years oil importers among developing countries logged average yearly real GDP growth of 4.35 per cent.[20] Among developing countries, neither oil exporters as a group, nor oil importers as a group, saw real GDP growth drop into negative territory for even one year between 1978 and 1981. A comparison of average yearly growth in per capita GDP between a World Bank grouping of oil exporting countries and a World Bank grouping of severely indebted middle-income countries throws light from another angle. Oil exporting countries saw yearly per capita growth average a lively 7.3 per cent between 1965 and 1973. That yearly average percentage fell back to 4.9 per cent between 1973 and 1980. Severely indebted middle-income countries enjoyed marginally less yearly growth between 1965 and 1973, posting a healthy average of 6.4 per cent. It is noteworthy that these latter countries underwent a gentler drop off in per capita growth between 1973 and 1980, posting a still sound average of 5.2 per cent.

EAST ASIA STANDS AT THE THRESHOLD

One set of numbers stands out as a clear portent of the future. From 1965 through 1973 only one group of countries posted average yearly per capita real GDP growth above the 5.2 per cent average rate of severely indebted middle-income countries. The bustling countries of East Asia between 1973 and 1980 roared to an average annual per capita real GDP growth of 6.5 per cent, outdistancing the average per capita growth of 4.9 per cent for the oil exporting countries.[21] Growth among a galaxy of exuberant nations in East Asia would later lift the per capita income of Hong Kong above the per capita income of Great Britain, holding up for the world's eyes the singular case of a colony logging higher per capita income than the parent country. This quirky but intelligible incongruity lasted until possession of Hong Kong passed over to China in 1997.

The advance of the East Asian countries to the frontlines of economic growth offered the most fruitful and illuminating clues and hints about what the future held in store for laissez-faire capitalism. The secret of the birth and flowering of capitalism probably lies in the history of Hong Kong and Singapore in the second half of the twentieth century. Like Venice at the dawn of capitalism, and Amsterdam in the early days, Hong Kong and Singapore are city-states. Capitalism may be a means of maximizing productivity and spurring economic development in small states battling to uphold independence from a neighbouring empire on the make. Venice had the Ottoman Turks for a rival, and Amsterdam worried about France with good reason. The growth of an aggressive communist state in China may have flung down a grim challenge that stung Hong Kong, Singapore, Taiwan and South Korea into forward growth.

Whatever the impetus that ignited economic development, it stirred alive an area once thought culturally and philosophically fated to sleepy backwardness and lassitude. Confucian philosophy accorded only a low order of talent to individuals engaged in commercial and trading activity. The worship of ancestors was not calculated to promote modernization. Confucian philosophy favoured contentment and order over change and excitement, scholarship over scientific and technical prowess, and courtesy and wisdom over greed, litigation and the scramble for wealth. Confucian-trained government officials coached governments to follow isolationist policies. Europeans saw in Confucian philosophy the symptom of a dry and inert civilization. Some argued that European capitalism owed its zesty dynamics and growth to finer cultural and philosophical values and ideas. While Europeans observed that Confucian-trained government officials scored few marks for progressive leadership, they did not grasp that workers reared on Confucian values made good-natured and intelligent employees. Confucian exaltation of hard work, frugality, discipline, order, family, courtesy and education yielded tantalizing dividends in the workforce, even if it missed the Western-style education vital for leadership at the uppermost levels.

Other factors may also be at the bottom of the spirited economic growth in East Asia. When distributing foreign aid, the United States favoured countries that neighboured and defied communist countries. East Asia was an area where the war between capitalism and socialism raged white-hot and seemed everlasting. Whatever the underlying causes, East Asia would be the seat of another economic miracle before the century was out.

In summary, the global economy turned a corner about 1972 and entered a new era. Economic growth in the developed world faced more headwinds. Governments cast aside the last remnants of the gold standard. Conservative governments in the United States and the United Kingdom pulled off a sudden about face, and championed wage and price controls in a bid to keep alive a long and unprecedented post-war prosperity. Tightening supplies of foodstuffs, raw materials and energy opened investment opportunities in the developing world. Intoxicating progress in global communication and transportation multiplied the impetus to globalization from these opportunities. Rank and file workers in developed countries saw setbacks in real wages and hopes evaporate of forever rising living standards. The newest in the ranks of the conspicuously rich were royal families in resource-rich developing countries rather than the successful inventors and entrepreneurs in the developed countries. Venice and Amsterdam, legends of early capitalism, struggled uphill against a natural resource void. The city-states of Hong Kong and Singapore, outshone in resource endowment by the oil-rich Middle Eastern countries, put their houses in order to become the 'economic miracles' of later decades.

Chapter 6

A Tug of War between Inflation and Economic Controls

THE RISING TIDE OF INFLATION

To the devout disciples of conservative doctrine, the gold standard belonged with the holy of holies. Casting aside some economic policies might be short-sighted and unwise, but casting aside the gold standard was taboo. Outrage remained muted merely because the gold standard's undoing came to fruition under the watch of an avowedly conservative president. Many observers chalked it up as passing expedient.

The economics profession barely found the issue worth mentioning in textbooks. One thousand members of the American Economic Association signed a petition decrying the Smoot-Hawley Tariff of 1930, but few economists did honour to the fallen gold standard. Mainstream economists probably viewed dumping the gold standard a benchmark of progress rather than a red flag of alarm. According to the best economic thinking of the day the gold standard was something that got in the way more often than not. It stood at odds with implementation of policies that were direct corollaries of modern advances in economic science. Those who resurrected remembrances of Germany's post World War I hyperinflation were dismissed as crackpots.

Gold standard loyalists seemed to have little knowledge of the mechanics and intricacies of the global financial system or of approved doctrines in economics. If their dire warnings of inflation turned out to be on target, it could only be by chance, since they could not know what they were talking about. Stalwarts of the gold standard seemed innocently unaware that their economic theories had long been consigned to oblivion. Three decades of economic events have now passed since the break with the gold standard. In these three decades economies have been studied as never before, yet nothing has turned up among economists to trim opinions on the gold standard. In the eye of economics, it remains a dead artefact of a less informed era. It outlived its usefulness.

While ousting the gold standard squared with mainstream economic thinking then and now, it must be conceded that global inflation rates climbed steadily after 1971. The fault may lie with other missteps in economic policy rather than abbreviation of the gold standard, but the 1970s became a decade of inflation. Maybe it took time to fathom the intricacies and forge the methods of a workable inconvertible paper standard. Disciples of the gold standard might argue that the verdict of history remained a better guide than economic theory.

The United States had an average annual inflation rate of 3.5 per cent between 1963 and 1972. That was the average growth rate of the GNP price deflator for those years. The GNP deflator habitually reported a smaller inflation rate than the consumer price index. Using the GNP deflator, United States inflation rate inched up to 5.7 per cent in 1973, and to 8.8 and 9.3 per cent respectively in 1974 and 1975. Recession dragged inflation down to 5.2 per cent in 1976 and 5.8 per cent in 1977 before it heated up to 7.4 per cent in 1978, blazed through 8 per cent in 1979, and logged 9.3 and 9.4 per cent respectively in 1980 and 1981. Inflation headed into remission in 1982.

Steep and unyielding inflation was not unique to the United States. The trend echoed in other developed countries although the levels varied. Between 1963 and 1972 the United Kingdom weathered an average annual growth of 5.2 per cent in its GNP price deflator. Inflation flared up to 7.0 per cent in 1973, and to 14.9 and 26.9 per cent respectively in 1974 and 1975. Then it retreated to the 14 per cent range for 1976 and 1977, dipped to 10.9 per cent for 1978, and turned up to reach a peak of 19.2 per cent in 1980. Then the inflation rate sank, logging in at 8 per cent in 1982. France averaged 4.8 per cent annual inflation of the GDP deflator between 1973 and 1972, accelerated to 7.8 per cent in

1973, 11.2 per cent in 1974 and 13.3 per cent in 1975. Then it dropped to the 9 per cent range between 1976 and 1978 before posting modest yearly advances, touching 12.1 per cent in 1982.

Japan's inflation graphed a paralleling contour with a small twist. After averaging yearly rates of 4.7 per cent between 1963 and 1972, Japan saw inflation swiftly spiral upwards to 11.7 per cent in 1973 and 20.6 per cent in 1974. Worldwide tightening of foodstuff, raw material and energy supplies hit the Japanese economy hard. In 1973 a 'food supply crisis' reverberated in the Japanese media. In the space of a year soybean prices more than tripled. The United States, combating inflation at home, had banned exports of soybeans to Japan. Japanese supermarkets became scenes of panic buying for cooking oil, sugar, soy sauce, toilet paper and salt. Supplies of construction materials and industrial raw materials dried up, and prices soared. Land prices spiralled upwards. The public raised a howl about 'crazy prices', and in 1974 workers won hikes of 32.9 per cent in basic wages.[1] The government inflicted a stringent monetary policy, including restrictions on real estate financing. Inflation scares inspired the monetary backbone to dispatch inflation without delay. Japanese inflation fell back to 8.1 per cent in 1975, and steadily inched downward every year. From a 2.6 per cent rate in 1979, Japanese inflation bumped up to 2.8 per cent in 1980 and then retreated to 2.0 per cent in 1982.

In the 1970s even West Germany, the most inflation-wary of the developed countries, faced trouble keeping a lid on inflation. West Germany was the one country that handed its central bank the sole mission of watchdog over the integrity of its currency. Between 1963 and 1972 West Germany rode out average annual inflation rates on the GDP deflator of 4.1 per cent, slightly above the US average in the same time span. West German inflation remained a few points above the US average in 1973 at 6.5 per cent. At this point West Germany's early assimilation of monetarist economics began to pay dividends. In 1974 West German inflation crept up only 0.3 per cent to 6.8 per cent, while inflation in the United States rose 3.1 percentage points above the rate the previous year, and France, the United Kingdom and Japan saw more glaring increments. Between 1974 and 1978, West Germany logged milder inflation rates than any of these countries. West German inflation ranged between 3.4 per cent in 1976 and 4.8 per cent in 1982. Between 1979 and 1982 West Germany scored the lowest inflation record of these countries, aside from Japan.[2]

The rising tide of inflation overran the developing world as well. In Argentina annual inflation averaged over 50 per cent in the 1940s, then softened to 23 per cent annually between 1961 and 1965. Inflation really took off in the early 1970s, averaging a wild 293 per cent annually between 1974 and 1976. When the decade was out, Argentine inflation had fallen back to the 170 per cent range. It escalated again in the 1980s. Through the 1950s and 60s annual inflation in Chile pulsated between 20 and 40 per cent. In 1971 the Chilean government clamped down with wage and price controls. In 1972 inflation galloped to 163.4 per cent, reached an unnerving 508.1 per cent in 1973, and cooled to 375 and 340.7 per cent respectively in 1974 and 1975. A right-wing military government gave Chile a sobering dose of monetarist discipline, and inflation retreated to 35.1 per cent by 1981.[3] Brazil saw inflation rates rise from the 20 per cent range at the end of the 1960s to 77 per cent by 1979. Inflation rallied to an 83 per cent annual average in Uruguay between 1971 and 1974.

These severe inflation episodes were symptomatic of a general rising inflationary tide in developing countries, where between 1965 and 1971 consumer price inflation averaged 13 per cent.[4] During 1972 consumer price inflation averaged 6.6 per cent in Asia, 19.4 per cent in the Western hemisphere, 4.8 per cent in Africa, 9.6 per cent in Europe and 6 per cent in the Middle East.[5] By 1979 inflation had more than trebled from pre-1973 levels in Africa and the developing countries of Europe, more than doubled in Western hemisphere developing countries, and multiplied fivefold in Middle Eastern countries. After averaging 17.2 per cent between 1973 and 1975, inflation in Asia fell back to 6.1 per cent in 1979, but climbed to 11.1 per cent in 1980. In 1980 consumer price inflation stood at 14.7 per cent in oil exporting countries against 32 per cent in non-oil exporting developing countries. Between 1973 and 1980 inflation rates in oil-exporting countries remained roughly half of inflation rates in non-oil exporting countries.

Another food shortage bubbled up in 1979 and 1980. Tons of food grain shipped into Bangladesh nearly trebled between 1977 and 1980.

Pakistan saw imported tons of food grain more than double between 1978 and 1979. Food shortages vexed the whole developing world: India doubled imported tons of food grain between 1970 and 1975; Pakistan expanded tenfold imported tons of food grain and in South Korea government prices for rice procurement rose 45 per cent in 1973 and another 25 per cent in 1974 and 1975.[6]

It must be conceded that the data clearly authenticates quickening of inflation worldwide in the 1970s. Inflation shot up in every corner of the globe. In older times deafening cries to bring back the gold standard would have risen up amid this scourge of inflation. In the 1970s countries pinned the blame on official inexperience at managing money stocks without a disciplining gold standard. Bullish tactics of workers striving to recover lost purchasing power bore a share of the blame. One way or another inflation signified a foreordained penalty for misguided, maybe undisciplined economic policy and the solution lay in more modern policies, not in reinstatement of primitive anachronisms. President Ford articulated the subterranean change gradually taking hold in the social consciousness when he branded inflation 'public enemy number one'.[7] In time fear of inflation displaced fear of unemployment as the psychosis driving economic policy, but the psychology changed slowly. President Ford lost the next election and inflation fears were not at once exalted above unemployment fears in the social consciousness.

A LOCOMOTIVE FOR THE GLOBAL ECONOMIC SYSTEM

The idea of reinstating the gold standard was roundly put out of court. The gold standard as an enemy to economic growth had aroused suspicion even in the nineteenth-century United States. Developing and newly fledged countries feared that economic growth would be the prime casualty, and economic growth kept hope alive for them. It held the answer to breaking the bonds of mass misery. Inflation came under less criticism. Rural agricultural societies can turn to barter when money breaks down. The highest worry among policy makers worldwide centred upon lethargic and irregular growth in the global economy. They assumed all boats rose and fell with the tide. Unfortunately, the return to economic growth in the mid 1970s proved to be a short-lived affair.

The favoured theory for stoking the furnace of the global economy was the 'locomotive' theory, a species of demand management theory. Most of the world's governments pressed the powerful and advanced economies, the locomotives of the global economy, for expansionary monetary and fiscal policies, hoping to ignite a worldwide growth surge. The United States, West Germany and Japan belonged in the locomotive class. Advancing income in these countries, the theory held, multiplied world demand for exports from smaller and cruder economies. Assuming imports kept abreast with advancing income in the United States, West Germany and Japan, prosperity in these countries opened a better market for products of developing countries.

The locomotive theory met with a chilly welcome in West Germany and Japan. These countries pledged themselves to suffocating inflation even at the cost of domestic economic growth. Keeping a lid on inflation at home ran foul of a policy that nurtured a climate of strong spending at home. Kindling a domestic prosperity that spilled over to other countries held no charm for West Germany and Japan.

The United States threw itself with more heartiness into the role of economic locomotive. In January 1977 President Carter unveiled a fiscal stimulus package with a rebate of personal income taxes. The tax cut was later withdrawn after reports of heady economic growth beat expectations. Federal Reserve officials zeroed the monetary sights in on a desired federal funds rate (the interest rate at which commercial banks can borrow reserves from other commercial banks) and money stocks were expanded as needed to realize that rate. The Federal Reserve permitted the federal funds rate to rise over much of 1977 and then level off until mid 1978. Inflation advanced parallel with the federal funds rate, neutralizing any monetary tightness attending rises in the federal funds rate. A 1 percentage point addition to interest rates coupled with a 1 percentage point addition to inflation left real interest rates, that is, inflation-adjusted interest rates, untouched. Through 1977 and 1978 US money stocks grew at a pace that ratified and fed inflation.

The clearest barometer of lax monetary expansion appeared in exchange rates for the dollar. Imports leaped in front of exports, advancing the outflow of dollars against the inflow and undercutting the value of the dollar. At first the dollar held its ground against key currencies under the flexible exchange rate regime. Against the Japanese yen it remained roughly even between 1972 and 1976. It lost ground against the Deutsche Mark and gained ground against the pound sterling. In 1977 the US government spared no pains reminding the world that it believed the flexible exchange rate system was working intelligently, and that the US would take no steps out of the ordinary to shore up the dollar in foreign exchange markets. It sounded as if US officials felt that West Germany and Japan should do their part and enlarge their imports by raising the value of their currencies. Japan above all lay under the suspicion of keeping the yen cheap in foreign exchange markets. A cheap yen aided Japanese exports, and made foreign goods costly in Japan. The United States saw that a sinking dollar effectively lifted the value of the Deutsche Mark and the yen, leaving West German and Japanese exports more costly against exports priced in dollars. As West Germany and Japan exported less, they imported more. Imports became less costly as domestic currency gained value against other currencies in foreign exchange markets.

US officials denied signalling a preference for a weaker dollar, but that was the signal that foreign exchange markets heard. The dollar commenced declining in 1977. The last half of 1977 saw the dollar sink 10 per cent against the Deutsche Mark, 10.3 per cent against the yen, and 18.7 per cent against the Swiss franc.[8] The strong currencies overtook the dollar. Against a wider spectrum of currencies the dollar sank only 5 per cent. At first a deepening current account deficit on the balance of payments belied the expected useful effects of a sinking dollar. In balance of payments maladjustments, matters tend to worsen before they improve even when the necessary adjustments are in the right direction. Sales of Japanese automobiles in the United States kept growing in the face of a rising yen, which pushed up the cost of Japanese goods. Cheaper prices of US exports of foodstuffs and raw materials failed to raise demand proportionately.

In 1978 worry about a sagging dollar mounted at home and abroad. The Federal Reserve started nudging up interest rates, easing selling pressure on the dollar and toughening the assault on inflation. The United States also sold off gold stocks to prop up the dollar. At an economic summit in Bonn, Germany, in July 1978, the West German government pledged legislation to boost government spending at home. Japan vowed to whittle down its trade surplus by beefing up domestic spending and voluntarily holding back exports. The United States promised attention to reduction of oil imports and inflation.

In October 1978, Congress stamped approval on an overhauled version of legislation that the Carter administration had unveiled in April 1977, tackling energy dependence and usage. Debate and negotiations over energy policy brought to light a mood drift favouring free markets. The cornerstone of the Carter plan lay in conservation. Earlier President Ford proposed decontrol of domestic oil prices. Congress turned up its nose at Ford's full deregulation, still harbouring distrust of free markets, and enacted gradual deregulation of domestic crude oil prices. Under Carter's energy proposal, oil from existing wells remained regulated, but oil from new wells went unregulated. Tinkering with this provision in Carter's proposal led to a plan for graduated deregulation of all oil prices, but deregulation came faster for oil from new wells than oil from old wells. Congress also gave the nod to gradual deregulation of natural gas prices over Carter's proposal to elevate the regulated price. Hints of confidence in economic planning show in Carter's address on 20 April 1977 in the words: 'With proper planning, economic growth, enhanced job opportunities, and a higher quality of life can result even while we eliminate the waste of energy.' Carter's proposal embraced a gas-guzzler tax on automobiles. Among the celebrated offspring of energy legislation under the Carter administration are a cabinet level Department of Energy and a windfall profits tax against oil companies, which stood to gain massively from rising domestic oil prices.

The Carter administration welcomed the use of controls to attack energy problems, but stood firmly against compulsory wage and price controls. After inflation boiled over the Carter administration in October 1978 launched a programme of voluntary wage and price guidelines. Price escalation of cost of living expenses reached scary proportions by US standards. In 1978 the price of meat rose roughly 20 per cent, homeownership climbed 12.4 per cent, and used cars rose 13 per cent.[9] The guidelines counted on willing compliance, but spawned an administering bureaucratic programme headed by Alfred Kahn, former chairman of the Civil Aeronautics Board. The guidelines called upon companies and unions to hold pay hikes within an average of 7 per cent, and price hikes within an average of 6–6.5 per cent.

The catch-22 the United States faced was how to stamp out inflation and underpin the dollar without strangling economic growth. Under the Carter administration's watch the unemployment rate shrank, and a busy economy soaked up the swelling ranks of impatient baby boomers in the workforce. However, as the US economy broke the inflationary speed limit, its unemployment rate still lingered above the low levels achieved in the 1960s. Faced with a choice between tight monetary and fiscal policies and mandatory controls, the Carter administration opted for a middle path, mixing judicious tightening of monetary and fiscal policies with wage and price guidelines.

DEREGULATION BECOMES A VIABLE OPTION

Conflicting threads in the Carter administration's economic policy heralded the first fitful movement in a full and unforeseen pendulum swing toward free market policies. In January 1978 Congress passed a fresh minimum wage bill, hiking the minimum wage in graduated steps from $2.30 to $3.35 per hour by 1981. Congress liked a provision that permitted a lesser minimum wage for teenagers, but the administration culled it. The same year, however, President Carter signed a bill to deregulate the airline industry. Since 1938 the Civil Aeronautics Board had fixed airline fares and picked and pruned the routes that individual airlines served. After deregulation airline fares tumbled, proving that free markets outperformed regulated markets, at least on occasion. In 1980 Carter signed legislation deregulating the trucking industry. In the trucking case, the Interstate Commerce Commission had quietly settled in as a secret ally of monopoly pricing. It was a mark of the times that policies favouring free markets worked better than policies requiring regulated markets. Later that year Carter introduced legislation deregulating the railroad industry. The Depository Institutions Deregulation and Monetary Control Act of 1980 took strides towards deregulating the banking industry, allowing commercial banks to pay interest on personal accounts and thrift institutions to enter the fields of consumer lending and commercial lending. It also freed many loans from state usury laws that put ceilings on interest rates.

It is illuminating that deregulation in trucking, railroads and banking sprouted up in the wake of another blast of inflation. Before the year 1978 was out another explosion in oil prices splintered the Carter administration's plan for breaking inflation. Late in 1978 revolution in Iran constricted the flow of Iranian oil and sent world oil prices scurrying upwards. Within six months world oil prices shot up from $14 to $25 per barrel. Between December 1978 and April 1979, prices of meat, home heating oil and gasoline hit annual rates above 40 per cent. The cost of homeownership leaped up 17 per cent at an annual rate, and the cost of financing homes jumped 28 per cent at an annual rate.[10] With real wages coming under pressure, President Carter refused to postpone minimum wage hikes slated for January 1979.

THE UNITED STATES TAKES THE ROAD TO TIGHT MONEY

In July 1979 President Carter nominated Paul Volcker, President of the New York Federal Reserve Bank, to serve as Chairman of the Board of Governors of the Federal Reserve System. This action passed the sceptre of monetary policy to the experienced hands of a stout-hearted and conservative central banker who let it be known that the lone goal of monetary policy would be price stability. Volcker assumed office on 6 August and straight away interest rate graphs curled upwards. Money stocks and credit still advanced and foreign exchange and gold speculation emasculated the dollar. On 6 October Volcker announced a new and more stiff-necked strategy for monetary policy. The linchpin in this fresh line of attack highlighted money stock growth as the key variable to be targeted, rather than interest rate levels. This meant the Federal Reserve sided with the monetarist economic theories that first won converts among West German central bankers in the early 1970s. At the insistence of Congress the Federal Reserve had been announcing targets for money stock growth since 1975, but in practice it was outside the target range half the time. On the other hand, the Federal Reserve usually met interest rate targets. Keeping a tight rein on monetary policy necessitated letting interest rates climb to unexpected and unprecedented levels, and the Federal Reserve had dreaded doing that for fear of sparking a recession. Now the Federal Reserve steeled itself to turn a blind eye toward interest rates. It still announced targets for the federal funds rate, the market interest rate for borrowed bank reserves, but hitting these targets held a lesser place in monetary policy. The new policy zeroed in on growth of non-borrowed bank reserves rather than interest rates as the variable. In the last quarter of 1979 prime interest rates climbed from 13.5 per cent to an unforeseen record of 15.5 per cent. In the spring of 1980 the federal funds rate saw an unparalleled 20 per cent. Startled and anxious observers asked how high Volcker would let interest rates go. The dollar quickly gained 3 per cent value against the German mark, French franc and Dutch guilder.[11]

Murderous interest rates held the key to checking monetary growth because under inflation real interest rates, inflation-adjusted interest rates, become negative whenever inflation rates overleap interest rates. With negative real interest rates, simply borrowing money turns a profit as long as borrowed funds are invested in an inflation hedge. The financial system meets a heavy loan demand by finding clever ways to multiply bank deposits against bank reserves. Bank deposits pyramid out of bank reserves, and the money stock, which includes bank deposits, grows. To drive a stake into the heart of this monetary harlotry interest rates must edge above inflation rates.

Tight money policies broke the back of inflation but it was a long and mutilating process. Inflation retreated at a leisurely pace. In 1977 and 1978 the growth rate of M1, an elementary money stock measure, surpassed the upper bounds of the targeted growth range by 0.7 and 1.4 per cent respectively. In 1979 the Federal Reserves succeeded in bringing M1 growth within a targeted range between 4.5 and 7.5 per cent. In

1980 M1 growth crept above the targeted upper bounds by 0.4 per cent, and in 1982 it stopped short of the lower bounds for targeted growth by 1.1 per cent.[12]

Several things made disinflation bitter and corrosive. As mentioned earlier, interest rates rocketed to stratospheric heights. Home mortgage rates ominously climbed to 18 per cent by mid 1981. Spikes in short term interest rates loomed no less unprecedented and merciless. The interest rate on 90-day Treasury bills topped 16 per cent in May 1981. Not only did interest rates rise to unspeakable levels, but they seesawed and meandered like never before. Soaring and chaotic interest rates threw the US economy into the deepest and lengthiest recession since the Depression of the 1930s, ratcheting the unemployment rate above 10 per cent by the second half of 1982. Economic growth in the United States slumped to 2.8 per cent in 1979 and went into negative at -0.4 per cent growth in 1980. In 1981 growth inched up to 1.9 per cent positive before reeling back to -1.7 per cent in 1982.[13]

Federal Reserve policies awakened public criticism. Fuming farmers besieged the Federal Reserve building in Washington DC, waving signs such as 'Help American Agriculture – Eat an Economist'. In December 1981 authorities arrested a man after he threatened to take hostage members of the Board of Governors. Members of Congress lashed out against the independence of the Federal Reserve System, and talked of curbing it. The Chairman of the Board of Governors served a fixed number of years, not at the pleasure of elected officials. When asked at a Congressional hearing what it would take to get the Federal Reserve to loosen up money stock growth, Paul Volcker replied: 'Impeachment'.[14] Only the 1930s had seen businesses fail as fast as they failed in 1980 and 1981.

A diet of grudging money stock growth reels inflation in but not without hitting one snag. Output momentum holds far less ballast and is more fickle than inflation momentum. A dose of monetary stoicism at first does little to put inflation on a leash, but instead reroutes the economy on a treacherous detour of recession and rising unemployment. This starves actual inflation, opening a gap between actual and expected inflation at the cost of economic pain. Matching reductions in both actual and expected inflation clear the field for a return to full employment and price stability. As output in the United States staggered between 1979 and 1982, inflation went on climbing. As already indicated the GDP deflator logged yearly advances between 1977 and 1981. After peaking in 1981, inflation retreated in 1982, but only after the economy had been injured by a brutal recession. President Carter happened to be running for re-election just when the Federal Reserve put an iron clamp on money stock growth, dooming the economy to an economic hell of spreading unemployment coupled with rising inflation. Candidate Carter had cheerfully hurled at President Ford the 'misery index', a stinging cocktail of the unemployment rate and inflation rate added together. During the election between Ford and Carter, the misery index stood well above where it was under the previous Democratic administration. In 1980 and 1981 it was on the upward march again, and Ronald Reagan pirated Carter's own weapon and turned it against him. The misery index reached grimmer heights under Carter than under Ford, and Reagan minced no words.

The US economy sailed through foul economic weather while the Federal Reserve with small success wrestled to hold money stock growth within targeted ranges. In March 1980 the Federal Reserve, facing pressure from the White House and a panicky financial community, slapped on credit controls that curbed access to certain types of credit. Soaring long-term interest rates bit a hefty chunk out of market values of bonds issued at lower interest rates, and losses mounted at financial institutions holding bonds. Ayatollah Khomeini's government further roiled financial markets when Iran repudiated its foreign debt. The voluntary but effectual credit controls counselled banks against underwriting speculative holdings of commodities and precious metals, takeovers and mergers, and backup lines of credit for large borrowers. They also set forth special deposit requirements that stunted the multiplication of consumer credit from credit cards, unsecured personal loans, and so forth. These controls aimed to rechannel available credit into more intelligent and productive purposes at more workable interest rates. Both money supply growth and interest rates hit the skids after credit controls, and real GDP growth tumbled sharply negative. An uneasy Federal Reserve quickly lifted credit controls a mere four months later in July 1980, and interest rates shot straight up again.

The United States owed the upward drift in the misery index to an economic disease commonly billed stagflation, a predicament of leaky productivity allied with inflation. The United States, however, exhibited shallow symptoms of stagflation compared to the United Kingdom, which explains why the UK beat the US by a few months in unfurling the banner of monetarism. In 1976 the United Kingdom, at the bidding of the IMF, started reporting monetary growth targets, nudging the UK toward monetarism. It was all part of a stabilization plan to buttress the pound sterling. The IMF extended a loan to rescue the pound sterling in a humbling episode more characteristic of troubled developing countries. A Labour government clung to wage and price guideposts, struggling to keep inflation away, but a volcanic political reaction to stagflation turned Labour out of doors in 1979. As an assault on stagflation, a new Conservative government led by Margaret Thatcher launched a broad revival of free market economics. One prong of the assault was monetarism. Between 1973 and 1978 real GNP in the United Kingdom averaged a poor annual growth of 2.2 per cent. Two of those years rode out air pockets of deeply negative growth. In 1976 the United States, West Germany, France and Japan all rebounded from recession with growth rates above 5 per cent. The United Kingdom lagged at a prosaic 3.4 per cent growth. Between 1976 and 1977, the United Kingdom registered the sorriest annual growth rates and by far the hottest inflation rates of these countries. By 1978 economic growth in the UK caught up to competitive levels, but the inflation rate ranged far above rates in the United States, West Germany, France and Japan, and the world economy teetered at the edge of another recession.

The Thatcher government recruited monetarism as a weapon safe for subduing inflation without market controls that ruled out unhampered operation of free markets. It saw in the revival of free markets the secret to the resurrection of productivity and growth. In June 1979 the Thatcher government unveiled its first budget, which included a stern promise to the hold the annual growth of M3 (a monetary aggregate that encompasses currency plus all sterling deposits from public and private sectors) within an orderly groove of 7 to 11 per cent. Historically the growth of this aggregate tracked in step with the inflation rate. What appeared as a piece of airtight and unimpeachable logic held that stingier growth in M3 would be mirrored in a quieter inflation.

As the United States later discovered, constriction of the monetary noose assails output first and inflation afterwards. Interest rates spiralled skywards. Higher interest rates sweetened the income earned from holding sterling financial assets, rendering the pound sterling more inviting to foreign investors and speculators. The value of the pound sterling rose in foreign exchange markets, leaving United Kingdom exports more costly, and imports of foreign goods into the United Kingdom less costly. These economic pressures cornered United Kingdom producers into enduring whatever adjustments were necessary to soften price hikes, outflanking domestic inflationary pressures. Impatient business allies of the Conservative government voiced bitter complaints, but the government stuck to its plan. Critics censored it 'punk monetarism'. Doubling oil prices slipped an economic cog that might have been deadly to the government's strategy, but coincided with North Sea oil making the UK self-sufficient in oil. Cabinet ministers split into two groups, 'wets' and 'drys'. The wets were at odds with hefty cuts on social programmes, citing worries over unemployment. The drys pushed for sterner monetary policies. In 1980 real GNP growth tumbled to -2.1 per cent, a deeper setback than witnessed in the recession years of 1974 and 1975. Only the Depression of the 1930s seemed a worthy comparison. While real GDP growth floundered inflation topped 19 per cent, surpassing the inflation rate of a year earlier by 4 per cent. The United Kingdom sank into its own nightmare of economic pain, but throughout 1980 the government remained loyal to the monetary target range of 7–11 per cent.

Towards the end of 1980 the United Kingdom's inflation weakened. In March 1981 the Thatcher government brought forward a severely tightened budget for its third year in office. Inflation grudgingly inched downwards. For the year 1981 growth in the GNP deflator averaged 12.2 per cent, and real GNP still shrank, measuring growth of -0.2 per cent. The United States, West Germany, France and Japan weathered negative growth sometime in the 1970s, but in none of these cases had negative growth in the order of 2 per cent lasted for a whole year.

After steadily rising since mid 1979, the pound sterling in 1981 turned downwards in foreign exchange markets, arousing more inflation fears from costlier imports. The government lessened its reliance upon growth in M3 as a guide to monetary policy, and rehabilitated interest rates. Monetary authorities tinkered with interest rates while keeping an eye on the foreign exchange value of the pound, another measure of monetary tightness. Interest rates underwent adjustment to smooth and modulate fluctuations in the pound and fortify its value.

The severity of the downturn barred all hopes of a swift and healthy recovery. In 1982 real GNP growth staggered into positive territory at 0.7 per cent. Inflation yielded another 4 percentage points to come in at 8 per cent. Both West Germany and Japan saw small advances in inflation in 1982, while the United States and the United Kingdom saw inflation give ground.

The new monetary policy adopted by the United Kingdom and the United States marked the second time during the 1970s that the global economic system abandoned habits of thinking and policy inherited from the Depression of the 1930s. The start of the 1970s oversaw the undoing of the Bretton Woods system and the gold standard. From then on, the free markets dictated the value of currencies rather than officially pegged prices. The 1970s closed with the United States dumping wage and price regulation as legitimate therapy for inflation. Inflation came to be viewed solely as a market phenomenon, a barometer of and reciprocal to the value of money. Inflation signalled money was losing its value, which is what happens to market values of commodities when supply outruns demand. By seemingly infallible logic taming inflation became a simple matter of subtracting money supply, opening a deflationary imbalance between the supply and demand for money.

The Depression-born fear of markets as favourite hunting grounds for clever middlemen and minefields for price wars melted away before a fresh mode of economic thinking. In this new paradigm explanations and solutions lay in free markets. President Carter's energy proposals wore aspects of the Depression mode of thinking that looked to economic planning as an instrument of national foresight and control. Conservation measures were counted on to make sure industry had the energy lifeblood it needed. From the 1930s through the 1960s government and industry tackled economic problems by paralysing and side-stepping markets. Maintaining stable prices helped individual firms undertake economic planning. Government-sponsored price supports in agriculture kept prices propped up, emboldening farmers to shoulder higher debt loads and buy costlier machinery financed over longer stretches of time. The mission of a national energy policy lay in pledging a reliable flow of energy to industry at prices that did not upset planning and long-term investment. Wage and price guidelines were an eleventh-hour try at keeping a sticky price structure that had evolved over years of planning. The fact that stock market prices remained flat during the 1970s held a clue that the economic system born of the Depression had taken a deadly hit. Economists and policy makers turned their faces to the rising sun of free markets.

JAPAN PREPARES TO BECOME A WORLD FINANCIAL CENTRE

As the United States and United Kingdom wriggled free of wage and price controls, and welcomed the discipline of tight money and unemployment, Japan took steps to reform and deregulate one of the most closely regimented financial systems in the developed world. Japan turned to monetary targeting soon after West Germany became a devotee, and both Japan and West Germany generally enjoyed clearer success holding back inflation. Still, a switch in monetary policies equated to a small matter against a quieter but unstoppable financial revolution that was budding in Japan. This revolution bulldozed aside rigid and across-the-board control in favour of free markets in Japan's financial sector, educating and grooming it for graduation to a global financial centre. In the 1970s Japan's growth rates were about half of what they had been in the previous two decades, but still far surpassing growth rates in the United States, West Germany, France and United Kingdom. Japan's racy growth coupled with stumbling economies in the United States and Europe elevated Japan to the rank of a global economic powerhouse and heir apparent to the sceptre of global financial leadership. In financial matters Japan had remained subservient to broadly controlled and isolationist policies, but its newly exalted economic status invited outside pressure to liberalize its financial markets. Financial liberalization smoothed the path for Japan's metamorphosis into a global financial centre, putting the yen on the road to becoming second only to the dollar as a world currency. In the 1980s Japan headquartered nine of the ten largest banks in the world.

Before the 1970s Japan was without a long-term government bond market spanning maturities of seven years or more. The Japanese government nearly always ran budget surpluses until the 1970s. The Bank of Japan went without open market operations in government securities or private securities because the market for these issues bordered on non-existent. The dual levers of discount rate and resolute moral suasion monopolized monetary policy. The corporate sector turned to banks when external financing was needed, and interest rates remained low as a matter of monetary policy. Narrow and shallow competition between financial institutions helped keep interest rates pinned down. Monetary policy relied upon direct controls, quantitative quotas and ceiling rather than market forces. Open capital markets remained stunted and underdeveloped. Monopolistic concentration in the banking industry invited the Bank of Japan and the Ministry of Finance to rigidly regulate interest rates. Foreign access to capital markets faced prickly hurdles. As part of a policy to maintain a fixed value of the yen under the Bretton Woods fixed exchange regime, capital flows, both inflows and outflows, met with close-knit restrictions. Neither could Japanese households with savings shop for fatter interest rates abroad, nor could Japanese corporations borrow abroad to sidestep credit restraint at home. As late as 1976 a mere handful of foreign stocks traded on the Tokyo Stock Exchange. In the 1970s the Japanese government began running sizeable budget deficits, casting up a supply of bonds that spawned a secondary bond market.

Another factor spurred financial development and liberalization in Japan. Until the 1970s exuberant postwar Japanese industry soaked up all domestic savings to finance the Japanese economic miracle. A lack of saving ranked high as a growth retardant. In the 1970s Japanese industrialization finished its drive to maturity, dulling business appetite for capital while an affluent and ageing population boosted savings. Japan swam in domestic savings, and stood ready to export capital, a tantalizing prospect with double-digit interest rates abroad.

Integration of Japan's financial sector with the global financial system loosened the Bank of Japan's hold on interest rates at home, and exalted the role of market forces in setting Japanese interest rates. At the start of the 1970s Japan ventured a few steps toward freer interaction and linkage with the global financial system. As the Bretton Woods system broke apart, unleashed market forces put upward pressure on the yen. To vent and redirect this upward pressure, Japan beefed up controls on inflows of foreign capital. Foreign exchange holders and speculators intelligently expected the yen to appreciate, and wanted to enlarge holdings of yen bank deposits at the expense of deposit holdings of other currencies, widening the demand for yen in foreign exchange markets. Tighter controls on inflows of short-term foreign capital neutralized the added demand for yen from this quarter. Wider repercussions for financial liberation sprang from the obverse, which was lighter controls on capital outflows. Japanese companies and households wanting to invest in the other countries had to sell yen for other currencies. The sale of yen in foreign exchange markets attended capital outflows, venting upward pressure on the foreign exchange value of the yen. In 1972 Japanese long-term capital outflows measured US $4.5 billion, outdistancing by a factor of four the capital outflows of the previous year. These capital outflows shored up the value of the dollar and abbreviated escalation of the yen.

Between 1973 and 1974 rocketing oil prices swelled the volume of Japanese imports. Japanese industry was a slave to imported oil, and more yen went up for sale to buy dollars. Imported oil came priced in dollars. The heavier outflow of yen dragged down the yen in foreign exchange markets, persuading Japanese authorities to reverse the actions of 1971. To prop up the yen, Japanese authorities clamped down on capital outflows and loosened controls on capital inflows. Between 1975 and 1978 market forces again pulled the yen upward, and Japanese authorities flip-flopped, liberalizing capital outflows and putting a check on capital inflows.

Japan still sucked in a river of imported oil in 1979 when another oil shock undermined the yen. Again the Japanese authorities lightened up controls on capital inflows. In February 1979 Japanese authorities nullified a ban against non-residents purchasing yen-denominated bonds. March 1979 saw the first issue of unsecured yen-denominated bonds by a foreign private company. In May 1979 foreigners won permission to purchase yen-denominated CDs, and Japanese households and businesses won permission to contract loans of foreign currency. Into 1980 regulation step-by-step came unwound. In March 1980 Japanese authorities further dissolved controls on loans in foreign currency, and deregulated interest rates on yen deposits held by foreign central banks and other public authorities. In December 1980 a new Foreign Exchange and Foreign Trade Control Law went into effect. The underlying and pioneering principle in this law held that the authorities would not inflict controls on capital flows to orchestrate exchange rates. The law awarded foreigners permission to hold yen bank deposits and Japanese residents permission to hold interest-bearing foreign currency accounts in Japanese banks. It also softened restrictions limiting foreign ownership in a Japanese corporation to 25 per cent of the company's assets, and subject to ceilings it freed Japanese banks to join in syndicated yen-denominated loans abroad.

Parallel with opening the Japanese financial sector to international transactions, Japanese authorities brushed aside domestic regulations that diluted competition between financial institutions and squashed the role of market forces in financial markets. Interest rates still felt the controlling hand of regulation, but fluctuations widened. Between 1978 and 1981 market yields on central government bonds fluttered between 6 and 10 per cent while call money interest rates bounced between 4 and 12 per cent.

Japan opened the 1980s still an adolescent in financial liberalization, but the foundation of financial regulation had buckled and cracks radiated in every direction. Between 1979 and 1982 foreign ownership of stock in Japanese corporations multiplied from 2.5 per cent of the total market to 5.1 per cent, and foreign ownership of Japanese bonds multiplied from 3.9 per cent to 6.7 per cent.[15] Japanese banks abroad more than doubled holdings of CDs and deposits. By 1982 the yen was the third largest reserve currency in the world at 3.9 per cent of official reserves, behind the dollar at 71.4 per cent and the Deutsche Mark at 11.6 per cent.

In summary the 1970s saw the planning paradigm in economics splintered and jettisoned in the face of market pressures and inflation. Through the 1930s, 40s, 50s and 60s governments looked for ways to master prices and markets, and businesses prayed for stable prices over price competition, itching to overpower market forces. Businesses favoured prices controlled by themselves or government regulation over market prices that magnified the risks to long-term planning. The escalating inflation of the 1970s surpassed the tolerances of the planning paradigm for managing change. The foresight of planning no longer rivalled supply and demand for intelligent and useful resource allocation. Futures markets could hedge the risk of long-term planning. The trouble lay not only with sizzling inflation rates but also with the volatility and unpredictability of inflation. Between 1973 and 1980 annual inflation varied between 20.6 and 2.6 per cent in Japan, between 7 and 26.9 per cent in the United Kingdom, between 5.7 and 9.3 per cent in the United States, and between 7.8 and 11.8 per cent in France. The loftier the inflation rate, the wider the variability, it seemed. West Germany boasted enviable success at subduing inflation, holding it between 6.5 and 3.4 per cent. Apart from variations over time, inflation also varied widely across commodities, further clouding business decision-making with risk and uncertainty. Some governments and electorates welcomed a return to free markets. A climate of unpredictable inflation left free markets the safest bet, the truest guide to realistic choices and thinking.

Chapter 7

The Political Pendulum Suddenly Swings

THE REPERCUSSIONS OF DEFLATION AND INFLATION

We have discussed the idea that economies assimilate waves of deflation by developing habits, practices, customs, institutions and laws that hamper price flexibility. During deflation households and businesses come to view free markets as the enemy rather than the friend, as chaotic rather than intelligent. Governments grow large, inviting government spending to act as ballast and balance wheel, cancelling the impact of private sector fluctuations. Monetary and fiscal policies elevate total spending to a level that spares businesses all need to slash prices and risk price wars. A stable price structure emboldens businesses to undertake costly and long-term planning and investment that guarantee the supplies of goods and services at current prices. Under the planning paradigm a thin supply arouses added research and development rather than spikes in prices.

The obverse of this argument holds that waves of inflation tilt the outlook and attitude of households, businesses and governments in favour of free markets. Free markets become unbeatable insurance against shortages. If a product dries up in supply, its price escalates, multiplying the penalty for consuming the product, and the reward for producing it. The only logical explanation for a shortage lies in unwillingness to let markets work. Inflation implies that households and businesses buying products can nearly always sell them for more than they paid for them. Selling things for a profit day in and day out dispels Depression-born images of cut-throat competition and piggish middle men. If households and businesses lay awake at night for anything, it was for fear for being cheated of the market price of their product. They blamed their worries on anachronistic government regulations favouring special interests. As the wildly inflationary decade of the 1970s unfolded, one country after another cast off ageing and worn market controls and regulations in favour of freer markets. Even governments not ideologically loyal to free-market policies drifted in that direction.

A mess of social, political, and economic consequences from prolonged deflation or inflation comes to light with the passage of time. In the United States a long span of deflation around the late 1800s stirred up a political whirlwind known as the Free Silver Movement. William Jennings Bryan won the Democratic nomination for the presidency after delivering his famous 'Cross of Gold' speech. He compared the gold standard with crucifying mankind on a cross of gold. The gold standard rightly bore the guilt for deflation. Frank Baum published his famous book *The Wizard of Oz* in 1896 as an allegorical defence of the Free Silver Movement and William Jennings Bryan ran for president three times without success. After 1896 new discoveries of gold in Alaska, Australia and South Africa cured the deflation, but when deflation snapped back to life in the Depression the same populist political forces rebounded triumphant.

This populist political movement owed its growth to prolonged deflation and the discordant redistribution of income that attends inflation or deflation. A wave of unforeseen deflation batters debtors and speculators with income losses while creditors make windfall gains. In the late 1880s the lucky creditors were Eastern bankers, and the harassed debtors and speculators Midwest farmers and land dealers. Deflation made it hard for land dealers to sell land for more than they paid for it, and farmers saw grain and commodity prices fall while overhanging debt to banks stood fixed. The Free Silver people worshipped silver as the saviour. An infusion of silver into the economy would enlarge the money stock, leading to an inflation of prices.

The post World War II era embodied a long wave of inflation rising to unforeseen levels, creating fertile ground to spawn a grass roots political reaction, a polar opposite to the Free Silver Movement. Unforeseen inflation enriches debtors and speculators at the expense of creditors and savers. Creditors face impoverishment, but speculators grow wealthy borrowing money to invest and speculate in real estate, precious metals and assorted collectables. The business heroes of an inflation economy are real estate moguls such as Donald Trump rather than industrial technology entrepreneurs such as Henry Ford or Bill Gates. Investing in real estate and precious metals turns out more millionaires than exploiting and advancing the newest technology. The aroma of capital gains lures teachers, professors, engineers, nurses and beauticians to take up buying, fixing up and renting houses. Fear of poverty and unemployment is lost in the glare of hopes of riches, and disciples of capitalism's gospel multiply. Since getting rich on borrowed money seems easy, voters grow impatient with government programmes to aid the unemployed and impoverished. Frontrunners in this speculative lottery proudly credit their triumph to hard work and thrifty values when they really owe much of it to a hidden boost from inflation. In truth they waged an insolent bet that society could not rally the discipline to master inflation, and they won. When disinflation sets in, they meet with disaster, but that comes later. For the time being, the ranks of millionaires swell with self-made individuals who started out with no inheritance, social connections or high-tech and prestigious education, but only with such ordinary knowledge as how to build houses, or buy and sell antiques. A new breed of voters struts and frets about greedy government taxing away the wealth it earns or hopes to earn, and pays no mind to the kind aid of a good-natured government that might be needed in the face of economic ruin. As money from these newly earned inflation profits pours into the political process, governments veer to the capitalist end of the political spectrum. The more people trusting free markets to gratify future hopes, the more rightwing and pro-capitalist the government. In the United States a tax revolt sprang up when property holders awakened to the escalation of property taxes on inflation-appreciated property.

A disinterested observer would have to say that inflation only tips the odds in favour of debtors and speculators, and as always not every eager soul who plays the game wins. A number of individuals may dignify the other side of the ledger. One headline grabbing case was the Hunt brothers. The Hunt brothers shared in one of the largest Texas oil fortunes, but in the late 1970s they cast their lot with silver speculation. With the reservations about democracy often encountered in wealthy families, the Hunts had concluded that democratic societies suffered a defect where inflation was concerned. Fickle and restless voters would never impose stern discipline upon themselves to stamp out inflation. Precious metals were a historic hedge against inflation. As with other commodities the silver market tightened in the late 1960s and early 1970s. In 1965 Congress passed legislation largely removing the silver content from coinage. It feared that rising silver prices would create temptations to melt down silver coinage for the silver content. In the 1960s the US government sold off silver reserves to hold down silver prices. Government stocks of silver had reached a peak of 2.1 billion ounces in 1959 before the government started liquidating silver to meet private demand. Much of the liquidated silver went to private investment. Between 1971 and 1974 the average price of silver abruptly rose from $1.55 to $4.74 per ounce. Prices levelled off between 1974 and 1978. Silver production lagged behind industrial demand for silver, but investors willingly sold off silver holdings stored up in the 1960s. In January 1979 silver stood at $6 per ounce, and it entered a hurried climb, passing the $10 benchmark in August, and reaching $17 per ounce in September. From October 1979 the Federal Reserve frowned upon commercial banks loaning money to finance speculation. Later Nelson and Herbert Hunt through their commodities firm borrowed $115 million from Citibank to purchase silver. Brushing aside Volcker's whips and scorns, the First Bank of Chicago advanced them $70 million and the First National Bank of Dallas $30 million.[1] Foreign banks also joined in the lending. An ambition to corner the silver market drove the Hunts' highflying financial wizardry. The First National Bank of Dallas along with 29 other banks shared in the financial malpractice, lending $450 million to the Hunts' oil company. The Hunts' oil company in turn loaned the money to the Hunt brothers to buy silver. What the Hunts paid brokers equalled only a fraction of the amount of silver bought since the silver was bought on margin. The brokers directly financed the margin purchases, but broker financing was backed up by bank credit at places such as First National Bank of Chicago. Merrill Lynch advanced $492 million and E.F. Hutton $104 million. Bache Halsey Stuart advanced the brothers $233 million and narrowly missed bankruptcy after the silver market crumbled and the Hunt brothers sank into insolvency. Between twelve banks and five brokerage houses, the Hunts pulled together $800 million of credit for speculation, amounting to 10 per cent of all the bank loans of the previous two months.

In January 1980 the price of silver lost upward momentum at the dizzy height of $52 per ounce. The price fizzled into a stupefying downward slide. On 27 March 1980, otherwise known as 'silver Thursday', the price tumbled from $15.80 to $10.80 per ounce. Before 'silver Thursday' Volcker heard grim rumblings that crashing silver prices could wreck large banks such as First National of Chicago, the ninth largest bank in the country. Federal Reserve officials and bank regulators worried that a speculative debacle in silver might unleash ominous repercussions rivalling the stock market crash of 1929, shattering the whole financial system and touching off another dreary Depression. Word passed that if the price of silver fell to $7 per ounce, the value of silver held by banks as collateral would sink below the value of bank loans advanced for silver purchases. Just as the Hunts stared into the financial abyss, the Federal Reserve gave the nod to a private bail out of exposed banks by other banks. The Hunts brokered a reprieve from bankruptcy and rolled over silver debts to a loan with a longer pay out. The Federal Reserve gave its blessing out of fear of repercussions if a string of large banks suddenly failed. The price of silver rebounded moderately through September before renewing a downward slide. In June 1982 silver prices sank to $4.98 per ounce, and in August 2003 it traded in the $5 range.

POLITICAL TREMORS

The Hunt brothers finished losers in speculation's game, but small and adventurous winners abounded. Some bought houses and resold them for a tidy profit before mortgage closing reached completion. In the mid 1970s political distempers brewing over two decades of non-stop inflation oozed to the surface. Out of Australia came a portent of the future in December 1975 when a coalition of the Liberal party and the National party unseated the Australian Labour party. As leader of the new conservative coalition, Liberal Prime Minister Malcolm Fraser backed less government spending and more orthodox monetary and fiscal policies. Between 1965 and 1980 inflation averaged 9.3 per cent in Australia, and it stood at 15 per cent when Fraser took office. The new government pitched its economic policy as an 'inflation first' strategy, spotlighting the tranquillization of inflation as top priority. In its 1977–8 budget it proposed a modest tax cut and a freeze on real government spending, that is, government spending adjusted for inflation. The proposal scaled back the maximum tax rate from 66 to 60 per cent. In 1976 the Fraser government had unveiled a proposal to index taxable income to inflation, but later withdrew it.

The stricter fiscal policy came after a brief unfruitful flirtation with a voluntary wage and price freeze. The Fraser government assailed indexation of wage to the consumer price index. It succeeded in putting ceilings on adjustments, shutting off full indexation for higher paid workers. The government met with difficulties restraining a defiant monetary growth, but inflation quietly inched downward until the 1978–9 hikes in crude oil unleashed it again. From mid 1978 until mid 1979 the inflation rate measured 8.8 per cent. In 1980 the government sponsored a study on ancillary government functions. The report of the study made the case for downsizing or closing down certain functions that could fall within the province of states or private enterprise. In March 1983 the Fraser government was defeated by the Australian Labour party. Fraser's Liberal Party–National Party coalition signalled no sharp u-turn in government policy, more a hint of shifting political ground that would later resurrect a purer species of capitalism.

In September 1976 a clearer and larger shift in political ground sharpened into focus for Sweden, when the socialist government was turned out of office for the first time in four decades. Between 1965 and 1980 inflation averaged 8 per cent in Sweden. A coalition of Sweden's three non-socialist parties, the Centre party, the Liberal party and the Conservative party, ousted the Social Democratic party, which had ruled Sweden for 44 years and fathered Sweden's far-reaching welfare system. Thorbjorn Falldin assumed office as prime minister, replacing Olof Palme, prime minister from 1969 to 1976. Parliament enacted the new government's first budgetary proposals, which included modest cuts on personal income tax rates. The cut in income taxes came with offsetting hikes in payroll and indirect taxes. Prolonged labour disputes plagued the new government's first year. In 1978 inflation slackened to a gentler 5 per cent range, and Ola Ullsten of the Liberal party replaced Falldin of the Centre party as prime minister. The government left Sweden's welfare programme largely intact, but trimmed food subsidies and boosted household fuel taxes.

In 1981 the coalition fell to pieces after it failed to reach agreement on a tax plan, which would have gradually pared back the highest marginal tax rate from 80 to 50 per cent. Briefly a Centre-Liberal coalition sought to spur economic growth with cuts in government spending and tax sweeteners for personal savings. By 1981 unions and employers began settling wage disputes on quieter and friendlier terms. Earlier, the unions burned with resentment against a Centre, Liberal, Conservative government that sided with employers trying to hold the line on wage increases, and that held out tax cuts to coax workers into softening wage demands. The following year the Social Democrats returned to power, with Olof Palme as prime minister. The chastened Social Democrats were now much more willing to appease the non-socialist parties.

Another domino fell in May 1979 when Margaret Thatcher and the Conservative party dethroned the Labour party in the United Kingdom. The empowerment of the Conservatives heralded more than the newest twist in a political drama. Margaret Thatcher led the Conservative party to victory mincing no words about the United Kingdom's indulgent slide toward socialism. She remembered how the Conservatives lost power in 1974 after Conservative prime minister Edward Heath grabbed the wage and price control lever in a skirmish against inflation. Margaret Thatcher was the very flame of determination. She pledged to find answers to stagflation in freer markets, less government control and ownership, and unstinted reliance upon disciplined monetary growth as a lasting cure for inflation. Under Margaret Thatcher the United Kingdom turned to the Conservative party for leadership, and the Conservative party turned to its rightwing grassroots for ideas. The rightwing reaction that had been gathering strength since World War II caught its stride with the election of Thatcher. Her election signified a more passionate and unyielding bid to overturn the existing state of affairs than the elections of Falldin and Fraser, and the repercussions rippled wider and deeper within the global economic system.

We have already seen how Thatcher's government welcomed the theories of monetarism, and changed its intermediate targets in the conduct of monetary policy. Changes in the methods and spirit of monetary policy were technical and narrow against the sum of changes Thatcher envisaged for the United Kingdom. She set out to rewrite social and economic norms in favour of self-reliance over government dependence, profits and business over government controls, and an entrepreneurial and can do spirit over lassitude and defeatism. The first step to kick-starting a confident entrepreneurial spirit lay in enrichment of economic incentives. In a budget unveiled the month after the election, the new government restructured the tax system to lessen the burden of income taxes. To offset income tax reductions, value added taxes went up. Value added taxes levy taxes on individual firms. The amount subject to a value added tax is the difference between the value of the goods sold by a firm, and the value of the goods and resources purchased by a firm. The basic rate on the income tax saw a mere 3 per cent shaved off, cutting it from 33 to 30 per cent, but marginal tax rates underwent more than fine-tuning. The marginal tax bite on the top income bracket shrank from 83 to 60 per cent.[2] The new budget indexed all personal income tax brackets to inflation.

Perhaps no actions of the Conservative government symbolized the will to revitalize and unfetter capitalism more than the privatization of nationalized industries. Such industrial notables as British Rail, English Channel Ferry Service, Jaguar, British Petroleum, British Aerospace, Britoil, British Telecom, British Gas and the British Airports Authority graced the roster of nationalized companies returned to the private sector.

Equally bold was legislation that curbed the power and militancy of labour unions. The Employment Acts of 1980 and 1982 put unions under some restrictions, and nullified the immunity unions had enjoyed from civil damages for unlawful activities since 1906. The Trade Union Act of 1984 sought to check the political activity of trade unions. Prime Minister Thatcher wanted to evolve an American style arrangement in which trade unions held no single affiliation with one party. The legislation did not effectively control union activity in the political process, but the cooperative effects of legislation and a deep recession went far to soften union militancy.

Margaret Thatcher held the post of Prime Minister until 1990. A reputation for unrepentant stubbornness and insensitivity inspired standing ovations when the United Kingdom's economic problems appeared obstinate and intractable, but these qualities cost her friends in a political party comfortably in power. The Conservative party turned its back on her in 1990. In 1997 the Labour party ousted the Conservatives, but victorious Labour bore silent testimony to the capitalist revolution launched by Margaret Thatcher. Gone were the socialist ideology and the tight alliance with unions. A chastened and rejuvenated Labour party elevated a young and stylish Tony Blair to prime minister and charted a centralist course.

Margaret Thatcher kept her popularity while remaining loyal to policies that a few years earlier belonged at the outposts of rightwing extremism. Before Margaret Thatcher even the Conservatives dismissed individuals mouthing those extremist views as a crackpots. Such was the shift in attitudes that confidence in free markets and capitalism left the marshes of outdated, unimproved and discredited economics and blossomed into a fresh and trendy orthodoxy. Issues centring on income disparities between the rich and poor were ignored in favour of newer issues of privatization, deregulation and incentive or supply-side economics. Awarding entrepreneurs enticements and opportunities to rise as far above the poor as possible ranked above dreams of a contented egalitarian society. Electorates were suddenly more interested in strengthening society than in changing it, more concerned with arresting decay, lassitude and chaos than with progress toward an idealized future, and were less fearful of returning to the past than of losing the future.

No turn of events bore healthier and broader testament to the social momentum behind a global renaissance of capitalism than the United States presidential election in November 1980. In the past the Republican party had smugly shaken its head at Ronald Reagan's bid for nomination. In 1980 party moderates laughed at his economics as 'voodoo economics' but his sleek campaign aroused wide grassroots support. He won the election. He resembled Margaret Thatcher in that the passion of his convictions overrode political instincts when it came to trimming sails for the sake of consensus. Ronald Reagan inherited an economic topography free of large nationalized industries inviting privatization, and President Carter served as the thin edge of the wedge for deregulation and tight monetary policies. The large issue for Ronald Reagan narrowed down to tax cuts, and that is what he spotlighted as a fair and safe remedy for stagflation. The political gust of a grassroots tax rebellion had helped sweep Reagan into office. In 1978 a California 'taxpayers revolt' had led to passage of Proposition 13, a constitutional amendment put before bristling voters and ratified. This audacious amendment cut local property taxes by more than two thirds. In presidential campaign rhetoric Reagan vowed to cut taxes, enlarge military spending and balance the budget. These seemingly conflicting goals became possibilities if tax cuts adequately spurred economic growth, and if fatter tax revenues from a zestier economy cancelled the blow to tax revenues from tax cuts. As taxes fell, the tax base widened, and total tax revenue might grow.

THE THEORY OF VOODOO ECONOMICS

Critics savaged 'voodoo economics' but economists who warmed to the idea ceded it some dignity, christening it 'supply-side economics' and elucidating it with a graph. The graph was called the Laffer Curve after Arthur Laffer, a theoretical economist who won notoriety as the chief originator and prophet of the new economics. The contours of the graph traced the vertical trajectory of tax revenue as tax rates expanded horizontally. It is hardly a theoretical breakthrough to suggest that larger tax rates yield heftier tax revenues. It is self-evident that zero tax revenue gives a dry and inescapable corollary of zero tax rates. As tax rates rise above zero, tax revenue rises parallel to the rise in tax rates. How could governments confidently expect tax revenue to go up if tax rates were cut? Arthur Laffer reminded economists and policy makers of the other horizontal point where tax revenue sank to zero. If the tax rate stood at 100 per cent, all incentives to work and take risks evaporated since all profits and wages went straight to the government. Nothing would be produced except in the underground economy. Tax revenue therefore equals zero at two extremities, a zero tax rate and a 100 per cent rate. Between these extremities tax revenue reaches a summit at one tax rate. A wasteful and pointless loss in tax revenue attends either a positive or negative change from that one ideal rate. Therefore we can say with mathematical certainty that a fixed range of tax rates exists in which tax cuts bolster tax revenue. Starting at the point of a 100 per cent tax rate, falling tax rates yield larger tax revenues. This is a necessary corollary, but history has observed few or no unmistakable cases of governments cutting taxes under the happy expectation of raising more tax revenue. It may have happened that tax revenue went up shortly after a tax cut in the face of an expanding economy. Economies rally and retreat for many reasons. If we may believe supply-side economists, tax cuts fathered the economic expansions that multiplied tax revenues.

The idea that tax cuts could stimulate a recession-ridden economy was not new. Cutting taxes gave households more money to spend on goods, activating idle factories and unemployed workers. It widened and deepened the market for goods and services, and production and employment thrived. This line of thinking, however, held that the government would not want to cut taxes in a booming economy. If production had already expanded against the full employment boundary, cutting taxes only bred a redundant and overbearing demand against an unchangeable supply of goods and services. Rather than a horizontal expansion in output and employment, the economy saw a vertical adjustment in prices.

Supply-side economists disagreed, reasoning that tax cuts held out the only intelligible and fruitful form of economic stimulus for an economy already at full employment. Cutting taxes enlarged after-tax incomes and rewards, exciting eagerness for work. It enlarged the supply of goods relative to demand, clearing the field for full-employment production to grow without inflation. A supply-side post-mortem on the 1970s underscored soaring inflation as an unerring sign of a booming economy. The elevated unemployment rates mattered little in this diagnosis. Dreary productivity numbers lurked behind the scenes, and sagging productivity amidst a booming economy hinted at stagnation on the supply side. Supply-side economists pointed the finger of blame at steeply graduated marginal tax rates. If rising affluence stemmed from the kinds of enterprising activities that made individuals rich, then rapacious marginal tax rates dulled and enervated the edge of forward progress. The symptom of inflation in the 1970s betrayed an economic policy blind to the supply side of the economic equation, fuelling the demand for goods while choking the supply. In the 1930s the supply of goods far outdistanced the demand, and an economic policy zeroing in on the demand side was what the doctor ordered. Inflation flared up in the 1970s because governments myopically clung to demand-side policies when supply-side policies fitted the circumstances. In the 1970s the key problem distilled to shortages, shortages of crude oil, shortages of food. When shortages became a worse ill than idle capacity, supply-side economics blossomed in the theoretical sphere, and in the practical realm political power passed from labour unions to people who managed production.

The honour for best reading the needs and trends of the times went appropriately to an economist who cut his theoretical teeth in the field of international economics. Robert A. Mundell won the Nobel Prize for economics in 1999, earning him a tardy fame characteristic of inventive thinkers who herald the future. Professor Mundell saw clearly the issues surrounding monetary and fiscal policy under an international monetary system of floating exchange rates and unfettered capital mobility across national borders. He wrote up his findings in the early 1960s, a time when none of the world's major trading partners gave a minute's thought to scrapping the Bretton Woods fixed exchange rate regime for a regime of floating exchange rates. The better part of three busy decades passed before financial liberalization of capital flows became orthodox policy in the capitalist quarter of the world's economies. Professor Mundell also brought up the subject of the optimal currency area in the early 1960s, nearly four decades before Europe's euro saw light. This arcane subject has to do with the economic traits and circumstances of an area that stands to gain from having its own sovereign currency. The Nobel Committee cited his theoretical work on the analysis of monetary and fiscal policy under different exchange rates and on the criteria for an optimal currency area as reasons for his selection.

In the 1980s Professor Mundell was largely unknown against the exalted celebrity status of Arthur Laffer. Economists named no curves after him. His broader international perspective and deeper theoretical penetration kept the big picture in view and lifted his analysis far above the impassioned and one-sided rhetoric that invades shallow analysis of taxation issues. Mundell argued in favour of a two-pronged policy – an expansionary fiscal policy rooted in large tax cuts, and a tight money policy. Orthodox economics saw this discordant and irregular policy mix as analogous to driving a car with one foot on the accelerator and one foot on the brake. The pressed accelerator pedal stood for the expansionary fiscal policy, and the pressed brake pedal the tight money policy. Under the fixed exchange rate regime such a policy seemed unintelligible and incongruent with a pledge to hold exchange rates fixed. Under the fixed exchange rate regime an expansionary fiscal policy dictated an easy monetary policy to keep exchange rates locked in place, and a contracting fiscal policy evoked a tight money policy for the same reasons. The Reagan economic policy condensed to the Mundell prescriptions.

To make these conflicting policies, a stimulating fiscal policy and a retarding monetary policy, intelligible and credible it helps to think about what went awry after the United States was enlisted as the global economy's locomotive. As the United States rebounded from the 1974–5 recession, US imports outgrew exports, enlarging the world market for goods and services and propelling the global economic system into an upswing. The excess of outflowing dollars over inflowing dollars undercut the value of the dollar in foreign exchange markets, resulting in a sinking foreign exchange value of the dollar between 1977 and 1978. Once monetary policy tightened up under Volcker, the dollar stopped sinking and stabilized, but well below 1976 levels. Cheap dollars in foreign exchange markets bloated the cost of imported goods, notching up US inflation. Cheaper dollars also left US goods cheaper in foreign markets, and rechannelling production into foreign markets multiplied shortages at home.

It is hard to appreciate the rationale for tight money paired with large tax cuts without revisiting the airy and abstract realms of economic theory. A healthy and unwavering operation of the economic system implies that the aggregated demand for goods roughly matches the aggregated supply of goods. The odds are slanted in favour of such an equilibrating balance since supply and demand share a common ancestry. Whenever an individual produces a good, that individual earns the right to consume the good, or sell it and buy other goods of equal market value. A one-sidedness can arise when individuals produce goods and sell them, but do not use the income from selling goods to buy other goods.

In other words, if households and businesses put nothing into savings, paid no taxes and bought no imported goods, then the demand for all goods and services produced domestically would equal the total supply of goods and services produced domestically. An excess demand for one good precisely equals and counterbalances an excess supply of another good. Over time relative prices come under pressure to smooth out and cure inescapable but passing gaps and disparities. If the economy only produced two goods, apples and oranges, then the market value of the pooled demand of apples and oranges equals the market value of the pooled supply of apples and oranges. This subtle and delicate state of macroeconomic balance could be met even if an excess supply of oranges and a matching shortage of apples coexisted.

Of course people do save, pay taxes and buy imports, but the total demand for goods and services still balances the total supply if government spending exactly offsets tax revenue, exports exactly offset imports, and all the savings go to underwrite domestic investment spending, neutralizing savings with equal investment spending. In practice things do not come together quite that neatly, and the economic system settles at a point where an imbalance in one area, say savings and investment, offsets an imbalance in another area, say government spending and taxes. That is, the effect of too much saving relative to investment spending may be cancelled out by too little tax relative to government spending. What economists call fiscal policy has to do with consciously opening a gap between taxes and government spending to offset gaps at full employment between savings and investment or exports and imports. Only gaps at full employment matter.

It is easy to grasp the *raison d'être* for large tax cuts. By the 1970s the United States required a vast amount of imported oil. As oil prices soared, US imports dwarfed exports. The United States lavished more on imports and other countries spent hard won dollars on oil rather than US exports. Oil was priced in dollars, the international currency. Thus in the second half of the 1970s imports widely outdistanced exports in the United States, and outflowing dollars outnumbered inflowing dollars, which triggered a tumbling dollar in foreign exchange markets. A timely subtraction from tax revenue was needed to counterbalance an unwelcome addition to imports. When total demand matches total supply, the sum of imports, savings, and taxes matches the sum of exports, investment spending and government spending. If the combined measure of exports, investment spending and government spending remains constant, then swollen imports can be offset by a matching shrinkage in taxes.

THE ECONOMIC RECOVERY TAX ACT OF 1981

Professor Mundell advanced the idea of tight money and expansionary fiscal policy in 1974, but not until 1981 did the United States opt for this mongrel policy mix. In 1978 a defiant Congress bulldozed over President Carter's resistance and shot back a tax bill with a cut in capital gains taxes. Windfall profits from the inflation of asset values made themselves heard in the counsels of government. The chief tax cut awaited the forward urgency of President Reagan's lobbying and political midwifery. Congress, perhaps with a twinkle in the eye, named it the Economic Recovery Tax Act of 1981. This act generously assimilated such sweeping reforms as exempting all estates under $600,000 from estate taxes, shielding about 99 per cent of all estates at the time from taxation. Over a four year span this watershed legislation scaled back from 70 to 50 per cent the highest tax rate on estates above $5 million. It was billed as the largest tax cut in US history, pruning across the board tax rates on personal income by 25 per cent over two years. The touted 25 per cent cut stood for a heftier percentage tax cut at high-income brackets than at low-income brackets. For the first year individuals and families in the highest income bracket saved 20 per cent in taxes. The act also sweetened individual retirement accounts, allowing individuals a maximum of $2,000 tax-exempted savings, and couples a maximum of $4,000.

The Economic Recovery Act levelled another swipe at capital gains taxes, with a ceiling of 20 per cent as the uppermost tax rate on capital gains. Capital gains were the profits earned from the sale of assets held beyond one year. The act exempted 60 per cent of capital gains from taxation, and subjected the remaining 40 per cent to taxation as ordinary income.[3]

The act effectively cut taxes for businesses, allowing them to write off the depreciation costs of plant and equipment sooner. Depreciation registers as a cost for measuring taxable income, but involves no payments to outside suppliers of resources. This accelerated depreciation radically enlarged yearly depreciation deductions for measuring taxable profits. Congress threw in an added investment aphrodisiac in the shape of a 10 per cent tax credit for newly purchased equipment. Equipment fully written down to zero within three years fell within the guidelines of yet another 6 per cent tax credit, enriching the first 10 per cent credit with another 6 per cent. These business tax cuts were aimed at hurrying the tempo of investment spending on new plant and equipment. Out of all this tax legislation the investment tax cuts stood the best chance to bear quick dividends for economic recovery. Aside from investment tax cuts, small corporations reaped handsome cuts in corporate income tax.

The dose of large built-in deficits and tight monetary policy bore the expected fruit. During the 1970s, interest rates mostly remained in single-digit territory. In 1979 interest rates on 30-year FHA mortgages were in the 10 per cent range with brief detours into 11 and 12 per cent territory. In the 1980s this interest rate rarely sank to single-digit territory. In October 1981 it logged an 18.55 per cent rate, and in 1982 only retreated to the 16–17 per cent range. Falling inflation rates subtracted some inflation premium, clearing the path for interest rates to veer downward, but unlike the 1970s interest rates hovered far above inflation rates. Still, interest rates inched downwards, falling through the 10 per cent range in 1986. They stood at comparable levels in 1979 and 1986, but whereas inflation stood at 11.3 per cent in 1979, it was 1.9 per cent in 1986. In real terms interest rates were much higher in 1986 than in 1979. Not only did lenders earn appetizing interest rates, but loaned money surrendered little value to inflation before it was repaid. Ten per cent interest rates hold small charm if the loaned money loses ten per cent of its value before the lender receives it back in repayment. The 30-year FHA mortgage interest rate dipped below 10 per cent in 1986 because inflation was unusually low. The rate crawled up again, momentarily topping 11 per cent in 1987, and floated down to the 9 per cent range by 1989. In 1990 it flickered around 10 per cent.

Lofty inflation-adjusted interest rates in the United States opened up tempting opportunities to the nomadic capital of the world. Between 1981 and 1985 interest rates in the United States hovered far above foreign interest rates.[4] Before foreigners could buy US financial assets, they had first to buy US dollars in foreign exchange markets. In 1980 forces pushing the dollar down caved in to forces lifting the dollar up. By the end of 1984 the dollar against other currencies was on average 40 per cent above its 1973 level in inflation-adjusted numbers. By 1986 the inflation-adjusted value of the dollar sank back to 1973 levels, and it hung at that level, give or take 10 per cent, until the decade was out. The strength of the dollar's upward drift varied between currencies. In July 1979 it took $2.25 to buy £1 sterling. In February 1985 it took only $1.09 to buy £1.

The outcome of tight monetary policy and expansionary fiscal policy unfolded along contours outlined by Professor Mundell as early as 1974. Mundell also saw lower taxes inviting an inflow of capital. The enactment of a heavy tax cut, he argued, would straightaway notify capital markets that doing business in the United States had suddenly grown more lucrative and rewarding, at least when judged against other countries. A corollary followed that domestic capital would stay at home instead of migrating to foreign countries. The enrichment of capital investment in the United States would accelerate economic growth, and widen the US trade deficit. The higher outflow of dollars from imports did not undermine the dollar in foreign exchange markets. Foreigners were eager to buy dollars, angling for financial investments in the United States at tantalizing interest rates. Swelling US imports multiplied demand for goods produced in foreign countries, quickening and revitalizing economies around the world and exalting the United States into a Herculean locomotive that pulled the global economy along no matter what.

Tight monetary policy paired with fiscal stimulus crushed inflation in the United States. A rise in the foreign exchange value of the dollar cheapened the cost of imports. A stronger dollar meant it took fewer dollars to buy a Toyota. US businesses facing stiffer foreign competition balked at raising prices. The rest of the world, seeing dollars as the ticket to interest rates unrivalled anywhere, were eager to sell goods in the United States. They sold products in the United States at ruthlessly competitive prices and still came out ahead after earning interest on the money. Crude oil prices hit a bruising $35 a barrel in 1981. Worldwide recession and energy conservation eroded oil demand. OPEC laboured to stabilize prices by withholding production, but to no avail. Eagerness to sell crude oil for dollars ran roughshod over OPEC, whose members slyly expanded production above quota levels. In 1985 crude oil prices crashed to $10 per barrel, and the long wave of global inflation died.

The complementary and fertilizing role the United States played in bringing alive global financial markets during the 1980s can be gleamed from Japanese statistics on foreign portfolio investment. In 1970 the flow of Japanese foreign portfolio investment measured $252 billion in US dollars.[5] In 1979 it stood at $2,072 billion. It topped a record $11,000 billion in 1980 and again in 1981.The flow slumped to $8,485 billion by 1983, and then tumbled faster, registering $3,851 billion in 1985.

Before the United States, Japan had tackled the economic storms and dilemmas of the 1970s with tax cuts and tight monetary policy. Japan slashed taxes in 1974, touted as the deepest tax cut in Japanese history. Japanese government bond issues and borrowing doubled from 1974 to 1975, and trebled between 1975 and 1980. A 25 per cent rise in government spending between 1971 and 1972 preceded the tax cut.[6] In 1974 the Bank of Japan retooled monetary policy and broadcast its intent to concentrate on money stock growth rather than interest rates as the intermediate target of monetary policy. Under the Bretton Woods system 360 yen equalled one dollar. When the Bretton Woods system fell apart, the yen spiralled upwards, topping out around 260 yen per dollar before descending in 1973. In 1975 the yen bottomed out in foreign exchange markets at 300 yen per dollar before turning up. By 1978 it took only 200 yen to purchase a dollar, the yen gaining strength while the dollar lost.

Japan not only numbered among the first to opt for new economic strategies, but also weathered the economic turbulence of the 1970s without the political somersaults seen in other countries. Japan stood better situated and fortified politically to handle the slippery economic challenges of the time. The conservative end of its political spectrum already ruled the country. The Liberal Democratic party, a conservative coalition of factions, had governed Japan since 1955 when it was formed. In the 1970s it muddled through disquieting turnover among prime ministers but kept the upper hand. In 1976 it lost a majority in the lower house, but retained a majority in the upper. It clung to power aided by conservative independents, but lost its freedom of independent action. It faced its broadest challenge since 1955, and owed it to an electorate turned chilly and uneasy toward a conservative establishment. The Japanese Communist party gained parliamentary seats in 1974 but surrendered them in 1976, when the Japanese Socialist party gained seats. In 1980 a prime minister lost a no confidence vote, the first time that had ever happened to the Liberal Democratic party. The motion for the no confidence vote issued from the Japanese Socialist party. In 1993 a scandal-ridden and embattled Liberal Democratic party fell from power after governing Japan for 38 years. A speculative debacle helped to bring down the Liberal Democratic Party. The Japanese Nikkei stock index peaked at 39,000 in 1989 before faltering. By 1992 the index read 15,000. Following speculative mania scandals entangled and tainted Japanese politicians.

THE POLITICAL UPHEAVAL RADIATES

The political quake that jarred Japan fanned out wider after the election of Ronald Reagan in the United States. In 1981 a coalition of socialist and communist voters swept François Mitterrand into the presidency of France, making him the first socialist president of the Fifth Republic. For two years Mitterrand pressed ahead with a one-sided socialist agenda, shortening the working week, giving workers more holidays, ratcheting up the minimum wage and welfare benefits, levying a wealth tax and nationalizing banks and industries. Uglier unemployment and inflation statistics spoke volumes about the wisdom of these policies. In 1983 a monetary crisis rendered the final verdict and dictated a u-turn in Mitterrand's policies. Monetary policy sternly swung around, buttressing the franc and maintaining France's standing in the European Community. The French government went for a leaner budget. Budget deficits ran high despite a tight-fisted and austere government, and state-owned enterprises thirsted for an infusion of capital. The government opened the door for state-owned companies to sell stock and raise capital. In some cases the government sold stock in state-owned enterprises to raise funds for itself.

Mitterrand learned to content himself with international affairs and left management of the French economy to ministers, some of whom were rightwingers. When conservatives won control of parliament in 1986 he cooperated with a conservative prime minister. In 1988 he defeated a conservative challenger, but withdrew bit by bit from political infighting over economic issues. Suffering from cancer, he declined to run for re-election in 1995.

The winds of change infected Spain with a passion for capitalist revolution. The Spanish Socialist Workers party had never gripped the levers of power until Felipe González led them to victory in 1982. Mitterrand's experience in France may have shared in redirecting González and his socialist party toward conservative, free-market policies. In the 1970s Spain's economy felt all the ills of stagflation. High unemployment, inflation, bank failures, balance-of-payment deficits, slow growth and investment could be studied in Spain. The new government reined in money stock growth, and sought to wean itself from the habit of buying out failing businesses to save jobs. It also encouraged privatization of businesses already owned by the government. The socialist government removed monopoly privileges enjoyed by many state-owned companies, loosened labour laws, and liberalized criteria for establishing new companies. In the last half of the 1980s Spain joined the ranks of economic miracles. Deregulation of Spain's economy under a socialist government continued into the 1990s. In 1996 the centre-right Popular party ousted the socialist government.

Germany shared in the political upheavals bred by the economic difficulties of the 1970s. In 1969 the Social Democratic party for the first time became the governing party of Germany, and remained in power until 1983 when the Christian Democratic party in coalition with the Christian Social Union returned to power. Helmut Kohl of the Christian Democratic party led the coalition to victory stressing opposition to socialism and support of NATO troops and weapons on West German soil. Chancellor Kohl worked for leaner government budgets and welfare programmes and cuts in taxes, but squabbles within the coalition undercut his efforts. Later the focus shifted to the unification of Germany, the achievement for which Kohl will be remembered. Kohl became the longest serving German Chancellor of the twentieth century, serving from 1983 until 1998.

Spreading from one country to another the thin edge of the wedge of capitalism cracked through the shackles of economic planning and control. The early 1980s witnessed the dawning of a capitalism revolution that ended with a worldwide victory of capitalism over socialism. Before the century was out communist stalwarts such as Eastern Europe, China and Russia placed their confidence in market reforms to solve economic problems, and stockmarkets sprouted on the ash heaps of socialism.

Chapter 8

The Floodtide of the Capitalist Revolution

The crest of the global inflationary wave toppled and dissipated in the early 1980s. The United Kingdom registered a 19.2 per cent inflation rate in 1980, but averaged a 5.8 per cent annual rate for the period 1980–91. The United States opened the decade at 9.3 per cent inflation for 1980, but posted a sedate 4.2 per cent annual average for the period 1980–91. France chalked up double-digit annual inflation between 1980 and 1982, but passed through the period 1980–91 averaging yearly inflation of 5.7 per cent. West Germany reported annual inflation above 4 per cent for the years 1980–82, but averaged a mere 2.8 per cent for 1980–91. Japan logged an enviable 2–3 per cent inflation for the years 1980–82, and brought average inflation down to an all but inert 1.5 per cent for the years 1980–91.[1]

When a global wave of inflation suddenly retreated at the end of the Korean War, terms of trade soured and deteriorated for the developing world where production of foodstuffs, raw materials and fuel accounted for most economic activity. At the same time, the terms of trade strengthened for the developed and industrialized world. A similar economic change of phase unfolded in the 1980s. Based upon a terms of trade index set at 100 for the year 1987, the terms of trade for low-income countries skidded from 106 in 1985 to 94 in 1991.[2] Among these countries Uganda sagged from 143 to 48, Egypt from 131 to 93, and Pakistan from 90 to 80. Middle-income economies saw terms of trade droop from 109 to 103 between 1985 and 1991. Within the ranks of these countries Bolivia watched its terms of trade take a spiral downward from 167 to 73. Terms of trade crumbled from 153 to 90 for Ecuador, from 108 to 103 for Guatemala, and from 126 to 103 for El Salvador. Terms of trade among upper middle-income countries between 1985 and 1991 turned against South Africa, Mexico and Saudi Arabia. On average middle-income countries gave up ground, dragging down the index from 117 to 105 between 1985 and 1991. Again the scale puts these index numbers at 100 for 1987.

For Latin America and the Caribbean as a whole terms of trade caved in from 111 to 105 over the same time frame. Sub-Saharan Africa saw a slip from 107 to 87 between 1985 and 1991. As a group fuel-exporting countries suffered a savage hit, scaling back the index from 167 to 85 between 1985 and 1991. One clue to the future development of the global economic system loomed up during this time frame. Terms of trade for East Asia and the Pacific crept up from 96 to 108.

Wilting terms of trade for less developed countries correlated with healthier ones for developed and industrialized countries. Between 1985 and 1991 the high-income countries saw the index inch up from 97 to 101. Terms of trade drifted up for wealthy countries still widely involved in production of foodstuffs, raw materials and energy. The United States belonged in this category. Between 1985 and 1991 Japan's terms of trade were buoyant, jumping from 71 to 99. West Germany's index went up from 82 to 95 between 1985 and 1991. Spain, Italy, Switzerland, Finland and Denmark saw their terms of trade index climb by ten points or more between 1985 and 1991.

A glance at the Consumer Price Index (CPI) statistics for the United States authenticates the easing in foodstuffs and energy supplies. Food prices crested later than energy prices but longer-term trends stamp their signatures early in the next decade. The CPI index numbers measured from a base period between 1982 and 1984 furnish a barometer of relative prices shifts between the early 1980s and the early 1990s. By December 1992 the all items CPI index scaled a height of 142.3, signalling a 42.3 per cent boost in prices from the base period. The meat, poultry, fish and eggs sub-index logged a value of 132 in

December 1992, showing a quieter 32 per cent escalation in these prices. The all-inclusive food index for December 1992 came in a bit higher at 138.8, clearly measuring slower growth in food prices against CPI prices overall. The most telling of all, the index for the energy component in the CPI, only logged 105.3 in December 1992, an unhurried 5.3 per cent growth in prices over nearly a decade. The Producer Price Index (PPI), also calculated by the Bureau of Labor Statistics, leaped from 100.5 to 117.6 between December 1982 and December 1992. The crude materials index, representing the crude materials portion of the PPI, remained flat over the same time period, merely edging up from 97.9 to 100.9. The PPI includes crude materials as well as manufactured chemicals, plastic products, metal products and wood products.

The terms of trade, CPI and PPI statistics chart a global economy that turned a corner in the 1980s analogous to the corner it turned at the close of the Korean War. Once again leading sectors shifted into high gear on the back of bargain prices for foodstuffs, raw materials and energy. Two meaningful differences distinguished the period following the Korean War from the mid 1980s. First, households and businesses by the 1980s were no longer naïve about the hazards of inflation. By mid 1980 the global economy had floundered through two episodes of hyperactive inflation since the Great Depression. Moreover, the inflation of the 1970s lasted a decade and brought in its wake higher unemployment. Depression no longer bore all the guilt for unemployment. Inflation had also become the enemy of full employment. The lasting legacy of the 1970s displaced fear of depression by fear of inflation. The deflation during the early 1930s was forgotten. Policy makers nervously watched every increase in the inflation rate rather than every increase in unemployment numbers. All the energies and strategies of economic policy went into subduing inflation.

One upshot of the Great Depression was distrust of markets. Depression era government regulations hampered price flexibility, particularly downward price flexibility. Corporations shunned price moves that might ignite a price war. In the mid 1980s markets shrugged off these fetters. Markets were what allowed households to buy houses and later sell them for a higher price. Markets were what lifted households and businesses out of debt. In sum, the global economy stood at the threshold of expansion just as a global capitalist revolution picked up momentum.

As fear of depression cast a fading spell, governments came under less pressure to underwrite and enlarge programmes that softened economic insecurity. Voters thought the poor and unemployed merely needed more encouragement and incentives to find jobs, or better jobs. They saw less need for minimum wage laws and welfare benefits. Governments met with wider freedom to hold taxes down. Hefty government spending seemed redundant as a prop and ballast for economic prosperity. Free markets ordained prosperity apart from levels of government spending. Economic insecurity wielded small sway in the social consciousness anyway. In the 1950s and 60s capitalist nations thought answers to economic problems lay in the spirit and methods of socialism, whereas in the 1980s and 90s socialist countries looked for answers and cures in the dynamics and intelligence of free markets.

THE VICISSITUDES OF CREDITORS AND DEBTORS

It will be recalled that inflation arbitrarily rearranges income in favour of debtors and speculators and against savers and creditors. It enlarges the number of self-made millionaires relative to millionaires by inheritance, exalting the prestige of capitalism as the friend of the common man. Deflation works in the opposite direction. The global economy underwent no deflation after the 1970s inflation, but it did exhibit disinflation. Unexpected drops in the inflation rate give the same income rearrangements as deflation, rewarding creditors and savers and penalizing debtors and speculators. When creditors become habituated to inflation, they take to charging higher interest rates as inflation insurance. Higher interest rates recoup the purchasing power creditors lose to borrowers under inflation, neutralizing the tendency for a rearrangement of income in favour of debtors. They equate to insurance against inflation and when inflation fails to arrive, creditors win.

Creditors gain from disinflation but banks and savings institutions are more likely to lose than gain. These institutions bestride depositors and borrowers, caught in the middle but bearing more resemblance to speculators than creditors. They issue short-term claims against themselves in the form of deposits. The public deposits funds and banks and savings institutions promise to redeem these deposits with small notice. Funds in personal accounts or demand deposits await withdrawal at any time without notice. While banks and savings institutions issue short-term liabilities against themselves, they accept longer-term liabilities against borrowing customers. Depositing customers hold the right to all show up on a given day and in chorus demand to withdraw all deposits, but a lending institution cannot on a given day command all borrowing customers to repay loans. When borrowing customers are unable to repay loans and disinflation despoils the value of collateral, both depositing customers and the banks stand to lose, but deposit insurance spares the depositors. Premium interest rates atone for losses that savers sustain, but lending institutions remain squeezed in a vice between depositors and borrowers. The Hunt brothers were an example. Others include savings and loan institutions in Texas investing depositors' money in real estate loans. Once the price of oil crashed, collateral values of real estate withered. When borrowers were unable to repay loans at bloated interest rates, lending institutions sank into insolvency.

Therefore a few years of decelerating inflation leaves the economic countryside littered with bankrupt lending institutions. Between 1985 and 1991 bank insolvencies within the ranks of industrialized countries decelerated the economic growth in the United States, Germany, Finland, Sweden, New Zealand and Norway. The United States rode out a tide of bank insolvencies throughout the 1980s, cresting between 1988 and 1991 when roughly one third of all savings and loan institutions in the United States went bust. Bank insolvencies cropped up earlier in Spain, climbing to scorching levels between 1977 and 1985. A rash of bank insolvencies arrived late in France, spiking between 1994 and 1995. The bank insolvency wave paid a tardy but lasting visit to Japan in the 1990s.[3]

East Asian countries that later chalked up jaw-dropping rates of economic growth shared in the global wave of bank insolvencies. Hong

Kong underwent a steep and sobering spike in bank insolvencies between 1982 and 1983 and again between 1983 and 1986. A procession of bank insolvencies occurred in Indonesia in 1994, in Malaysia between 1985 and 1988, in Singapore in 1982, and in Taiwan between 1983 and 1984.

Between 1980 and 1995 periods of bank insolvencies lasting one to three years affected the economic topography of Latin America. On the roster of Latin American countries jolted by banking crises belong Argentina, Bolivia, Brazil, Chile, Colombia, Costa Rica, Ecuador, Mexico, Uruguay and Venezuela. During three separate time spans, 1981–2, 1991–2 and 1995, Mexico reeled from banking crises.

In Africa short-lived or longer episodes of bank insolvencies hit more than twenty sovereign countries between 1980 and 1995. Egypt had a double dose of bitter banking crises, one in the early 1980s and another between 1990 and 1991. South Africa was spared, perhaps because of its abundant gold reserves. Mauritania felt the sting of three separate episodes, one in 1984, another in 1988 and a third in 1993.

The roster of countries jarred by banking crises between 1980–95 also includes Kuwait, Turkey, Thailand, the Philippines, Nepal, India and Bangladesh. In the early 1990s the transitional socialist economies also met with banking crises. Between 1990 and 1995 Estonia, Latvia, Hungary and Romania were all affected.

Indebted governments and countries also faced taller hurdles in the 1980s. Remember that developing countries began shouldering larger debt burdens in the 1970s. Debt went to pay for costlier oil imports and to finance investment opportunities afforded by rising prices of basic commodities. The external debt of developing countries (the debt of governments, households and businesses to foreign creditors) mushroomed threefold and more between 1976 and 1986 and sustained a shallower climb until 1991.[4] By then the volume of bad debts worried foreign lenders, and lending slumped. Foreign lenders could only count on receiving interest payments when governments in debtor countries kept reserves of dollars and other hard currencies. These hard currency reserves guaranteed that foreign lenders could repatriate interest and other payments in the currency of their home country. If reserves run too low, a debtor country must devalue its currency, or let it float downward. A debtor country can calm a currency crisis by spurring exports or luring more foreign capital, but these options usually recede beyond reach once the crisis looms in view. If the currency of a debtor country depreciates, foreign lenders lose. Borrowers in the debtor country are unable to line up sufficient domestic currency to pay off debt in hard currency. After depreciation debts denominated in the currency of the debtor country translate into less hard currency when the time comes for repayment.

Debt troubles first flared up in Mexico, which had sidestepped a crisis in 1976 when speculators sold Mexican pesos, betting devaluation was on the cards. Mexico's foreign exchange reserves were depleting rapidly. Interest rates were fairly low in 1976 and Mexico negotiated foreign loans adequate to soothe the crisis. As a sacrificial offering to lenders the Mexican government consented to hold down budget deficits. The expectations of future oil discoveries and exploding oil prices loosened budgetary discipline, and the government relaxed. Foreign borrowing underwrote government deficits along with printing money. In 1978 roughly 50 per cent of Mexico's gross fixed investment stemmed from government investment activity.[5]

Mexico's reserves and liquidity were again stretched in the early 1980s. As the government shouldered more debt and refinanced maturing debt at near usurious interest rates, external interest payments owed in dollars soared. Global economic recession cut a chunk out of Mexico's oil revenues. In 1981 Mexico slashed oil prices $4 per barrel to plug a haemorrhaging demand.[6] Rumours circulated touching the government's financial soundness and likely devaluation of the peso. Foreign investors, facing a windfall loss if Mexico devalued, pulled funds out of Mexico. The redemption of fleeing capital into dollars siphoned off Mexico's international reserves. In February 1982 the Mexican government suspended redemption of pesos into hard currency, equivalent to floating the peso. Foreign exchange markets quickly sheared 40 per cent off the peso's value. The devaluation vented pressure to empty out Mexico's international reserves, but the peso's future value still stood in jeopardy. Mexico's external debt-servicing payments continued to mount, and its balance of payments never left the negative column. To stabilize the foreign exchange market for pesos Mexico looked to the

IMF, Federal Reserve and other Western central banks for help. A new round of agreements opened the way for Mexico to delay debt-service payments and enlarge foreign exchange reserves.

Mexico exemplifies a wider epidemic of third world debt crises that plagued the global financial system after global disinflation. Mexico scared foreign investors in all developing countries, adding to debt troubles. Impending debt and currency crises in less developed countries habitually grabbed front-page news coverage.[7] Relief from the IMF and reschedules of interest payments paved the road for most countries to skirt outright defaults. Agreements worked out with the IMF dictated some austerity measures to debtor governments, and news of IMF agreements and rescheduling agreements won roaring applause from all corners.

One barometer of the gravity of the debt crisis was the discount rates at which Latin American bank debt traded in secondhand markets. In May 1986, Argentine loans in New York traded at 63 cents on the dollar, Bolivian loans at 7 cents, Brazilian loans at 76 cents, Chilean loans at 68 cents, Colombian loans at 85 cents, Ecuadorian loans at 64 cents, Mexican loans at 60 cents, Peruvian loans at 20 cents, Uruguayan loans at 64 cents and Venezuelan loans at 77 cents.[8]

Some blame for debt crises in developing countries can be pinned on the United States. Wide budget deficits in the United States swallowed a handsome slice of global financial capital. US government bonds paid appetizing interest rates for slim risks. The United States, sweetening the invitation to foreign capital, cancelled the withholding tax on non-residents holding financial assets in the United States. This lubricated the grooves for foreigners to use the United States as a tax haven. The economic forces that fortified and pushed up the US dollar weakened and dragged down other currencies. The shakier currencies belonged to the developing world.

GLOBAL CAPITAL WINS NEW FREEDOM AND PRESTIGE

For the first three decades after World War II capitalism was on the defensive, but well before the century was out it was back on the offensive. Just as declining terms of trade in the 1950s and 60s disgraced and undercut capitalism in developing countries, in the 1980s and 90s declining terms of trade and debt crises brought socialism into disrepute. Post-mortems for economic failures cited an overgrowth of socialism and economic regulation. Developing countries pored over the canons of capitalist doctrine to find inspiration and guidance. The United States had upped the bid on returns to capital, leaving other countries uncompetitive in capital markets unless they remoulded their economies to curry favour with capital. Economic policies kinder to capital equated to survival.

In the 1980s the developed world still had nooks and crannies to explore where liberalization of capital flows was concerned. Progress went in baby steps. In 1984 the United States lifted the 30 per cent withholding tax on interest on income paid to foreigners. The same year Germany eradicated the tax on foreign investors' income from German bonds, and in 1981 lifted temporarily imposed controls on capital flows. In 1986 France partially liberated capital flows. Also in 1986 the New York Stock Exchange, the American Stock Exchange and NASDAQ opened the way for foreign issuers to list stock if they abided by home country regulations. That year also saw the conclusion of interest rate deregulation in the United States, and France liberalizing interest rate regulations on deposits held longer than three months. In 1986 the Tokyo Stock Exchange admitted six foreign members, and restrictions on Japanese purchases of foreign securities went by the board. In 1987 Ontario and British Columbia legalized foreign ownership of security dealers incorporated in these two provinces. The same year the Chicago Board of Trade opened evening trading. In 1988 Germany stamped approval for foreign investors to purchase five-year Federal bonds in the primary market, and four Japanese security firms entered the field of primary dealers in US government securities. That year Japan also scaled down taxes on bond transactions. In 1989 Canada loosened restrictions on foreign banking in Canada. In 1990 France dissolved all controls on foreign exchange, a step the United Kingdom had taken in 1979. Also in 1990 foreign investors unlocked access to Italy's government securities market, and Italy dismantled its last controls on foreign exchange. In 1991 Germany scrapped a tax on security transactions. In 1992 the Chicago Mercantile Exchange launched GLOBEX, the first global electronic trading platform.[9]

The changing atmospherics for economic policy poured into the outposts of the developed world. New Zealand stands out, a classic example of a developed country that navigated the switch from a highly regulated financial system to one driven by market forces. Following the 1984 election the government overhauled economic strategy to lay emphasis on freer markets, committing itself to undoing trade barriers, reforming labour markets, restoring fiscal discipline and reforming or privatizing state-owned enterprises. To unleash the financial sector into the orbit of market forces, the government did away with all interest rate controls, let the exchange rate float freely and brought forward market based tenders for government securities.[10] The government opened the banking industry for new entrants regardless of domicile, and granted non-banking institutions the right to deal in foreign exchange markets. Controls on inflow and outflow of capital were removed.

By 1989 several developing countries (Argentina, Chile, Malaysia, Mexico, the Philippines, Thailand, Uruguay and Francophone Africa) permitted wide freedom for capital flows.[11] In the 1990s momentum for financial liberation overflowed into developing countries. Advances in information and communication technologies widened investors' radar screen, enabling them to access and track asset prices around the world. These advances defied and undermined the initiatives of governments trying to enforce capital controls. Mutual funds and pension funds in developed countries were willing to spread risk across a wider spectrum of assets by investing in foreign countries. Also, capital inflows promised to finance accelerated economic development and raise living standards.

Lastly, the carrots and whips of the World Bank and IMF steered countries toward financial openness. Without a gold standard propping up a world monetary system, currencies have value if households and businesses have reasons to hold them. If a currency passes as a ticket to promising returns on capital, then it embodies value. One means of shoring up the value of a currency is to award capital denominated in that currency the widest and most unfettered opportunities to earn income.

For decades India flirted with socialism, counting heavily upon inward-looking and regulation-focused policies to spur economic development. In the 1980s and particularly in the 1990s it warmed to market-opening policies. Until 1991 a maze of restrictions shackled most private capital transactions, including direct foreign investment, portfolio equity investment, borrowing from foreign sources, non-residents deposits, short-term credit and investment in foreign countries. Like many developing countries India, under the approving eye of the IMF, liberalized capital flows to fix balance of payments problems. In 1991 India consented to 51 per cent direct foreign investment equity in priority industries. India also opened equity markets to foreign portfolio investment. In the early 1990s inflows of portfolio investment outdistanced direct foreign investment, a common trend at the time for developing countries. External portfolio investment jumped from 0.1 to 1.2 per cent of GDP between 1990 and 1993. In 1992 Indian companies obtained permission to issue equity abroad. Controls on external borrowing lightened up without going away. Within the ranks of developing countries India, even after these reforms, stood low on the ladder of economic openness according to mid 1990s data.[12] Indonesia, Korea, Malaysia and Thailand liberalized international capital flows before India and scored livelier growth. These countries also went further in liberalizing capital flows.

The case of Malaysia deserves study. Based upon 1994–8 data, Malaysia was one of the most open economies in the world. Exports plus imports added up to over 175 per cent of Malaysian GDP.[13] Running a distant second by this measure went the Philippines, where exports plus imports equalled roughly 90 per cent of GDP. This measure fell below 25 per cent for the United States, India, Japan, Argentina and Brazil. Exports plus imports were just more than 50 per cent for the United Kingdom, and just less than 50 per cent for Germany.

Malaysia went all out for liberalization of capital flows, and staged hasty retreats on two occasions, the last in 1998 with the imposition of capital outflow controls. In 1986–7 Malaysia liberalized capital flows and set to work deregulating its financial system, freeing interest rates to move with market forces, doing away with credit controls, and nurturing competition and efficiency in the system.[14] Inflows of capital gathered a heady momentum between 1990 and 1993, sending Malaysian authorities scurrying to put curbs on portfolio investment inflows. Earlier Malaysian authorities pushed up interest rates to combat inflation, but economic fundamentals remained inviting. A gust of foreign capital swept down, drawn by excellent returns. A sudden and unforeseen inflow of foreign capital exposes a host economy to a risk of destabilization. Rather than cut interest rates, Malaysian authorities reached for controls over capital inflows. Malaysian residents no longer sold securities with maturity less than one year to non-residents. Offshore investors met with less access to Malaysian commercial banks when seeking backing for speculative activities. Malaysian banks coped with size restrictions on deposit liabilities to non-residents and stiffer reserves requirements on foreign bank deposits of Malaysian currency. Most of these controls went out of effect by the close of 1994. In 1998 a destabilizing exodus of foreign capital led Malaysian authorities to install curbs on capital outflows. These curbs limited the ability of non-residents to convert Malaysian currency into another currency, and required prior approval for residents engaging in any species of foreign investment.

THE PRIVATIZATION REVOLUTION

The dissolution of controls on international capital flows holds a high place within the wake trailing a deeper capitalist revolution, but privatization goes straight to the heart of it. The term 'privatization' covers all government divestiture of property and activities that can be owned and run by the private sector. Margaret Thatcher's Conservative government started a global wave of privatization that rippled throughout the 1980s. After World War II the United Kingdom, the soul of global capitalism at the dawn of the twentieth century, had become infected with a passion for nationalization. In the 1980s it swung around to the opposite ideological pole, and pressed forward with privatization. In the UK's case the more fitting term is denationalization, since most of the privatized firms had earlier undergone nationalization. An inefficient constellation of nationalized industries made happy hunting grounds for believers in privatization. Remember the list of firms the conservative government sold to the private sector included Jaguar, British Rail, English Channel Ferry Service, British Petroleum, British Telecom, British Gas and the British Airport Authority.[15] The government also sold all or part of its stake in British Sugar, British Aerospace, British Petroleum and British Steel. Roughly 1 million public housing units and assorted public utilities went into the private sphere.[16]

Other European governments shared in the privatization movement. Mitterrand's government in France sold off Saint-Gobain, a materials producer, and Paribas, a key bank. The first socialist government of Spain privatized SEAT, an automobile manufacturer, and the Italian government let Alfa Romeo go to the private sector, along with its stake in Alitalia and other public assets.

The United States and Japan also hoisted the banner of privatization. The Japanese government privatized Japanese Airlines, Nippon Telegraph and Telephone, and other public operations. In 1987 the federal government put its 85 per cent stake in Conrail, a non-profit government corporation stitched together from bankrupt railroads of the northeastern United States, on the auction block.[17] This public stock offering raised $165 million before underwriting fees. The US government entertained proposals to privatize air traffic control, the postal service, low-income housing, federal loan programmes, military commissaries and prisons, and Medicare, but these never graduated into action. The federal government enlarged the use of private contractors to perform background checks for government job applicants, collect on bad debts owed the government, and audit books of the General Services Administration. Nearly all industry in the United States, even telecommunications, already belonged to private investors, leaving little publicly owned industry ripe to privatize. The United States owed state and local governments for the broadest sweep toward privatization.[18] Housekeeping services, building maintenance, vehicle fleet management, lawn care, data processing and engineering services were custom-made for privatization. States also privatized prisons.

Among OECD (Organization for Economic Cooperation and Development) countries, the United Kingdom between 1975 and 1990 reported the widest shrinkage in state ownership of traditionally regulated industries – airlines, road transport, telecommunications, postal services and utilities.[19] Japan, New Zealand and Finland also made hefty cuts in government ownership during that time frame. The US and Australia settled for small progress, but more progress occurred in Austria, Belgium, Denmark, Finland, Germany, Ireland, Norway, Spain, Sweden, Switzerland, Turkey and Canada.

It is illuminating of the times that developing countries were not too poor to reverence the privatization movement. In poorer countries socialism and government ownership of private property generally appeal. Ownership of property transfigured into a prime social marker, and a classless society equated to one without private property. Many poor citizens opted to take their chances with a concrete equality of wealth rather than an abstract equality of votes promised by democracy. The straightest path to equality of wealth lay in government confiscation and ownership. No one expected socialism to help the few who were rich. When socialism lent no succour to the poor, it surrendered its rationale for existence. From 1995 Chile privatized airlines, urban transport, telecommunications and ports. Mexico took strides in this sphere as well, and India made a sound showing. Korea, the Philippines, Egypt and Turkey made measurable progress. Egypt's warmth toward privatization grew to importance when laid aside against that country's friendly ties with Eastern Bloc countries. These findings applied to transportation and communication industries. Shifting the spotlight to common product-oriented industries (petroleum, fertilizer, mining, sugar, textiles, cement and steel) gives a similar picture. For these industries Chile missed by only two places top ranking among developing countries for privatization in product-oriented industries. Korea chalked up the largest gains in privatization for these industries and Ghana trailed close behind, though scoring zero progress toward privatization in the transportation and telecommunication fields. Mexico showcased privatization triumphs in product-oriented industries, matching its privatization performance in transportation and telecommunication fields. Egypt split about even between privatization in transportation and communication industries and in product-oriented industries. Compared to privatization in transportation and telecommunication fields, India orchestrated less and the Philippines and Turkey more privatization in the product-oriented industries. Senegal went without privatization in the transportation and telecommunication fields, but assimilated substantial privatization in product-oriented industries.[20]

In the 1980s Jamaica cast its lot with privatization after a long flirtation with socialism. The World Bank and the IMF nudged it towards privatization after entering into short-term adjustment lending to the Jamaican government. Jamaica in the 1980s belonged in the same league as the United Kingdom when it came to progress and commitment to privatization.[21] By 1990 it had a phalanx of 41 privatized companies. Numerous hotels underwent privatization. Companies in banking and finance, transportation and telecommunication, mining and agriculture went to the private sector. A sentence of privatization overhung another 50 firms. The Jamaican Stock Exchange (JSE) came alive in the wake of privatization. In the 1970s only four firms issued new shares on the JSE. Between 1982 and 1990 ten firms issued new shares. Thanks partly to a long bull market, market capitalization as a percentage of GDP rose from 2.5 per cent in 1980 to 28.1 in 1989. Trading volume went up tenfold between 1984 and 1989.

Malaysia's privatization record sounded a discordant note partly because it was home to a highly developed equity market and a thriving private sector when it opted for privatization. Its stock market was one of the liveliest emerging stock markets in the world. Outside observers envisaged Malaysia in the frontline of privatization among developing countries, but the reality was different. By 1990 Malaysia listed a mere 24 companies spun off to the private sphere. Thirteen of the companies were in commerce, manufacturing and services. Banking and finance supplied the other two. Agriculture accounted for five privatizations and transportation and communication for four.

At first observers saw Malaysia as a standard-bearer of privatization in the developing world. Government officials talked of establishing 'Malaysia Inc'. In the Malaysia Inc. vision of Malaysia, the government contented itself with furnishing infrastructure, deregulation, liberalization and macroeconomic stability, and the private sector played the part of economic dynamo. Economic plans are usually wedded to central planning, regulation and socialism, but Malaysian economic plans touted privatization as a goal. Given savings rates at nearly 30 per cent of GDP and boasting a large sector of state-owned enterprises, Malaysia flaunted the signs of a country groomed for privatization, but the process was slow.

Privatization initiatives cropped up in most developing countries. Argentina, Brazil, Trinidad and Tobago, Papua New Guinea, Sri Lanka, Kenya and Malawi undertook privatization. In most countries privatization imparted a fertilizing ingredient in a wider programme of reform aimed at deregulation, free markets, freer international trade and more open financial markets. In many countries revenue raised from selling off state-owned enterprises went to balancing the government's budget. In 1993 a new government in Peru outlined an economic policy that called for privatizing large slices of the state-owned sector. The same year a new rightwing government in Ecuador received congressional approval but showed no hurry to take action on privatization of 160 state-owned enterprises. In 1995 the Bolivian government netted $920 million in sales of state-owned enterprises, and in 1996 laid out plans to privatize more.

The Bolivian case illustrates why in some countries privatization inched forward without hurry. Out of anger over privatization and in solidarity with striking teachers, the Central Obrera Boliviana, a central labour organization, called a general strike in March 1996, persuading the government to shelve plans for privatization of the state-owned oil company. The company later underwent privatization with the government retaining a minority interest. In Mexico privatization could not go forward without a constitutional amendment.[22] In Turkey the courts threw out some sales of privatized companies.

Perhaps no turn of events measures the social and economic power at the bottom of the capitalist revolution better than the rapid displacement of centrally planned economies with market economies in Eastern Europe. Privatization clashed against sturdier hurdles in socialist countries, but these countries came under internal political fire since the blame for economic failure lay squarely at the feet of central planning. In the former German Democratic Republic, favourable financial, legal and technical conditions lubricated the mechanics of privatization, but snags remained to gum up progress.[23] The 9,000 state enterprises slated for privatization dissolved into 30,000 to 40,000 firms in a market economy. These nurslings went to private buyers at a rate of 300 per month. The government consented to settle the prices by arbitration after the sale out of indecision over the worth of privatized companies.

Privatization utterly overturned state ownership in Eastern Bloc countries. Between 1990 and 1995 the share of GDP flowing from the private sector doubled in Poland, multiplied threefold in Hungary, sevenfold in the Czech Republic and sixfold in Russia, Estonia and the Slovak Republic. By 1995 the share of GDP churned out by the private sector topped 50 per cent in Poland, Hungary, the Czech Republic, the Slovak Republic, Estonia, Lithuania, Latvia, Albania, Mongolia and Russia.

Czechoslovakia doled out free shares of stock to diversify and multiply shareholders of privatized companies and quicken privatization. Poland's privatization plan revamped large state-owned enterprises into corporations, and distributed shareholder stock between workers, pension funds, banks and other financial institutions. Some stock went to private buyers.

China lagged far behind Eastern Europe when it came to privatization, but reform of agriculture in 1978 achieved some of the same goals. Collective farms were torn apart and a system of household responsibility usurped decision-making authority, vesting households with user rights over land they cultivated. The reform ditched price and marketing controls that discriminated against agriculture. As food shortages and rising food prices bedevilled the era of the 1970s, rising agricultural production and rural incomes radiated an animating growth surge throughout the Chinese economy. Vietnam overhauled agriculture along similar lines in the mid 1980s and within a few years graduated from a rice importer to a rice exporter.[24]

Privatization sowed the seeds for stock market development. By 1995 Russia, China, Poland, Hungary, the Czech Republic, the Slovak Republic, Croatia, Lithuania and Romania boasted stripling stock markets. In most of these countries stock ownership turnover was low by the standards of developed countries, but in China a highflying turnover rate echoed a growing passion for speculation.

It hardly needs to be said that countries alive with privatization eagerly flocked to the less radical standard of price deregulation. Between 1975 and 1990 New Zealand among developed countries took the longest strides towards dismantling entry restrictions on new firms. The United States merited mention for deregulation of airlines, railroads and telecommunications. Australia, Austria, Canada, Germany, Ireland, Norway, Japan, Turkey and the United Kingdom saw measurable progress over this time span. Small change occurred in Belgium, Denmark, Sweden and Switzerland, but all these countries, except for Belgium, disentangled markets from price deregulation. No OECD country strengthened entry restrictions or price regulations.[25]

Among developing countries Chile, Korea, Mexico, Philippines, Egypt, Ghana, India, Senegal and Turkey markedly loosened the regulatory grip on product industries. Deregulation of services industries went less uniformly, but all deregulated them to some degree.

THE PROTECTION OF THE GLOBAL COMMONS

As the virtues of private ownership drew applause from governments worldwide, fresh concerns arose surrounding the fate of resources held in common. The gospel of capitalism held that private property supplied the keystone in a system of rewards and penalties that favoured the conservation of resources. Privately owned resources multiplied the owner's income and wealth when employed in a manner that preserved value. Owners who let resources go to waste faced sure punishment thanks to a costly depreciation in the value of those resources. Capitalism was innocent until proven guilty of the charge that short-sighted and greedy owners permitted an accelerated exploitation of resources for quick gains. Leaving this issue aside, owners, thinking in the long term, reaped the fattest profits by positive stewardship over resources, shielding them from abuse and harnessing them to produce goods and services that society most needed. Moreover, the craziest exploitation decimated resources that belonged to no one. The sorry fate of the American buffalo comes to mind as a case of reckless and greedy exploitation, and it was lack of private ownership that left the buffalo unprotected. Rustling a rancher's cow was a hanging offence, while shooting and skinning buffalo wore the sanitized aspect of an honest living.

Capitalism that triumphed harnessing greed for higher good has yet to lose an ill repute for mishandling the use of resources held in common. Now socialist societies also have to live down a chequered past for exploitation of resources shared in common with capitalist countries. Whales, with the same Achilles heel as the buffalo, are being hunted to extinction with twentieth century technology.

In 1946 the United States hosted the International Whaling Conference, which led to the organization of the International Whaling Commission (IWC). The mission of the IWC lay in developing an industrial code pledged to shielding the whale from over-exploitation and extinction. As postwar economic growth charged ahead, the whale transfigured into a symbol of man's greedy and unintelligent exploitation of collectively held resources. In 1972 the United Nations sponsored the Stockholm Conference addressing global environmental issues. During the conference environmental activists held a celebration of the whale, including a whale march into Stockholm. Japan and the Soviet Union paid little heed to the IWC and pursued the whale to near extinction. Japan secretly underwrote whale pirates working under the flags of non-IWC countries. The timing seemed ironic that the IWC in 1982 voted to impose a five-year moratorium on whaling just as a worldwide capitalism and privatization revolution burst on the world. The same governments arousing capitalist greed to spur economic development clamoured for a watchdog to safeguard a global resource shared in common.

Whales belong to a class of resources that lie outside the jurisdiction of nations, and collectively go by the name 'global commons'. The global commons encompasses the atmosphere, Antarctica, the oceans, outer space, migrating birds, ocean mammals and fish. It covers the electromagnetic environment born of wireless transmission. Early on farming villages embraced habits, customs and practices for the intelligent management of communal grazing lands, safeguarding their fertility and usefulness for future generations. One unfinished and ongoing task of globalization comes down to the international community brokering rules for managing the global commons. Since the 1972 Stockholm Conference governments have struck more than 130 environmental treaties.[26] Several knotty issues rank high on the list of environmental worries that must be tackled in a multinational framework. Ozone depletion may breed a scourge of skin cancer. Greenhouse gas emissions lead to global warming, causing ice caps to melt and flood low-lying coasts and islands. Global warming can also blight agricultural production and multiply desert areas. Rainforest and coral reefs face a dreary future in developing countries. Depletion of rainforest and coral reefs, paired with degradation and desertification of land, lays waste to many biological species whose genetic material will be forever lost. Biodiversity is richer in developing countries, and this genetic material may be needed as medical knowledge unfolds. Unfortunately it is in developing countries that environmental concerns take a backseat to economic development.

Twenty years after the Stockholm conference, the United Nations Committee on Environment and Development held a second conference in Rio de Janeiro. The conferees adopted the Rio Declaration on Environment and Development, which acknowledged that all sovereign countries shared a communal responsibility to safeguard the earth's ecosystem. In December 1997, 160 nations met in Kyoto, Japan, and signed an agreement to limit greenhouse emissions. The US later pulled out of the agreement.

THE ORGANIZATION OF THE WORLD TRADE ORGANIZATION

Governments embracing private property and free markets at home aided and abetted forces pitching free trade between nations. Canada, Mexico and the United States ratified the North American Free Trade Agreement, providing for measured eradication of tariffs and trade restrictions on all goods traded in North America. The Treaty became effective on 1 January 1994. The treaty also afforded protection to patents, copyrights and trademarks. In United States Senate confirmation debates NAFTA drew fire from critics worried about environmental and labour issues. The treaty stirred fears that stiffer foreign competition would pressure the United States to dilute and slacken environmental and labour laws. The three governments gave grudging consent to treaty supplements that made NAFTA the environmentally friendliest of free trade organizations.

In 1994 Europe formed the European Economic Area, which unified and fused into one free trade area the countries of the European Union and the countries of the European Free Trade Association. In the same year the organization of the General Agreement on Tariffs and Trade (GATT) signed a trade pact dissolving itself and launching the World Trade Organization (WTO). The last GATT negotiations, the Uruguay Round, opened in 1986 and terminated in 1994. Aside from fathering the WTO, this round of talks pledged the contracting parties to scale down tariffs by 33 per cent over time, and undo other trade obstacles. The agreement also incorporated provisions to open up investment flows between countries and to protect patents, copyrights, trademarks and other intellectual property rights. Sound recordings and computer programs, easily duplicated, stood out among international concerns for intellectual property rights.

GATT and WTO coexisted in 1995 as governments shifted gears into the newer and broader organization. The WTO has a similar mission to GATT but its writ ranges wider. GATT's duties all came within the narrow orbit of merchandise trade, but WTO mounted the throne of watchdog over merchandise trade practices, trade practices in services such as international telephones, and practices regarding intellectual property rights. As part of administering and policing prior and freshly negotiated trade agreements the WTO settles trade disputes between member states, brandishing enforcement powers that GATT never wielded. The WTO can hand down trade sanctions on countries unwilling to revoke laws and practices that trespass and thwart WTO agreements.

Headquartered in Geneva, the WTO takes instructions and direction from a General Council. Member states send an ambassador to serve on the general council and assorted subsidiary and specialist committees. Every two years a ministerial conference meets and appoints a director-general. Wider liberalization of international trade and investment monopolizes the agenda at these meetings. The General

Council answers to an overseeing ministerial conference. The WTO began with a membership of 124 states, and grew that membership to 146 by 2003. Another 31 states participated as observers, and all but two of these observers had applied for membership.

The rules of the WTO carry the force of law on member states. A WTO arbitration panel hears the arguments of members locked in trade disputes. Unsatisfied disputants can appeal rulings of this panel to a WTO appellate body whose rulings are irrevocable. WTO rules prescribe time limits for resolution of disputes. The 'banana wars' illustrate the kinds of disputes brought before the WTO. Banana exporting countries of Latin American lodged a complaint against the EU for unfairly favouring banana-exporting countries in Africa, Caribbean and the Pacific. The favoured banana exporters enjoyed unique trade ties as former European colonies. The WTO ruled that the EU must level the banana market playing field and stop favouritism to former colonies.

The WTO serves as a focus for much of the criticism levelled against the flowering of global capitalism. Critics point an accusing finger at WTO trade rules for paying small notice to workers' rights, environmental issues or human health. They bewail the informal tyranny of an international agency that can hold the laws and regu-lations of sovereign nations a violation of trade rules, unleashing unbearable pressure to amend these laws. The press and public are shut out from hearings on trade disputes, kindling more scepticism and suspicion. Most WTO member countries belong to the ranks of democratic governments, but member electorates find the lines of democratic accountability hazy and unintelligible where trade policy is concerned.

Unhappiness with the WTO boiled over in late 1999 when over 30,000 activists swept down upon a WTO summit in Seattle, Washington. The activists wanted reforms that rendered the WTO more answerable to the voices of consumers, unionists, farmers and envi-ronmentalists. A parading army of activists became standard fare at WTO ministerial meetings. At the September 2003 WTO meeting in Cancun, Mexico, a South Korean protestor climbed a metal fence and plunged a knife into his heart. His suicide was a protest for small farmers around the world threatened by dissolution of agricultural subsidies and protectionist trade policies. In July 2001 a conference of industrialized nations held in Genoa ended with one protestor shot dead by Italian police.

Chapter 9

The Force of Speculation Enrolled in the Cause of Globalization

In September 1929 the Dow Jones Industrial Average (DJIA) touched a peak of 381.17, a giddy climax after six years of marching upwards. The DJIA first scored the 100 mark in 1906, and still dallied in the 100-range in 1924. Then it veered upward through a long stretch of record-breaking closings. As it mounted countless citizens flocked to the stock market buying stocks by the bucketload. The DJIA won an intoxicating notoriety with the man on the street. When the market crumbled, eyes were glued to the DJIA as a graphic measure of the carnage. The DJIA suffered a jolting slip in October 1929, and started a tumble downward, bottoming out at a stupefying 41.22. It only crept back to 150 before the next decade was out. It drooped below 100 in the months following Pearl Harbor but finished the war decade in the 220-range. It was in 1954, after a roughly 25-year valley, that a revitalized DJIA crossed into 400-territory, topping its fitful record of September 1929. In that year J. K. Galbraith published *The Great Crash*, chronicling the disaster of the 1929 crash and dissecting the speculative mania in cold, crystal-clear logic. The searing experience of 1929 lived as a memory in 1954, still stirring thought. The last two and a half decades had quenched the hope of quick gains from speculation.

Speculation boasts an aphrodisiac all its own. It calls for no official qualifications. Before an individual buys anything for speculation, the seller does not ask for evidence of a college degree, or high school diploma, or ability to read and write. Criminal records and health issues do not matter. The buyer does not have to ask anyone to write eloquent letters of recommendation testifying to a sound character and lofty social standing. Speculation can be a sideline and moonlighting activity and a speculator does not have to give up a day job or other sources of income. Speculators can go without telling employers, spouses or friends what they are doing. Since no esoteric or mysterious knowledge or training guarantees success, the playing field appears level for everyone, regardless of background. A victorious speculator can only be lucky, and anyone who is alive and hasn't worked himself out of health may well rate himself lucky. In highly commercialized societies speculation connotes a manly cleverness and boldness that bestows social prestige. In aristocratic and militaristic societies traders and speculators fill a low order of social caste. Samuel Johnson defined a stockjobber as 'a low wretch who gets money by buying and selling shares in funds'. In modern societies individuals without gainful employment may hide in the camouflaging mantle of stock market investors. Investing in the stock market perfumes the social standing of the unemployed and individuals stuck in low-paying careers.

In the 1950s and '60s memories of 1929 still chilled and envenomed the lure of speculation. As a muscular postwar boom gathered an unstoppable momentum, the DJIA again posted new records but not at the wild-eyed tempo of speculative fever. It crossed through the 500-benchmark in March 1956 and topped the 1000-benchmark in November 1972, doubling in just over 15 years. Standards of living grew rapidly, but the DJIA floated cautiously upwards. A doubling of the DJIA over 15 years stood a far cry from the stampeding growth that nearly quadrupled the DJIA over 6 years between 1924 and 1929. Fears of the stock market sprang to life again in the 1970s as economic growth hit the skids, and unemployment shot up. The DJIA skidded to 577.6 by 1974, and the 1000 milestone would not appear again until late 1982.

The stock market became a dull place to be in the 1970s, but doors of speculative teasers flew open in unexpected quarters. We have already seen how speculation in the silver market seduced the Hunt brothers, leaving them peering into a financial abyss. The gold market wooed speculators with equal hopes of rich speculative profits. Remember that the United States had fixed the value of the dollar at $35 per ounce of gold and banned the private ownership of gold for investment. The US government sold off gold stocks to uphold this price until 1968 when the free market price went free from official intervention. In 1971 the United States' suspension of dollar convertibility into gold severed the last official link to free market prices for gold. Precious metals had long served as safe havens from inflation, and now gold prices were free to fluctuate with haphazard shifts in inflation. Without official sales meeting higher gold demand, gold prices shot up, touching $195 an ounce by the end of 1974. Some investors, scared about inflation and abandonment of the gold standard, welcomed gold in investment portfolios. In the United States gold ownership remained illegal until 1 January 1975, but stock ownership in gold mines overcame that legal hurdle. After 1 January 1975 the US Treasury and central banks in other countries sold hefty quantities of gold to satisfy the new demand and to reap handsome profits from gold stocks. Official gold sales sent gold prices skidding to $103 an ounce by August 1976, blistering innumerable small investors. As gold prices rebounded the IMF joined the US Treasury in selling gold to hold prices down.

In 1977 the dollar slipped in foreign exchange markets, assailing confidence in it as a store of value. With all currencies floating and the chief international currency sinking in value, gold cast its spell on fretting investors. Gold seemed a surer choice for holding wealth than currencies or the stock market. From lows in August 1976, the price of gold erupted with seemingly unstoppable momentum. By July 1978 the price had retraced its steps back to the $195 level of December 1974. By February 1979 it was $250 per ounce. In April President Carter unveiled Treasury plans to sell 300,000 ounces of gold per month for the next year, but the price went on climbing, hitting $300 by July. On 6 October 1979 the Federal Reserves announced a switch in monetary regimes, favouring a regime that targeted monetary aggregates. October saw the price of gold hit $400. The last quarter of 1979 saw prime interest rates climb from 13.5 to 15.5 per cent, which increased the lure of money deposits as a rival to the enchantment of gold. The price of gold still soared, hitting an all-time summit of $850 on 21 January 1980, but as prime interest rates went on increasing, investors dumped gold. In July 1982 the price of gold sank to $296. It rebounded to $510, but then yielded to a longer-term trend downward. Before the century was out the price of gold sank into the $250 range.

The gold and silver markets came to the same sad end that awaits all speculative manias. True believers patiently held out hope of a rebounding market. *Business Week* carried an article acknowledging that the price of gold was depressed 'in relative terms', but hypothesizing that fears of political upheavals could send gold prices soaring again, maybe even catapulting the price of gold passed the $1,000 milestone.[1] The periodical *Commodities* carried an article counselling that the price of gold could rebound from a low of $388 to a high of $5,044 per ounce by 1987.[2] Deregulation heralded new and unsullied speculative opportunities. Adventurous souls who never bought in the gold market, who never knew what it was like to be burned alive as the price of gold tumbled, stood ready to act on blind instinct at the next speculative opportunity.

Soaring gold and silver prices were a glaring reminder that speculation could beguile individuals away from safer investments and that opportunities for sudden riches in speculation were not extinct. The Depression psychosis had left the brooding outlook that one should count oneself lucky just to sell something for more than it cost. A seller would sooner see prices crash than rake in windfall profits. That outlook slowly but surely lost its grip. Gold and silver speculation ensnared and burned numberless small investors. Still, it chiefly infected a narrow slice of the population whose attention was already sharpened to investment opportunities.

Highflying prices in another market enriched individuals innocent to speculative ambitions. Many never gave a minute's thought to investing in stocks, bonds or precious metals. In the United States the median sale price of single-family houses grew from $22,600 in September 1970 to $68,300 in September 1980, an escalation of over threefold. Consumer prices grew by a quieter factor of 2.11. In some regions housing prices boomed more, but California was unrivalled in skyrocketing house prices. In 1977 alone western states underwent an average 24.5 per cent rise in the median price of single-family houses. The purest of American dreams, owning a home, turned a handsomer rate of return than the stock market. Individuals bought houses, fixed them up, rented them out, and sold them for a lordly profit. The requisite grass roots talents of carpentry, plumbing and painting owed little to society's educational institutions or the human instinct for social prestige. Families bought instead of rented houses for children to live in at college. After graduation the house sold for a tidy profit, maybe enough to pay for a college education at a state-supported school. A couple marrying in 1970 and buying a house could a few years later divorce and sell the house for twice what they paid for it. Both husband and the wife rescued their investment out of the house, and underwent a friendlier divorce. Happier couples often sold their family home for a profit, and put the profit into a down payment for a more spacious and luxurious home. They moved on up, counting on selling the new home for a profit if necessary. Teachers, professors, postmen, white-collar industrial managers and housewives earned spare income on the side tinkering with rental property. In 1977 houses for rent in San Francisco outnumbered houses for sale. In normal times ten houses went up for sale for every one listed for rent.[3]

Borrowing money to purchase a commodity in speculative play holds a high place in the inventory of levers and manoeuvres beloved by speculators. By such stratagems, speculators pyramid small investments into towering profits. The Hunt brothers borrowed money to purchase silver after the Federal Reserve sternly warned commercial banks against loaning money to finance speculation. Entrenched connections permitted the Hunt brothers to turn up their noses at the Federal Reserve, but the humblest family needed no cosy relationships with lenders to purchase a house on credit. In the United States any mortgage company would gladly arrange a house loan for a mere 5 per cent down, putting the margin for speculating in houses far below the margin for speculating in the stock market. The government gave its loyalty to a credit system that helped families purchase homes.

Land prices made a parallel jump in prices. A study of Iowa farmland prices points to a doubling of land prices in inflation-adjusted numbers.[4] Measuring land prices in 1992 dollars as a benchmark put Iowa farmland in 1970 selling for roughly $1,500 per acre. By 1980 the price had climbed to roughly $3,400 per acre, more than doubling. What the land investment could buy in real purchasing power had more than doubled. Sticking to prices converted to 1992 dollars underscores the fall in land prices with disinflation. By this inflation-adjusted measure the price of Iowa farmland fell back to $1,500 per acre by the mid 1980s. Doctors, lawyers and dentists bought farms as hobbies, reaped windfall profits from soaring prices, and enjoyed a rustic country retreat.

The United States's housing statistics mirrored a worldwide housing market. In 1978 prices of houses, apartments and land in South Korea roughly doubled. In 1981 a burning issue in West Berlin surrounded a scarcity of low and medium-income houses. A housing deficiency festered in the shadows of numerous vacant buildings held by speculators. In West Germany, and particularly West Berlin, young people populated the buildings illegally as squatters. Forced evictions of squatters sparked brutal and noisy confrontations and property was smashed. In September 1981 riots erupted in several cities after a police bus crushed and killed an eighteen year old in one of these episodes. During the mid 1970s young couples in France and particularly Paris waited several years before getting an apartment. During Queen Beatrix's investiture as Queen of the Netherlands in 1980, angry squatters seized the festive occasion to hotly protest Amsterdam's housing shortage.

THE MAKING OF A SPECULATIVE DEBACLE

By the early 1980s households and businesses awoke to the possibility that towering profits could be earned from intelligent or lucky speculation. Real estate and precious metals persuaded a broad demographic spectrum that luscious profits awaited individuals who paid close attention to what they bought. Few sophisticated Wall Street types were given to soiling their hands restoring antiques or classic automobiles, but hardly a city in the United States was too small or poor to have citizens, maybe with scanty educations, doing just that, and they thrilled to handsome windfall profits. Good investments of all kinds sprang up that lay within the grasp of the most financially innocent of citizens. From gold, historically the most prestigious of financial assets, to antique furniture, a Niagara of profits poured in from speculation, and hopeful eyes scanned the economic horizon for fresh speculative opportunities.

The 1980s furnished just what the doctor ordered for a population primed to jump into a speculative mania. The stock market crash of 1929 had faded into a dull memory. Most stockbrokers and investors believed vulnerability to a crash of that scale went by the wayside long ago. Tight money and high interest rates invited foreign capital. Large flows of money swept in from Japan where financial liberalization was underway. High interest rates in the United States dealt blows to stock markets around the world. Nowhere could stocks compete against US treasury bonds earning 13–14 per cent interest. Lower tax rates further enriched the returns to capital, leaving the United States more than ever the darling of foreign capital. In 1982 the United States saw its way clear to ease monetary policy. Global stock and bond markets cheered when Paul Volcker announced plans to abbreviate the Federal Reserve's strategy of money supply targeting. The new economic strategy proposed to let interest rates drop, dragging down the value of the dollar in foreign exchange markets, making US goods more competitive in the global market place. An economic recovery in the world's economic locomotive would pull the rest of global economy out of recession.

The global economy basked in another shaft of sunlight in 1985 when the price of crude oil crashed to $10 per barrel, further cheering equity markets and dispelling inflationary forces and fears. In 1986 the Federal Reserve slashed the discount rate four times within six months.[5]

Between 1980 and 1982 the DJIA ranged between dips in the mid 760s and flirtations with 1,000. In late 1982 the DJIA put the 1,000 milestone beneath its feet and only looked up. The following year it invaded 1,200 territory, but remained flat in 1984, finishing in the 1,200 range. Toward the end of 1985 stock prices sprouted wings, crossing into 1,400 territory in November, and puncturing the 1,500 milestone in December. Fears of inflation died when oil prices crashed, freeing central banks to quicken growth of money stocks. As the market in 1986 climbed into the 1,600–1,700 ranges, bewildered investors could only wonder how much higher the market could go. The 1970s taught investors to sell when the DJIA bordered on record-breaking ground. It first crossed 1,000 in 1972 but not until 1982 did the market roar past 1,000 without retreating. Before 1986 was out the market gained new wind and mounted upwards, crossing through another milestone, 2,000, early in 1987. It took twelve years for the DJIA to climb from 1,000 to 1,500, but barely more than a year to leap from 1,500 to 2,000.

By 1987 stock market trading wore the aspect of a speculative frenzy. Cautious investors hoped and predicted that the market would take a breather, and settle into a quiet trading range between 1,800 and 2,200. Given the years the DJIA took to put the 1,000 signpost safely in the background, what investor could expect the market to long hold the fresh record of 2,000? But stock prices went on increasing. The DJIA opened 1987 at 1,895.95, and surged upwards 44 per cent, peaking at 2,722.42 on 25 August. While predictions of when the DJIA would crack 3,000 echoed down Wall Street, the market stumbled and then entered a steep decline, backtracking 1,000 points in two months. It had spent over a decade struggling to achieve and hold 1,000 points, and then lost 1,000 points in a mere two months. Half of the 1,000 points melted away on 19 October, when the market lost 508 points, the largest one-day drop ever. It ended the year near 2,000.

A radiating stock market boom infected the global economy. Between December 1986 and August 1987, stock markets in the New York, London and Tokyo, the three largest financial centres, saw parallel surges ranging between 42 and 46 per cent. Just as the DJIA trespassed 2,000 territory, Japan's Nikkei Dow burst through 20,000, and the London FTSE cracked through 1,800. French and West German stock markets broke records in the summer of 1987. European stock markets were buoyed by Japanese investors. The crash on Wall Street sparked a global wave of stock selling. The day after the Wall Street bubble burst, Tokyo saw stocks plunge 15 per cent. Hong Kong shut down its market for one week.

A post-mortem on a stock market crash is inescapable and not always reliable. Much blame was laid at the feet of program trading.

Computer programs, engineered to shield asset values, all pushed the sell button at once. The usual number of post-crash scandals oozed into the headlines. Another large underlying factor stemmed from the development of the global economic system. With financial liberalization Japanese investors became players in US financial markets. Between January and August 1987 Japanese investors bought $8 billion of US Treasury bonds per month.[6] In September sales to Japanese investors sank to $1 billion. In October Japanese investors hurriedly unloaded US Treasury bonds, driving bond prices down and the yield on 30-year Treasury bonds above 10 per cent. Why were thousands of Japanese investors selling US Treasuries, a safe investment? Perhaps economic expansion in the United States ignited fears of a declining dollar. In 1970 a dollar traded for 360 yen. Between 1982 and 1985, years of a strong dollar, it traded around 250 yen. Between 1985 and 1995 it sank against the yen, bottoming in a range of 100 yen per dollar. Another reason Japanese investors bailed out was fresh investing opportunities in Japan. The Japanese government phased in privatization of Japan's largest telecommunication company, NTT. These shares drew heavy investor and speculator interest, and another block of shares came up for sale in November 1987.[7] Japanese investors liquidated US Treasuries in anticipation of the next offering of NTT shares.

In defiance of many predictions, the global economy rebounded in haste from Wall Street's debacle. From the recession of 1981–2 the global economy grew on the re-employment of idle capacity. By 1988 ageing and outgrown capital stocks opened large gaps and opportunities for modern and unworn capital goods. The global economy sprang back to life fed by booming investment spending. In 1988 American and European monetary authorities began nudging up interest rates, aiming for a disciplined and healthy recovery with price stability. Japan was an exception among the largest economies. The Bank of Japan's discount rate remained pinned down to the postwar low of 2.5 per cent until May 1989.

Most world stock markets eked out slim recoveries before the end of 1987. Within four years the DJIA broke 3,000. A screeching economic deceleration never came about, but major industrial countries went on worrying about the weakening dollar. Recall that the United States embraced an economic policy pairing large budget deficits with large trade deficits. Japan sold the United States Toyotas and from the dollar proceeds bought US government bonds. A river of imports sent dollars out of the United States much faster than a trickle of exports drew dollars back. Unless foreigners had a reason to hold redundant dollars, they would sell them off, sending the dollar plummeting. High US interest rates persuaded foreigners to hold dollars. As long as US interest rates hovered in the upper reaches, the dollar had an unbeatable ally. Once inflation cooled, stratospheric interest rates held no charm for the United States, and a falling dollar only rendered US goods less costly in foreign markets and more competitive at home. The rest of the world stood to lose from a falling dollar that left US goods more competitive against foreign goods. In February 1987 finance ministers of the major industrialized countries met in the Louvre, Paris, and saw eye-to-eye on the need to jointly prop up the dollar. They undertook buying dollars with their own currencies, shoring up the demand and value of the dollar, and swelling money stocks of their own currencies.

THE TOKYO BUBBLE

The world was in for another wild speculative ride, this time in Japan, before the 1980s was out. Events leading up to the stock market crash of 1929 throw a telling light on the Tokyo Bubble. In the spring of 1927 Montagu Norman, Governor of the Bank of England, headed a delegation of European politicians who undertook to recruit the Federal Reserve on the side of looser monetary policies. Lower interest rates in the United States held the key for venting pressure on European currencies, clearing the field for easier monetary policies in Europe. The Federal Reserve pitched in and shaved its discount rate from 4.0 to 3.5 per cent,[8] and enlarged money stocks by buying government bonds, keeping interest rates pegged at low levels. Money from bond sales to the Federal Reserve spilled over to the stock market, touching off a speculative boom.

Substitute Japan in 1988 for the United States in 1927. In 1927 the British pound sterling belonged in the forefront of leading world currencies, and the United States eased monetary policy to bolster it. In 1988 the US dollar was the leading world currency, and Japan rallied to fortify it with easier monetary policy. In 1927 the United States was the world's largest creditor, giving it a distinctive stake in the value of the pound sterling. In 1988 Japan was the world's largest creditor, inspiring in that country an unthinking loyalty to the US dollar. The weakening of the dollar that started in 1985 mirrored itself in a strengthening of the yen. Exports supplied the engine and lifeblood of the Japanese economy and a highflying yen left Japanese exports more costly to foreign buyers. In 1986 Japanese growth turned sluggish. The Japanese government largely shunned the use of fiscal policy to reignite an ailing economy, relying instead upon monetary policy. Easy money policies kept interest rates down, and the yen cheap. A cheap yen translated as low-cost exports to foreign markets. Purchasing dollars with new yen, strengthening the dollar and weakening the yen, enlarged the Japanese money supply.

Early in 1986 the Bank of Japan's discount rate stood at 5 per cent. Within a year this was cut in half. At 2.5 per cent it logged a postwar low. Japanese financial liberalization also kicked in, inviting Japanese capital to hunt abroad for fatter interest rates, further undermining the yen and strengthening the dollar. Japanese investors sold yen and bought dollars to invest in the United States. The October 1987 crash evoked global nightmares of a 1930s replay, and governments world-wide unleashed domestic money stock growth. The Bank of Japan let the supply of yen grow faster to hold its value down against other currencies. The Japanese government wielded behind-the-scenes pressure on banks to curb lending for real estate speculation, but took no steps to dampen money stock growth. Despite pressure to starve lending on real estate speculation, residential and commercial property values doubled between 1986 and 1989.

All the global forces for expansion seemed to swarm in Japan, as if it siphoned them in. Real GDP growth in the United States went slack at a yearly 2.5 per cent in 1989 and 1 per cent in 1990. Japan logged 4.9 per cent real GDP growth in 1989 and 5.4 per cent in 1990. Japanese consumers spent. Households saw no point stashing away savings for a house they could never afford. The Nikkei stood roughly at 12,000 in

1986. After the October 1987 crash it fell to a post-crash low of 17,387, far above its value at the end of 1986. From that low the Nikkei index went on a euphoric tear, rocketing upwards 120 per cent within two years, marking a breathtaking peak of 38,915 in December 1989.[9] This speculative frenzy infected the market for works of art. In the late 1980s the Japanese proudly took home four out of every ten quality paintings auctioned off at the biggest events.[10] Companies also yielded to a capital-spending binge.

The Nikkei index fell only a little faster than it had climbed, never falling to pieces with a resounding crash. It sank to the 20,000-range in October 1990, but the sliding went unstopped. In 1992 it dipped within the neighbourhood of 15,000.[11] The Nikkei never retraced the lost ground to match past records. It opened 1999 below 15,000, and climbed past 20,000 in the first quarter of 2000 before slumping again, momentarily sinking below the 8,000-range in the second quarter of 2003. The Japanese talent for smoothly manipulating stock prices and escaping a complete crash may lie at the bottom of the market's failure to build a base and recover.

In the crash aftermath the usual rash of sham financial practices bubbled to the surface, ranging from secretly manipulating stock prices and covering losses of big investors to whitewashing real losses with sleight of hand accounting. A bursting bubble of stratospheric property prices sparked a gentler but lasting decline in property prices, leaving banks with an overhang of bad debts. Banks and insurance companies reported staggering losses after writing off bad loans. Many feared a collapse of the country's financial system lurked right around the corner. In 1995 depositors staged a sudden run on the Cosmos Shinyo Kumiai, the largest credit union in Tokyo. That year also saw short-term interest rates droop below 1 per cent amid the Bank of Japan's bid to reinflate the economy. In 1996 the government felt a need to offer assurance that none of the 21 largest banks would be allowed to fail. Aggressive monetary growth pushed interest rates to near zero and a hair's breadth of inflation lapsed to a touch of deflation as a new century opened. The Bank of Japan pegged Japanese interest rates bordering on zero, holding out to Japanese investors a golden opportunity. They could borrow yen at low interest rates, exchange them into dollars, and purchase higher-interest US Treasury bonds. By infusing liquidity into a global financial system, the Bank of Japan brewed a combustible mixture for igniting financial markets in other quarters.

Deep and lingering economic woes did little to soften Japan's pledge to financial liberalization. Foreign pressure helped keep Japan on track. In April 1998 a law took effect lifting the last restrictions on international financial transactions. Under a programme slated for implementation between 1997 and 2000, the government deregulated stock brokerage fees and other financial commissions, the provision of innovative financial instruments, and the range of business activities in banking, securities, trust and insurance.

THE PASSION FOR SPECULATION INFECTS EMERGING MARKETS

When the curtain descended on the 1980s, many investors were sharpened to attention at the prospect of sweeping speculative gains if they could only buy in and sell out at the right time. Speculative outbursts in the United States and Japan awakened a thirst for riches earned simply by owning things. It was what a person owned and not their profession or trade that counted. The enthusiasm of those who rode out speculative ecstasies skidded to a jolting and brutal halt. Their passion for speculation was cured, but spectators gazing from the sidelines burned with regret for not getting in at the first hint of speculative opportunity. They saw the problem as one of delicate timing, counting losing speculators as the ones who finished last in the competition for the best timing. Innocent to the passion that envelops investors swept up in speculative frenzy, they rated their chances high of selling out before the crash. On hearing that someone has started investing in Hong Kong, they wonder what that investor knows that they do not know. Getting in at the bottom requires hurried decisions and actions. Hong Kong is a long way off and no one has infallible real-time information about the situation there. A herd instinct grips investors. They bet that the first investors putting money into Hong Kong's stock market comprehend something that the rest do not. They all flock to Hong

Kong's market. When word is out that some investors are selling off Hong Kong holdings, hordes of investors panic to empty portfolios of Hong Kong holdings. Getting out before the crash is everything. In this context cautiousness means assuming that investors who act first have the best information. An impatient herd instinct usurps investor psychology, and investors do not give a minute's thought to jilting Hong Kong. Mutual fund managers know their mission is to buy in at the bottom and sell at the top. That is what is expected of them. Their compensation is bound up with it.

The herd instinct clearly seized the upper hand among mutual fund managers in the early 1990s. In 1992 the average return to investors investing in emerging markets measured 67 per cent. That has to be measured against a bland 15 per cent on funds invested in shares of large industrial countries. Emerging markets denote financial markets in such countries as Pakistan, the Philippines and Thailand where yearly stock market returns in dollars ranged between 69 and 74 per cent between December 1992 and December 1993. Market returns embody changes in stock prices and effects of currency fluctuations. In 1993 the Singapore index logged a 59.1 per cent increase.[12] Between April and September 1993, the composite Pacific Stock Index, minus Japan, exuberantly doubled in value.[13] For the first 11 months of 1993 market returns of stocks vaulted up 74 per cent in Malaysia, 73 per cent in Finland, and 70 per cent in Hong Kong.[14]

The passion for emerging market stocks suddenly turned chilly after Mexico's debt crisis in 1994, but a freshly negotiated NAFTA put a rainbow over Mexico's dreary and smudged economic outlook. On all sides investors thought favoured entrée to US and Canadian markets could only fire up a developing country such as Mexico. Undaunted investors worldwide open-handedly advanced loans to Mexico, both to the Mexican government and to Mexican corporations. The year 1994 opened with Mexico's sun in the ascent, but political developments soon triggered a somersault in these sunny expectations. A bloody uprising in the Chiapas region rocked the political state of affairs. A messy political situation darkened further after the assassination of the leading presidential candidate. Investors worldwide shied away from Mexico, and redeemed pesos for dollars. The Mexican government maintained a fixed exchange rate between dollars and pesos to render Mexico friendlier and safer for foreign investment. To maintain the fixed exchange rate, the government sold dollars for pesos. Put differently, the government bought pesos with dollars to buttress the peso. The government's reserves of dollars and foreign currency were too thin to ride out the crisis. The reserves of dollars ran dry as the year was out, and the government saw no choice but to devalue the peso, though it had promised this would never happen. The devaluation sparked a panicky retreat of foreign investors from Mexico. Between December 1994 and February 1995 market returns in dollars on Mexico's stock market plunged by 62 per cent.[15]

As Mexico's government debt came due and the government needed to roll it over in new debt, investors balked. The Mexican government trembled at the edge of bankruptcy. A mere few months had transformed Mexico from an emerging economy with a hopeful and radiant future to a disordered and risky economy with a government ready to default on its debt. The US government shuddered at the thought of economic collapse in Mexico. It could spark a colossal illegal immigration from Mexico into the United States and a panicky flight of capital from other developing countries. A cooperative initiative between the US government and the IMF spearheaded an international effort to bail out the Mexican government. The US government signed off on loan guarantees for debt to the Mexican government, permitting it to roll over its debt. The loan guarantees spruced up the outlook for the Mexican economy, soothing the fears and modulating the perceived risk of investing in that country, but did not spare the Mexican peso from devaluation. In August 1994 it took 30 cents in US dollars to buy a Mexican peso. A year later it took a mere 16 cents. The Mexican economy tumbled into recession but it had bounced back before the century was out.

Foreign investors saw the entanglements that crop up when too many foreign investors try to jump out of a developing country all at once. The dull, middling performance of stocks in the advanced industrialized countries recruited new customers from foreign investors in developing countries weary of risk and speculative pyrotechnics. Between December 1994 and February 1995 the International Finance

Corporation global composite index of emerging markets slumped 17 per cent.[16] Generally East Asia quickly shrugged off the trauma and gloom induced by the Mexican crisis. For 1994 stocks in South Korea finished up 18.6 per cent and stocks in Taiwan up 17.1 per cent.

Mexico's financial crisis educated new investors and observers in the humbling knowledge that even in a crisis a profit is in the cards for currency speculators. At the 1995 Halifax summit of the largest industrialized countries, the President of France, Jacques Chirac, remarked to reporters that foreign exchange 'speculation is the AIDS of the world economy'.[17] Foreign exchange markets are among the most free and least regulated markets. In the United States foreign exchange transactions fall outside the regulatory bounds of the Security and Exchange Commission and Commodities Futures Trading Commission.

Foreign exchange speculation unfolds along the following lines. Foreign exchange can be purchased either in a spot market or in a forward market. The spot market quotes the current price. The forward market quotes rates for foreign exchange deliverable in the future, three months or six months ahead. Suppose the three-month forward rate is 100 yen per dollar, but a speculator believes the spot rate three months ahead will be 110 yen per dollar. A speculator may borrow 100 million yen, and sell yen for dollars in the forward market at 100 yen per dollar. In three months each of those dollars can be converted back into yen at a rate of 110 yen per dollar. In the mid 1990s George Soros, a celebrated currency speculator, rose to worldwide fame on a flurry of profits reaped amid the collapse of Mexico's peso. Soros also won a grudging notoriety and a bonanza of speculative profits in 1992 after the British pound caved in. Currency crises in the order of Mexico's crisis walk hand-in-hand with currency speculation. Currency speculators have keen noses for the odour of weak currency. A whiff of possible devaluation sends speculators crowding upon a government, making demands to convert domestic currencies into dollars. By such action foreign exchange speculators may force devaluation.

Miscarried and backfiring foreign investments led investors to pause for thought, explaining why the mature and well worn US stock market scored highly in 1995. The Standard & Poor 500 climbed 34 per cent in 1995 while Morgan Stanley's EAFE index of foreign stocks crept up 9 per cent.[18] Investors doubted that the United States market could repeat that performance two years in a row, and again went looking for opportunities abroad. There were reasons to look abroad. Between 31 January 1995 and 31 January 1996 total market returns in dollars soared 56 per cent on the Hong Kong market, 22 per cent on the Singapore market, 32 per cent on Spain's market, 31 per cent in Canada, 18 per cent in New Zealand, 29 per cent in Sweden, 37 per cent in Switzerland, 41 per cent in Korea, 58 per cent in Poland and 32 per cent in Argentina. Even Mexico eked out a 13 per cent market return. The big losers, Venezuela at -27 per cent and India at -34 per cent, did little to dilute hopes for colossal gains.

DEVELOPING COUNTRIES IN THE AGE OF FINANCIAL
INTEGRATION

Statistics on stock market capitalization highlighted the debt owed to speculation for growth in developing countries. World Bank numbers on stock market capitalization measured the dollar value of all shares traded on a market. Between 1990 and 1998 the aggregated global economy stock market capitalization grew by a factor of 2.5. The United States boasted a strong stock market in the period and its stock market capitalization grew by a factor of 3.69. Japan's stock market capitalization for the period shrank, while Germany's stock market capitalization expanded by a factor of 2.3. French stock market capitalization grew by a factor of 2.1 over the same time, and the United Kingdom's stock market capitalization grew by a factor of 2.35.[19] Within the same time frame Australia's stock market capitalization multiplied by a factor of 6.47. Stock market capitalization in Hong Kong mushroomed by a factor of 4.95, in Argentina by 13.87, in Brazil by 9.8, in Chile by 3.8. The figure for low and middle-income countries in East Asia and the Pacific area stood more in line with world averages, chiefly because these markets crashed after a financial crisis in 1997 and 1998.

The world economy measured average real GDP growth of 2.4 per cent between 1990 and 1998, below the average of 3.2 per cent between 1980 and 1990. The United States, United Kingdom, France and

Germany recorded milder growth and Japan floundering growth in the later time frame. Above average growth between 1990 and 1998 chiefly surfaced in countries that beat their own economic growth rates for the previous decade. The developing world claimed its share of countries logging higher growth both against world averages, and against their own standard. Among these countries belonged Argentina, Bolivia, Brazil, Malaysia, Mexico and Chile. Among the fastest growing countries between 1990 and 1998 were Chile at 7.9 per cent, China at 11.1 per cent, Ireland at 7.5 per cent, Malaysia at 7.7 per cent, Singapore at 8 per cent, Thailand at 7.4 per cent, Uganda at 7.4 per cent and Vietnam at 8.6 per cent. Argentina, El Salvador, India and Indonesia were on the roster of countries averaging above twice the world GDP growth rate for the same time frame. Upper middle-income countries collectively tabulated faster growth in the 1990s than in the 80s. The same applied to countries in the lowest income category when China and India were included.

East Asian countries graduated into the elite order of economic miracles as the 1990s unfolded. Low and middle-income countries in East Asia and the Pacific averaged 8 per cent annual GDP growth between 1980 and 1990 and 8.1 per cent average annual growth between 1990 and 1998.[20] Singapore posted real GDP growth above 8 per cent for 1995, 1996 and 1997. Malaysia posted 9.8 and 10 per cent real GDP growth respectively for the years 1995 and 1996.[21] In 1996 South Korea simmered down to 6.8 per cent growth after averaging annual real GDP growth above 8 per cent for a decade. Taiwan thrilled to an average annual growth of 8 per cent before skidding to 6.4 per cent in 1995. Indonesia purred to busy growth rates above 8 per cent in 1995 and 1996.

With adventurous investors from developed countries fretting to be first to buy into promising ventures, the tempo of global capital flows to the developing world could only quicken. Kinder terms of trade also brightened investment prospects in developing countries. Between 1985 and 1994 the terms of trade for developing countries had sagged, undergoing yearly declines of 3.6 per cent, mainly owing to falling crude oil prices. In 1995 and 1996 the terms of trade for developing countries went up 2.8 and 3 per cent respectively. Among Asian developing countries only, the terms of trade drooped an average rate of 1.2 per cent between 1985 and 1994. In 1995 and 1996 the terms of trade edged up 0.4 and 1.4 per cent respectively for the Asian group.

In the 1990s the lure of speculation, liberalization of capital flows and strengthening terms of trade ignited an upsurge of private capital flows from advanced industrial countries to developing countries. The avalanche of global capital descending upon developing countries in the 1990s was unrivalled apart from the heavy capital flows of the late nineteenth century.[22] A hundred years transpired before capital gathered in developing countries on a scale equivalent to capital flows in the heyday of European imperialism. In the late nineteenth century European investors counted on European governments to patrol and shelter European investments in developing countries. European governments cooperatively shared in preserving order and political stability in developing countries. They also controlled and flaunted entrée to European capital as leverage over foreign governments, dangling loans as carrots to bend governments to Europe's will. Two world wars, worldwide Depression and the proliferation of Marxist ideology shut the door to global capital markets for numberless developing countries. The reconstruction of war-torn industrialized countries carved out a hefty chunk from mobile capital, squeezing the rest of the world. Developing countries turned to official sources of capital flows, foreign aid and loans from international agencies like the World Bank.

Between 1990 and 1998 official capital flows to developing countries measured in US dollars went from slightly over $50 billion to slightly under $50 billion.[23] Private debt flows grew from just shy of $10 billion to a shade above $50 billion. By 1998 private debt flows alone outdistanced official capital flows. Portfolio equity flows (investments in stocks and bonds) burgeoned from roughly $2 billion to $11 billion between 1990 and 1998. Direct foreign investment (when a company builds a facility in a foreign country, or buys controlling interest in an existing foreign facility) accounted for the largest slice of foreign capital flowing to developing countries. Between 1990 and 1998 direct foreign investment to developing countries multiplied from roughly $22 billion to roughly $150 billion. In 1990 direct foreign investment lagged behind official capital flows, but by 1998 it measured roughly three times official capital flows. Between 1970 and 1992 foreign portfolio investment growth and direct foreign investment growth stayed neck and neck. Between 1992 and 1993 foreign portfolio investment soared above $110 billion. Over the same time frame direct foreign investment scaled a height of roughly $60 billion. Portfolio investment peaked and slid back sharply amid marked volatility. Direct foreign investment went on climbing upward, far outrunning portfolio investment before the century was out.[24] In a nutshell the pace of combined debt, direct investment and portfolio private investment to developing countries increased hugely in the 1990s.

As the spirit of speculation fanned out across continents and social classes the range and tools of speculation multiplied. In the early 1980s worldwide trading in financial derivatives began shifting to fast forward. The Chicago Board of Trade (CBT) first gave the nod for trading in future contracts in 1972. In 1984 the CBT first signed off on trading in stock options, including options for stock indexes. Financial derivatives offer a means of hedging risks, but are also financial vehicles for high risk speculation. Derivatives imply high leverage, enabling a speculator to control assets far above an original investment in value. Towering profits are possible, but for every winner there is a loser. Trading in financial derivatives hit the headlines in 1994 after the Treasurer of Orange County, California, piled up losses in mortgage derivative trading that bankrupted the county. In 1995 Barings Bank, a British bank founded in 1763, which had handled the financing for the Louisiana Purchase, spiralled into bankruptcy after a 27-year-old Barings trader in Singapore traded in high stakes derivatives without authorization. The trader accrued billions of dollars in losses trading in stock index futures and sent the bank into receivership. The courts meted out a six and a half year prison sentence to the ambitious trader. Ownership of the bank had remained in the Baring family until 1995 when it was sold to a Dutch company. As Orange County and Barings slid over the edge of bankruptcy, political pressure in the United States mounted for permitting individuals to invest social security contributions in the stock market.

Chapter 10

Global Confidence and Global Panic

In the 1990s investors in developed countries cast financial nets farther afield for speculative prey, but always on the presumption that sound and intelligent economic policies in developing areas could not be routinely counted on. Mexico was a glaring admonition of how things get ugly when governments in developing countries enact conflicting and unsustainable policies. Latin America had furnished innumerable illustrations dating back to the 1970s, examples of profligate governments engaging in deficit spending underwritten by monetary expansion. Inflation always ignited, resulting in a trade deficit as imported goods became bargains. The trade deficit unleashed an outflow of domestic currency, undercutting the currency in foreign exchange markets. The offending government drained foreign exchange reserves in a bid to shore up the domestic currency in foreign markets. Once foreign exchange reserves ebbed to precariously thin margins, speculative sharks rushed in to finish things off. Investors' chances for dodging these crises lay in untiring attention to macroeconomic fundamentals. As a matter of course, countries with high inflation, slow economic growth, large government budgets, low savings and political instability held small enchantment to investors hunting foreign investments.

The muddled species of unbridled economic policies that bred financial debacles seemed unlikelier in societies moulded by

Confucian ethics. The Confucian stress on order and moderation hardly tallied with wild and reckless speculative fever, and unthinking and chaotic government extravagance. The Chinese enjoyed a reputation for exalting wisdom and courtesy above the scramble for power and wealth.

In 1996 upbeat macroeconomic fundamentals for East Asian countries stood out in glittering relief, clothing the area in the mantle of economic superstar. The previous chapter gave a statistical snapshot of economic growth in East Asia. Unemployment rates were low, and economic growth high. These indicators were a small pledge of lasting stability and macroeconomic strength, but other economic indicators fortified a picture of unimpeachable macroeconomic fundamentals in the East Asian area. Between 1991 and 1996 the central government of Hong Kong chalked up five annual budget surpluses and one budget deficit.[1] Between 1991 and 1996 budget surpluses lent dignity to the central governments of Thailand and Singapore without missing a year. The central governments of South Korea and Malaysia boasted unbroken strings of budget surpluses for the four years 1993 through 1996. The central governments of Indonesia and the Philippines logged budget surpluses for 1994, 1995 and 1996. These budget surpluses and small budget deficits may be laid next to the budget deficits of India, which exceeded 5 per cent of GDP every year between 1991 and 1996.

In 1996 savings as a percentage of GDP stood at 51.2 per cent for Singapore and at 42.6 per cent for Malaysia. Savings rates in Hong Kong, South Korea and Thailand ran in the 30–36 per cent range. For 1996 the Philippines made do with a decent 18.8 per cent savings rate. The East Asian countries enjoyed quiet inflation rates in light of heated growth in real GDP. In 1996 Hong Kong posted 4.3 per cent inflation of consumer prices, South Korea 6.3 per cent, Indonesia 7.9 per cent, Malaysia 3.5 per cent, Thailand 5.9 per cent and the Philippines 8.4 per cent.

Macroeconomic government policies in East Asia came under less fire and censure than policies in other developing regions. From this bedrock of fundamentals East Asian countries acted as magnets for the surging capital flows to developing countries that gathered energy as the 1990s unfolded. Between 1994 and 1996 net private capital inflows roughly doubled in Indonesia, Malaysia and Thailand. Japan's truncated interest rates and economic lassitude in the 1990s sent global capital exploring fresher pastures. Uninviting interest rates and tired economic growth dulled the investor appetite for Europe as well. The eyes of investors zeroed in on East Asia as one of the safer bets.

From a trough in early 1995, the fallout of the Mexican crisis, Hong Kong's Hang Seng stock market index more than doubled in roughly two and a half years, rising from the 8,000-range in 1995 to reach a closing zenith of 16,673 on 7 August 1997. Then an East Asian financial crisis overran Hong Kong. Between 20 and 23 October the Hang Seng index lost nearly a quarter of its value, its heaviest loss ever. It went on falling, sinking below the post-Mexican crisis levels. On 13 August 1998 the Hang Seng index closed at 6,660.42. Hong Kong suffered doubly from the economic strains of the region, and a political hand-over to the People's Republic of China. Other East Asian stock markets, not sinking as steeply after the Mexican crisis, never enjoyed quite the dizzy run up, and dropped off sooner. Between January and July 1997 stock markets in Thailand, Malaysia and the Philippines gave up about one third of their value in US dollars. From 1993 to 1997 the Malaysian stock market climbed from the 1,000-range to the 1,200-range, peaking in January 1997 in the 1,230-range. On 21 November 1997 it closed at 512.41. The Malaysian and Philippine markets topped out early in 1997, but the Thailand market entered a long twilight descent lasting throughout 1996 and 1997. Total returns in the Thailand stock market spiralled downward 48 per cent between July 1996 and July 1997. (Total returns, measured in dollars, incorporate the effects of changing exchange rates.) Between 31 May 1997 and 31 May 1998 total returns on the Korean stock market dropped 49 per cent. The Singapore stock market reached an apogee around 2,400 in April l996. It sputtered downward, posting a closing average of 1,605.10 on 3 March 1998. On 7 September 1998 it closed at 862.14. By 17 November 1998 it hovered way off its lows, but over the preceding 12 months it had lost a 29 per cent in total returns measured in dollars.[2]

These markets shared in a worldwide stock market boom in 1999, but in 2003 still traded below the index summits of 1996 and 1997. On 26 September 2003 the Hang Seng index closed at 11,290.15.

A post-mortem on the East Asian Financial Crisis unearthed hidden cracks that early in 1996 began to fan out within the foundation of East Asia's prosperity. These countries kept their currencies pegged to the us dollar, which was strengthening in value, lifting the real exchange rates for East Asian countries. In 1994 the Pacific Rim Countries devalued China's currency, the renminbi, further lifting East Asian currencies. The Japanese yen and the currencies of many European countries also yielded to depreciation. The escalation in real exchange rates for East Asian countries pushed up the cost of East Asian exports to foreign countries, and subtracted from the cost of foreign imports in East Asian markets. Lower wage Asian countries had a sound advantage in labour-intensive industries such as garments and footwear, edging out Malaysia and Thailand in export markets. The year 1996 saw the market for semiconductors and other electronic goods cave in, an untimely blow to East Asian exports.

Between June 1995 and June 1997 the Philippines saw a 21 per cent appreciation of its real exchange rate, Thailand 14 per cent, and Malaysia and Indonesia 12 per cent. South Korea saw a modest 1.5 per cent appreciation. Stronger currencies added to the drag on exports but also fired up imports. Swelling imports against exports raised the out-flow of currency against the inflow, undermining currencies in foreign exchange markets, an effect that was only cancelled out by inflows of foreign capital. In East Asia inflows of private capital kept the currencies strong for a while.

The currency trader George Soros says his company saw a glut of imports outgrowing private capital inflows, building market stresses fated to send East Asian currencies tumbling downward.[3] In January Soros's company began selling Thailand's baht and Malaysia's ringgit short, that is, the company borrowed bahts and ringgits and sold them for dollars in the confident expectation that the bahts and ringgits were overvalued and at risk of depreciation. After these currencies depreciated, bahts and ringgits would be bought back with fewer dollars. At depreciated values for bahts and ringgits, the dollar proceeds from the sales of borrowed bahts and ringgits far surpassed the dollars needed to buy back bahts and ringgits and pay off the loans and gave speculative profits.

In May 1997 currency traders widely shared the belief that the baht's value could not last. The Bank of Thailand shored up the baht with double-digit interest rates and the Thai stock market headed down. Within a couple of days currency traders let fly billions of dollars of sell contracts on the baht, flinging down a challenge to the Thai government to let the baht depreciate. In answer, the Bank of Thailand banned baht loans abroad, and rallied other Asian central banks behind the baht. The Thai central bank warded off the first assault on the baht, sending George Soros's company fleeing the market amid swelling losses. A battle was won but the war raged on. As June drew to a close the pressure to devalue the baht built to unstoppable proportions. On 2 July 1997 the Thai government commenced to float the baht. Speculative worries sparked a rapid depreciation of the baht, and flight of foreign capital.

The depreciation of the baht awakened forces for a parallel turn of events in other East Asian countries. Several factors contributed to the contagion. First, these countries shared kindred exports. A falling baht left Thai goods in foreign export markets less costly when measured against goods from Malaysia, Indonesia, the Philippines, Hong Kong and South Korea. These countries already faced the same imbalances and strains that heralded the currency collapse in Thailand. Rising competition in the export market now heightened currency pressures, and currency devaluation safeguarded exports. Second, in the eyes of foreign investors East Asian countries suffered from guilt by association. The Thai government floated the baht under pressure. Who could say with assurance that other harassed governments would stand firm against similar action? Panicky foreign investors wanted to exit the region. The aforementioned five East Asian countries saw a combined net outflow of private capital in 1997 in the order of $12 billion. That $12 billion outflow weighed against a $93 billion dollar net private capital inflow in 1996. Commercial banks faced the largest capital outflows.[4] Net foreign portfolio investment also crossed over to the negative column in no small numbers.

Third, the political cost of currency depreciation softened in other East Asian countries after Thailand took the first step. After Thailand floated the baht, currency depreciation suddenly became the path of least resistance. Lastly, Thailand's currency debacle may have owed part of its contagiousness to the way mutual fund managers earn compensation. Ignoring a warning could elicit crueller punishment than missing a long shot that paid off.

On 2 July 1997 the Bank of Thailand broadcast a decision to allow the baht to float, which sounded the opening of the East Asian crisis.[5] On 11 July the Philippine central bank freed its peso to float and bobble within a wider band against the US dollar. On 11 August the IMF announced a $17.2 billion bailout package for Thailand. The IMF, the Asian Development Bank, the World Bank and assorted Asian nations shared in funding the individual East Asian rescue efforts. On 14 August Indonesia scrapped its system of exchange rate management, and set its currency free to float. The IMF unveiled a $23 billion rescue package for Indonesia on 31 October, slightly more than a week after the Hong Kong stock market underwent its steepest plunge ever. Asian stocks on 7 November tumbled wholesale across the region as currency jitters infected South Korea, and Hong Kong reeled from damaging interest rates and diving property values. South Korean officials finalized negotiations with the IMF for a $57 billion loan to assist with its financial crisis on 3 December, and embarked on a managed float exchange rate regime on 16 December. When the year was out, the economies of Thailand, Indonesia, and South Korea faced a 40 per cent plunge in the exchange rates of domestic currencies against the US dollar. Moody's investor service downgraded the sovereign debt of Indonesia, Korea, Malaysia and Thailand on 22 December. The debt ratings of three of these countries sank to junk-bond status. The New Year opened with renewed selling of Indonesian, Malaysian and Philippine currencies. By 5 January the Thai government was begging the IMF for easier terms on its rescue package. Two days later the currencies of Indonesia, Malaysia, Philippines and Thailand skidded to new lows, and stocks across Asia retreated again.

Amid the crisis the prime minister of Malaysia criticized George Soros. He blamed him for attacks against East Asian currencies, damaging their values in foreign exchange markets. Soros, in his book *The Crisis of Global Capitalism*, grants that his company sold these currencies short several months before the crisis, but also says that it bought these currencies too soon after the currency depreciation first began. Soros immodestly intimates that when his company sold these currencies short, governments should have humbly inferred that the currencies were overvalued.[6] By acting on this early warning, East Asian governments could have enacted neutralizing and therapeutic policies to circumvent the crisis.

The deadliest wound to the East Asian economies centred on the crippled banking sector in the wake of the crisis. Before the crisis, foreign capital rained down upon East Asian banks in the form of loans denominated in dollars. Banks borrowed dollars, converted them into domestic currency, and funded loans to finance local investments in real estate and equities. A bubble factor puffed up the values of these assets. The banks held the real estate and equities as collateral. As embattled currencies depreciated, banks met with more difficulties buying dollars with domestic currency and paying off foreign loans. With banks unable to advance more loans to finance real estate and equity purchases, the value of these assets crumbled. While banks owed an Everest of debt in domestic currency, market prices of assets held as bank collateral sank into a tailspin. East Asian banks, unwisely counting on tight-knit relationships with governments to rescue them, had ensnared foreign capital for the sake of ever riskier investments.

THE GLOBAL SPECULATIVE DRAMA

The East Asian economic virus seemed contagious, kindling prophesies that the global economic system was doomed to infection. US monetary authorities passed the word not to expect monetary tightening from their corner. Other stock markets were hot and exuberant. Between 31 July 1996 and 31 July 1997 Russia's intoxicated stock market cast up a gripping 230 per cent in total returns measured in US dollars.[7] In July 1997 George Soros purchased a stake in a privatized Russian telecommunications firm. He suggested that Russia was the most interesting emerging market in the world. Venezuela's stock market gave total returns of 125 per cent for the same twelve months. Sweden, Finland and the Netherlands luxuriated in stock market total returns above 50 per cent for the same time period. Germany and Switzerland basked in total stock market returns of 39 and 34 per cent respectively for the same time frame. Between 25 January 1998 and 25 April 1998, the stock markets of Ireland, Italy, Finland and Spain piled up total market returns of 30 per cent or above. South Korea's stock market rebound lifted total market returns to 105 per cent for the same three-month period. The difference lay in the singular distinction that South Korea's stock market recovery still left that market down a merciless 39 per cent for the past 12 months. Animated stock markets in Italy and Spain chalked up gains in total market returns of over 80 per cent for the 12 months leading up to 25 April 1998.

The East Asian crisis was very directly felt in Russia where shaky finances already darkened the economic outlook. The direct problem lay in fading oil prices. Between 11 May 1998 and 11 August 1998 the Russian stock market plunged 64 per cent in total market returns.[8] Declining equity prices weakened Russian banks and worried foreign banks and investors, leaving the Russian government unable to roll over its debt. On 13 August George Soros published a letter in the *Financial Times* saying that the rouble should be devalued. Some observers laid the blame on Soros for triggering a run on the Russian rouble, but his company sustained big losses from what was about to happen. On 17 August 1998 the Russian government defaulted on its maturing debt to foreigners and announced it was allowing the rouble to float. The rouble fell until it was nearly worthless, and stock markets around the world recoiled. Within weeks the Dow Jones Industrial Average retreated 1,800 points. Between 17 August 1998 and 17 November 1998 the Russian stock market tumbled another 41 per cent in total market returns.[9] Soros bemoaned the fact that he had permitted himself to be sucked into Russia.

At the beginning of 1996 the Federal Reserve in the United States shaved its discount rate (the interest rate Federal Reserve banks charge to commercial banks) from 5.25 to 5 per cent. The discount rate remained at 5 per cent between January 1996 and September 1998. Then the Federal Reserve eased down the discount rate in small monthly steps, bringing it to 4.5 per cent by December 1998. It remained at 4.5 per cent until August 1999 when the Federal Reserve began raising it out of anxiety for a heated US economy. The Bank of Japan's discount rate was already at 0.5 per cent when Russia defaulted. It remained at 0.5 per cent until 2001 when the Bank of Japan lowered it again.

The DJIA had already displayed an uncharacteristic, irrepressible energy when the Federal Reserve cut the discount rate in October 1998. In 1994 it flirted with the 4,000-level benchmark but traded roughly flat for the year. Worries over Mexico kept it down as the year progressed. Early in 1995 it left the 4,000 benchmark behind. For the month of November 1995 the average closing price for the DJIA stood above 5,000. Further monetary easing in the United States let the momentum go unchecked. By October 1996 the average closing price for the month edged above the 6,000 milestone. It took the DJIA roughly 14 years to climb from 1,000 to 2,000, roughly 8 years to climb from 2,000 to 4,000, and roughly 5 years to climb from 3,000 to 6,000. The market held its muscular momentum, logging an average closing price above 7,000 for April 1997. The market soon roared past the 8,000 benchmark, finishing the month of July 1997 with a daily closing average above 8,200. The market stumbled below 8,000 as the East Asian crisis blemished the economic horizon. The daily closing average remained below 8,000 every month until February 1998 when it leaped above 8,500. The daily closing average finished above 8,800 for the month of July 1998. In August 1998 Russia defaulted on its treasury debt to foreigners. Daily closing averages measured below 8,000 for two months in a row, but stocks took wing again on the back of further monetary easing. For December 1998 the daily closing average for stocks passed 9,100. The DJIA went on climbing in 1999, registering for December 1999 a daily closing average above 11,400. In 2000 bullish momentum fell off and the DJIA meandered in the 10,000–11,000 range. In 2001 it started and ended with monthly closing averages in the 10,000 range. The daily closing average sank below 9,000 for September. In 2002 the DJIA veered downward, finishing December with a daily closing average in the 8,300 range.

The DJIA gently sagged to a sell-off in 2000, but the NASDAQ hosted a full-blown speculative debacle. In the shadow of Mexico's crisis the daily closing average for the NASDAQ measured 755 for January 1995. The daily closing average soared above 1,000 for September 1995. For

July 1997, the eve of the East Asian crisis, the NASDAQ logged a daily closing average in the 1,400 range. So far the NASDAQ had displayed gritty acceleration, but no unthinking subservience to wild speculative fever. Between December 1997 and December 1998 monthly closing averages rose from roughly 1,570 to roughly 2,190, an eye-catching rate of return in light of the Russian default, and general bewilderment over the global financial system. In 1999 the NASDAQ bulldozed over the pessimism induced by financial crises, and finished December with a daily closing average just above 4,000. On 10 March 2000 it topped out at a giddy 5,048.62. A stampeding sell-off sent the NASDAQ closing at 3,205.35 on 25 May 2000. For the month of December 2000 the NASDAQ's daily closing average finished in the 2,600 range. The grim slide wore on and for September 2002 the monthly closing average stood at 1,172.06.

The NASDAQ speculative debacle numbered the days of perhaps the longest economic expansion in US history. Stock markets around the world fizzled and slumped as the world braced for the dawn of global economic recession led by the United States. Recall that the Japanese NIKKEI peaked at roughly 39,000 in December 1989. The Japanese market floundered and drifted down through much of the 1990s. In January 1999 the daily closing average measured roughly 13,000. The NIKKEI turned up early in 1999 and rallied to a peak of 20,833.21 on 12 April 2000. The daily closing average for March 2000 stood above 20,000. It steadily sank for three years. In March 2003 the daily closing average broke below the 8,000 mark.

Between December 1998 and July 1999 the Federal Reserve held the discount rate at 4.5 per cent, small given inflation worries. In mid 1997 the unemployment rate dipped below 5 per cent, signalling a measure of tightness in the labour market previously linked with inflation. Not since the 1960s had the US unemployment rate sunk below 5 per cent without a burst of inflation heralding the onset of recession. Economists seemed confident that an unemployment rate of roughly 5.5 per cent was the lowest compatible with price stability. Fallout from the East Asian crisis helped counteract and vent inflation pressures. Between 1997 and 1998 the price of oil toppled from over $20 per barrel to $10 per barrel. An increasing average age of the workforce may have dragged down the inflation-triggering unemployment rate, consigning more workers to age groups with traditionally low unemployment rates. After mid 1997 US monetary authorities navigated new and uncharted territory, thinking inflation should be on the horizon – but it was not. Alan Greenspan, Chairman of the Board of Governors of the Federal Reserve System, made a stir blaming speculative mania in the stock market on 'irrational exuberance'.

The momentum behind Wall Street's stock market speculation can be gauged from the wild struggle waged by bullish speculators against unfavourable trends. The year 1999 opened with crude oil prices dipping below $10 a barrel, but prices turned up by the second quarter. By September 1999 oil prices had crept back to $20 per barrel. Consumer price inflation betrayed hints of perking up. For a two-year span between September 1997 and September 1999 consumer prices inched up 4 per cent. For a one-year span between September 1999 and September 2000 consumer prices grew at 3.4 per cent. This measurable quickening in inflation nudged monetary authorities toward tighter monetary policy. Between August and September 1999 the Federal Reserve notched up the discount rate from 4.5 to 4.75 per cent. By December 1999 the Federal Reserve had raised the discount rate another quarter point, to 5 per cent. The NASDAQ spiralled upwards as the Federal Reserve pushed up the discount rate. Then unemployment sank to levels not seen in 30 years, hitting 4 per cent in December 1999. Dismissing the hazard of inflation appeared on all sides to be unwise. The Federal Reserve kept the discount rate at 5 per cent until February 2000, but when neither the economy nor the stock market betrayed signs of cooling, upped the discount rate to 5.24 per cent.

One can only wonder what investors in the NASDAQ were thinking as February drew to a close. The Federal Reserve had notch-by-notch raised interest rates for seven months straight without NASDAQ investors blinking. It was as if reckless bulls in the stock market warred against the Federal Reserve. The Federal Reserve clamped the stock market in a vice between rising interest rates and an economy bound to decelerate. Investors in the NASDAQ could not win. In March the meteoric NASDAQ commenced a sudden retreat, but the Federal Reserve remained unfazed. By the end of April the discount rate stood at 5.5 per cent. In April the unemployment rate bottomed at 3.8 per cent. The Federal Reserve tightened further as the NASDAQ crashed and the unemployment rate hinted at inching upwards. By the end of June the discount rate stood at 6 per cent. The Federal Reserve kept the discount rate there until December 2000. In January 2001 the unemployment rate registered 4.1 per cent, but the NASDAQ was off its peak nearly 50 per cent. In February the daily closing average of the NASDAQ measured roughly 2,150. Inflation fears were lost in the glare of recession anxieties. By December 2000 the index of leading economic indicators had slipped four months in succession. In January 2001 the Federal Reserve slashed the discount rate by a half point.

THE UNITED STATES SINKS INTO RECESSION

The timeframe between late 1999 and the end of 2001 spans three of the more illuminating years in economic history. For seven months the highflying US economy stubbornly defied rising interest rates. The muted tones in which the economy answered the rising interest rate challenge insinuated that the interest rate hikes were barely enough to dampen economic activity. If interest rates dropped a half a point it might take flight again. As recently as 1996 the economy had exhibited lively strength at a 5 per cent discount rate. It seemed reasonable to expect that shaving the discount rate to 5.5 per cent should lead to measurable improvement. It could even be just what the doctor ordered to restore a lasting prosperity. When the Federal Reserve trimmed the discount rate to 5.5 per cent in January 2001, unemployment still stood at a historical low of 4.1 per cent.

The economy, however, exhibited the same belated response to falling interest rates as to rising interest rates. The half point cut in January became only the first in a 13-month string of cuts, leaving the discount rate at 1.25 per cent by January 2002. Many expected such aggressive discount rate cuts to touch off an explosive economic recovery. On the contrary, economic prosperity went on unwinding. The unemployment rate inched upwards throughout 2001, registering 5.8 per cent for December 2001. The NASDAQ little by little gave up ground.

In January 2002 it traded at a daily closing average of 1,934.03. Rock bottom interest rates offered small relief after a stock market crash had darkened business expectations. Given the economy's structure, a mere decrease in growth in output is often sufficient to trigger negative growth for investment spending, and all decreases in spending snowball. When one company lays off workers it narrows the market for goods and services, applying pressure on other companies to lay off workers. The downdraughts gain strength and momentum over the updraughts, dragging the economy into recession.

According to the National Bureau of Economic Research (NBER) the US economy crossed into recession in March 2001. An economy enters recession as decelerated growth in output and employment downshifts into negative growth. The previous recession hit a trough in March 1991. The 120-month expansion between March 1991 and March 2001 ranked as the United States' longest expansion recorded in the chronologies of the NBER, which stretches back 150 years. Sinking economic activity marks a recession, which means the recession phase of an economic cycle is usually brief. The United States recession of 2001 began in March and ended in November. The passage from sinking economic activity to level and then rising economic activity does not entail a sudden leap into rosier economic conditions. In the United States rising unemployment belied any economic recovery until June 2003 when the unemployment rate peaked at 6.4 per cent.

Amid the United States recession terrorists flew into the twin towers of the World Trade Center. Heroic firefighters whose first thought was saving the lives of others set a thought stirring example for the speculative world to ponder. Everyone sensed that at the fire station speeches on 'greed is good' were not welcomed and the ticker tape was not enshrined. Some hoped that the selfless firemen planted a seed of idealism in a world overrun with a myopic passion for speculative profits.

The US recession in 2002 hugged the contours of political business cycles. Annual real GDP growth rates graphed over time exhibit a jagged, irregular and unpredictable pattern. When the same data is reshuffled and ordered by year of presidential term, an unmistakable pattern sharpens into focus. Harry Truman began serving his first full term as president in 1949. He narrowly squeaked by re-election in the celebrated upset election of 1948. In 1949, the first year of his full term, real GDP annually grew at −0.6 per cent. That is the one and only time since 1949 that the United States faced minus GDP annual growth in the first year of a presidential term. The last half of the last century saw only one episode of minus real GDP annual growth in the fourth year of a presidential term. That happened in 1980, the fourth year of President Carter's first term. The voters abbreviated Carter's presidency to one term. The mere fact that the economy seemed headed for recession in 1948 throws light on Truman's uphill battle for re-election. He won by the slenderest of margins. In the same vein, the voters lived through only two episodes of minus real GDP annual growth in the third year of presidential terms. That happened with Nixon/Ford in 1975 and with George Bush Sr in 1991. The voters ousted both Ford and Bush after one term. All other years of minus real GDP annual growth cluster in the second year of presidential terms. Real GDP posted negative growth in the second year of Dwight Eisenhower's first term and in the second year of his second term. Eisenhower won re-election without a snag and the Republicans opened the 1960 presidential campaign way out front in the polls. Nixon/Ford saw minus GDP annual growth in the second year of that term also. That presidential term went doubly bedevilled with negative annual GDP growth in the third year too. Reagan presided over negative annual GDP growth in the second year of his first term, and won re-election in 1984. Negative growth never blemished a year of Reagan's second presidential term and the Republicans won the presidency again in 1988.

Since 1949 the United States economy had weathered eight episodes of negative real GDP annual growth. Half of these episodes belong in the second year of Republican presidential terms. Annual real GDP growth averaged 0.2 per cent in the second year of Republican presidential terms up through the second year of George Bush Sr's term. Economic doldrums go with the second year of Republican presidential terms, and George W. Bush's presidency fits that pattern.

An administration presiding over a recession pins the blame on blunders of the preceding administration. On average Democrats inherit a weaker and slacker economy, which they set to work firing up.

While the economy often sees weak growth or recession in the second year of Republican presidential terms, it often sees exuberant growth in the second year of Democratic terms. Ordered by presidential term, the second year of Democratic administrations registers the highest average growth rates, measuring 5.9 per cent from Truman through Carter. In the fourth year of presidential terms Republicans, vulnerable on the unemployment issue, go all out to speed up the economy before the election. Democrats, perceived as soft on inflation, worry that a booming economy will degenerate into an inflation riot. In the fourth year of a presidential term Democrats are content to see the economy decelerate. The fourth year of Republican presidential terms lays claim to the second highest average in real GDP annual growth.

THE SPECTRE OF GLOBAL DEFLATION

The global economy might brush aside the East Asian crisis, but economic troubles in the largest economies in the world mattered beyond measure. As a new century opened it became transparent that Japan lingered in a decade long slump without hint of recovery. Between 1995 and 2002 its average yearly growth in real GDP measured 1.12 per cent. This is for a country that miraculously averaged real GDP growth over 10 per cent between 1963 and 1972 and went unrivalled during the stagflation era, often logging real GDP growth above 5 per cent. In 1988 the peak of Japan's last boom, real GDP growth roughly measured 6 per cent. In 2001 and 2002 real GDP growth in Japan measured a scanty 0.04 and 0.02 per cent respectively. The IMF projected Japanese real GDP growth at 2 and 1.4 per cent respectively for the years 2003 and 2004.[10]

We saw how Japan's stock market never rebounded to its dizzy summit of 1989 a decade later. More puzzling was the ubiquitous wave of mild deflation that rippled through the 1990s and the opening years of the new century. Outbreaks of inflation have been worldwide a familiar, and of deflation a rare, turn of events in the post World War II era. To all appearances, history was given to inflation over deflation. Before World War II tightness in gold stocks bore the guilt for rare episodes of deflation. After dethronement of the gold standard, it was assumed in many quarters that the world had seen the last of deflation. Deflation gives governments a free hand to print more money, useful for democratic governments, eager to please the largest number of people. Inconvertible paper money walks hand in hand with inflation. Therefore the outbreak of deflation in Japan came unforeseen. Between 1995 and 2002 Japan registered negative growth in the GDP deflator for every year except 1997 when prices grew a mere 0.3 per cent. Evidence even insinuated a deepening of deflation. Between 1995 and 1996 Japanese deflation averaged 0.65 per cent per year, and between 1998 and 1999 1.7 per cent per year. In 2003 the IMF projected average deflation over 2 per cent for the years 2003 and 2004.[11]

Japan's deflation presented a riddle to the monetary theory that evolved out of the inflation-ridden 1970s, and may represent a rare potentiality of Depression-born monetary theory. Japan may have worked itself into a liquidity trap that muted and nullified monetary policy. Theories of a liquidity trap surfaced in the 1930s, but sank into the shadows amid post World War II prosperity. Over-investment in the late 1980s could have saturated the Japanese economy with fresh and modern capital goods, marginalizing the expected returns from remaining investment opportunities. Paralleling the boom in investment spending ran a stock market boom and then debacle. After the debacle, stock prices for a decade trailed downward rather than rebounding to earlier peaks. The stock market failure may have left Japanese investors enamoured of uncomplicated cash balances over longer term and less liquid financial assets. Interest rates sank to low levels after returns on purchases of new capital goods reduced. The number of bad loans bequeathed by the last speculative frenzy, paired with the stock market debacle, crushed any incentive to advance funds for low returns. As these conditions unfolded, Japanese households and businesses flocked to money balances as a safe investment. They came to idolize liquidity, and clung to cash balances as a surrogate for longer-term and riskier financial investments.

Deflation makes matters worse because it rewards holding cash rather than spending it. The longer cash is held, the more it buys, even though cash earns no interest. Economists measure what is called the real interest rate, or inflation-adjusted interest rate. The real interest rate equals the nominal interest rate minus the inflation rate. A thousand dollars deposited in an account earning 5 per cent interest mounts up to one thousand and fifty dollars over the course of a year. If inflation is also 5 per cent, however, what cost one thousand dollars when the cash goes on deposit, will cost one thousand and fifty dollars a year later. Inflation erases the increment in purchasing power owed to interest earnings, leaving the real purchasing power of the thousand-dollar deposit untouched. Therefore, economists would say the real interest rate is zero, 5 per cent minus 5 per cent.

Investment spending marches in step with real interest rates. A nominal interest rate of 50 per cent may seem prohibitive, but if prices are rising 50 per cent a year, businesses will be ready to finance plant and equipment at a 50 per cent interest rate. During inflation borrowing money opens the door for businesses to buy capital goods before prices go up. Borrowed funds are the ticket to beating the price increases.

Japan's quandary arises because this logic holds in reverse. The urgency to buy and finance capital goods melts away in the face of deflation. Existing capital goods can undergo refurbishment and repair to last longer. The longer the purchase of new capital goods is postponed, the lower the price. Under deflation, the real interest rate equals the nominal interest rate *plus* the deflation rate. Deflation lifts the real interest rate. Conflicting trends develop when real interest rates sit too high to invite investment spending, but not high enough to tantalize lenders. Businesses back away from real interest rates higher than expected returns on remaining investment opportunities. Lenders appraise real interest rates as too low given the rash of non-performing loans following the last speculative debacle.

A glance at short-term interest rates for advanced countries throws Japan into sharp relief. According to the IMF short-term interest rates in 2001 stood at 5 per cent in the United Kingdom, 3.5 per cent in the United States, 4.2 per cent in the Euro area, 3.9 per cent in Canada and 0 per cent in Japan. Japanese authorities cannot lower short-term interest rates. In 2001 Japanese long-term interest rates stood above zero at 1.3 per cent. That rate was far below the long-term rate of 5 per cent reported in the United States, the Euro area and the United Kingdom for 2001.[12]

Deflation is not out of the ordinary when real GDP growth far outdistances money supply growth. When the supply of goods races ahead of demand, prices fall. In the past Japan won applause for hearty and intelligent economic growth. At the close of the century Japanese money supply growth pulled out in front of real GDP growth. In 1999 the growth of the money stock in Japan, narrowly defined to exclude saving accounts and less liquid deposits, grew at an annual rate of 11.7 per cent. Japanese real GDP the same year posted a slight 0.2 per cent growth. Between 1995 and 2002 annual money stock growth averaged 11.1 per cent. Real GDP growth for the same time frame averaged 1.12 per cent. Deflation amid these conditions is a rare turn of events, unintelligible to many observers.

With deflation paying a visit to Japan, economists glued their eyes to price trends around the globe, mulling over the likelihood that the global economy could enter a phase of deflation. The late nineteenth century saw a global wave of deflation as the advanced countries rallied to the gold standard. When these same countries abandoned the gold standard in the 1930s, it was assumed that the problem of deflation disappeared. In the 1930s sinking prices were lashed to sinking output, but in the late nineteenth century mild deflation attended vigorous economic growth. In the twentieth century inflationary pressures ran side by side with economic growth, and tight money seemed a deadly poison to economic growth.

Aside from deflation fears the global economy appeared to be mending and pulling itself together as the new century unfurled. In the last quarter of 2003 it displayed wide evidence of a healthy and spirited recovery. Equity markets languished well below earlier peaks, but real GDP growth steered clear of negative territory. Of the advanced economies only Norway and Iceland reported negative growth for 2002. Three countries, the Netherlands, Portugal and Switzerland headed for negative growth for 2003, but the IMF predicted positive growth for all advanced countries in 2004.[13] Perkier economic growth eased worries about deflation without dispelling deflationary undertones. Over the 1980–84 timeframe only 0.9 per cent of all countries reported deflation.[14] Over the 1991–6 timeframe that statistic had grown to 1.2 per cent, and by 1997–9 to 9.7 per cent. Over the 2000–02 timeframe the percentage of countries reporting deflation was 13.1 per cent. Between 1980–84 and 2000–02 the percentage of industrial countries reporting deflation grew from 0 to 8.3 per cent. The same statistic for emerging countries grew from 1.6 to 16.3 per cent. A more glaring deflationary trend sharpens into focus when the scope is narrowed to producer prices. The percentage of industrial countries reporting deflation of producer prices grew from 2.6 per cent for 1980–84 to 29.9 per cent for 2000–02.

To date the drift toward deflation seems most at home in Japan, Hong Kong (SAR), Taiwan, China and Germany. Hong Kong reported deflation every year between 1999 and 2002. Germany reported deflation in 2000 but has since reported a trickle of inflation. Taiwan logged deflation in 1999 and 2000 and again in 2002. The People's Republic of China tasted gentle deflation in 1998 as fall out from the Asia Crisis and it lasted until 2000. Late in 2001 deflation resurfaced again in China but gave way to slight inflation in 2003. China has now overtaken Japan as the largest exporter to the United States. It can draw on a surplus of cheap labour and has excess capacity in some sectors. It could bud into an exporter of deflation.

Deflation casts the darkest shadow in the realm of goods as opposed to services. Around 2002 and 2003, the United States, France, Italy, South Korea, Thailand and Singapore witnessed deflation in prices of goods. Goods are more tradeable than services, a more capable vehicle for exporting deflation overseas.

Worldwide the forces of inflation still outweigh the forces of deflation, but the average global inflation rate is sinking. The average inflation rate for industrial economies between 2000 and 2003 sank below 2 per cent, measurably lower than the average inflation rate for the 1950s, 60s, 70s, 80s or 90s.[15] The US government enacted tax cuts and easy money policies to reignite economic growth, holding economic growth as the surest antidote against deflation.

THROWING LIGHT ON THE FUTURE

As this book catches up with the march of current events it is only natural to enquire what the future holds when current trends are viewed through the eye of economic history. What can be extracted from the half-century survey of economic history that can sharpen economic and financial foresight? First, the economy history of the last half century gives small reason to expect long-term deflation; it will probably be a passing matter. The terms of trade moved against developing countries between 1985 and 1998 but that downward drift appears to be reversing.[16] As terms of trade turn against developed countries, growth will slow. Monetary authorities in developed countries, tackling mushy growth and contagious deflation, will liberally enlarge money stocks. Global interest rates will remain in the bargain basement as the demand for capital slackens in the developed world. Rising foodstuff and raw material prices will vent downward pressure on general prices. As economic growth sags, governments in developed countries may face pressure to redistribute incomes. Robust economic growth buys broadmindedness for wider income inequality, helping poorer people stomach it. Deflation rearranges income distribution in a manner that undermines confidence in the fairness of the existing distribution of income and the evenness of the playing field.

The fear of deflation will outlive actual deflation, and last long enough to chill the worship of free markets. Recall that deflation in the 1930s rechannelled economic thinking away from faith in markets. The economy of the 1950s and 60s matured into prosperity on the back of expanding government sectors and scepticism about markets. In the dual shadows of deflation and depression markets aroused fear and uncertainty. Businesses turned to government regulation or mergers to tame risk-churning markets, and exalted planning and foresight. Just as inflation in the 1970s appeared to signal a failure of the planning mentality, deflation may wear the aspect of a failure of markets. Businesses will recruit and coach governments to prop up their own prices, unwilling to make costly and long-term investments without assurance that the bottom will not fall out of prices. They cannot usefully estimate an investment's profitability without knowing what the final output will bring in price.

Already signs are building that confidence in free markets and global capitalism is waning. Political leaders are lashing out against speculators, levelling accusations of shifty market manipulations for personal gain. Volatility in financial markets feeds the perception that free markets favour the fast learners over the slow learners, magnifying income inequality.

No less of a showcase of free markets than Hong Kong fell from grace in 1998. In August the government of Hong Kong in a desperate bid to keep stock prices up began purchasing shares of stock in its own stock market. When stocks rebounded a few months later Hong Kong's government officials triumphantly rejoiced in victory against greedy speculators. Government officials had concluded that Hong Kong's financial markets were the targets of synchronized and underhand assaults by packs of speculators. They envisioned a crafty scheme in which predatory speculators cleverly pressured Hong Kong's currency, forcing it to raise interest rates. High interest rates sent stock prices diving, rendering Hong Kong's stock market vulnerable to speculators who swarmed in and swept up truckloads of stock at bargain prices.

Recent talks over trade policies gave a few hints of what the future has in store. During the deflation of the late nineteenth century, and of the 1930s, tariff walls went up to shield domestic sellers. The last conference of the World Trade Organization, held in Cancún in September 2003, collapsed after delegates from developing nations walked out. They had joined hands demanding that rich countries slash agricultural subsidies, guilty of slumping agricultural prices. Some progress was reported in talks over subsidies, but the European Union unveiled proposals to further liberalize rules for foreign investment and to cut red tape that gummed up trade. Delegates from developing countries clamoured that the rules were already rigged against them. The conference was marked by pontification and little negotiation, a sign that feelings were heating up. For the time being developing countries will only cheer policies that boost their terms of trade.

These trends may tilt global capitalism to the capsizing point, leading to a new synthesis of economic ideas and systems, as happened in the 1930s. Governments and capitals around the world will succeed according to their ability to test and assimilate ideas that conflict with long cherished ideologies and theories.

References

Chapter 2: A Global Postwar Economy Takes Shape

1 N. Gregory Mankiw, *Macroeconomics*, 5th edn (New York, 2003), p. 407.
2 Brian Johnson, *The Politics of Money* (London, 1970), p. 51.
3 Kia-Ngau Chang, *The Inflationary Spiral: The Experience in China, 1939–1950* (Cambridge, 1958), p. 374.
4 Ian Shannon, *International Liquidity* (Chicago, 1966), p. 40.
5 Bank for International Settlements, *Eight European Central Banks* (New York, 1963), p. 59.
6 David McLean, 'Finance and Informal Empire before the First World War', *Economic History Review*, 2nd series, XXIX (1976), pp. 291–305.
7 Shannon, *International Liquidity*, p. 32.
8 Charles Kindleberger, *World Economic Primacy: 1500–1990* (London, 1996), p. 166.
9 Mark Harbison, trans., *Japan's Post-War Economy: An Insider's View of its History and its Future* (New York, 1983), p. 29.
10 T.F.M. Adams and Iwao Hoshaii, *A Financial History of the New Japan* (Tokyo, 1972), p. 31.
11 G. C. Allen, *Japan's Economic Expansion* (Oxford, 1965), p. 49.
12 Ibid., p. 50.
13 Harbison, *Japan's Post-War Economy*, p. 49.
14 Ibid., p. 52.

Chapter 3: Prosperity Born of Depression

1 Mark Harbison, trans., *Japan's Post-War Economy: An Insider's View of its History and its Future* (New York, 1983), p. 57.
2 Ibid., p. 61.

3 W.W. Rostow, *The World Economy: History and Prospect* (Austin, 1978), p. 110.
4 Bennett T. McCallum, *Monetary Economics: Theory and Policy* (New York, 1989), p. 4.
5 Rostow, *The World Economy: History and Prospect*, p. 248.
6 Ibid., p. 346.
7 Don Waldman, *The Economics of Antitrust: Cases and Analysis* (Boston, 1986), p. 53.
8 Richard Bernhard, 'English Law and American Law on Monopolies and Restraints of Trade', *Journal of Economics and Law*, III (1960), pp. 136–45.
9 John Kenneth Galbraith, *The New Industrial State* (Boston, 1971), p. 75.
10 John Kenneth Galbraith, *The Affluence Society* (Boston, 1956), p. 39.
11 Ibid., p. 39.
12 John Kenneth Galbraith, *Economics and the Public Purpose* (Boston, 1973), p. 46.
13 W. F. Bruck, *Social and Economic History of Germany* (1938, reprint New York, 1962), p. 78.
14 Malcolm MacLennan, Murray Forsyth and Geoffrey Denton, *Economic Planning and Policy in Britain, France, and Germany* (New York, 1968), p. 68.
15 Johannes Hirschmeir and Tsunehiko Yui, *The Development of Japanese Business* (Cambridge, 1975), p. 264.
16 Ibid., p. 269.
17 Rostow, *The World Economy: History and Prospect*, p. 68.
18 Benjamin Higgins, *Economic Development: Problems, Principles, and Policies* (New York, 1968), p. 486.

Chapter 4: The Thesis and Antithesis of Capitalism

1 W. W. Rostow, *The World Economy: History and Prospect* (Austin, 1978), pp. 94–5.
2 Ibid., p. 248.
3 Katheryn Morton and Peter Tulloch, *Trade and Developing Countries* (New York, 1977), p. 35.
4 Martin Bronfenbrenner, 'The Appeal of Confiscation in Economic Development', *Economic Development and Cultural Change*, III/ 3 (1955), pp. 201–18.
5 Franklin R. Root, *International Trade and Investment*, 4th edn (Cincinnati, 1978), p. 347.
6 Ibid., p. 355.
7 Root, *International Trade and Investment*, p. 267.
8 Everett E. Hagan, *The Economics of Development* (Homewood, IL, 1975), p. 368.
9 Benjamin Higgins, *Economic Development: Problems, Principles, and Policies* (New York, 1968), p. 486.
10 Hagan, *Economics of Development*, p. 232.
11 Ibid., p. 427.
12 Higgins, *Economic Development*, p. 197.

Chapter 5: The Ebbtide of Postwar Prosperity

1 W. W. Rostow, *The World Economy: History and Prospect* (Austin, 1978), p. 251.
2 Ibid., p. 255.
3 Ian Shannon, *International Liquidity* (Chicago, 1966), pp. 40, 73.
4 *Economic Report of the President* (Washington, DC, 1975), p. 359.
5 Edward J. Shapiro, *Macroeconomic Analysis*, 4th edn (New York, 1978), p. 482.
6 Alan Blinder, *Economic Policy and the Great Stagflation* (New York, 1981), p. 36.
7 Ibid.
8 Michael G. Rukstad, *Macroeconomic Decision Making in the World Economy*, 2nd edn (Chicago, 1989), p. 158.
9 Peter A. Johnson, *The Government of Money: Monetarism in Germany and the United States* (London, 1998), p. 84.
10 Ibid.
11 Ibid., p. 92
12 Franklin R. Root, *International Trade and Investment*, 4th edn (Cincinnati, 1978), p. 389.
13 Katheryn Morton and Peter Tulloch, *Trade and Developing Countries* (New York, 1977), p. 128.
14 Ibid., p. 102.
15 Francisco L. Rivera-Batiz and Luis Rivera-Batiz, *International Finance and Open Economy Macroeconomics* (New York, 1985), p 340.
16 Ibid., p. 361
17 United Nations, *Economic Survey of Latin America, 1981* (New York, 1981) p. 19.
18 Rivera-Batiz and Rivera-Batiz, *International Finance and Open Economy Macroeconomics*, p. 340.
19 United Nations, *Economic Survey of Latin America*, p. 19.
20 Ibid., p. 4.
21 World Bank, *World Development Report, 1990* (Oxford, 1990), p. 161.

Chapter 6: A Tug of War between Inflation and Economic Controls

1 Mark Harbison, trans., *Japan's Post-War Economy: An Insider's View of its History and its Future* (New York, 1983), p. 207.
2 Francisco L. Rivera-Batiz and Luis Rivera-Batiz, *International Finance and Open Economy Macroeconomics* (New York, 1985), p. 340.
3 Juan Gabriel Valdes, *Pinochet's Economists: The Chicago School in Chile* (New York, 1995), p. 25.
4 United Nations, *Economic and Social Survey of Asia and the Pacific, 1975* (Bangkok, 1976), p. 16.
5 United Nations, *Economic and Social Survey of Asia and the Pacific* (Bangkok, 1981), p. 14.
6 United Nations, *Economic and Social Survey of Asia and the Pacific* (Bangkok, 1982),

p. 174.

7 Alan Blinder, *Economic Policy and the Great Stagflation* (New York, 1981), p. 73.
8 Michael G. Rukstad, *Macroeconomic Decision Making in the World Economy*, 2nd edn (Chicago, 1989), p. 517.
9 Blinder, *Economic Policy and the Great Stagflation*, p. 215.
10 Ibid., p. 216
11 Rukstad, *Macroeconomic Decision Making in the World Economy*, p. 96.
12 Ibid., p. 96.
13 Rivera-Batiz and Rivera-Batiz, *International Finance and Open Economy Macroeconomics*, p. 340.
14 Rukstad, *Macroeconomic Decision Making in the World Economy*, p. 105.
15 Organization for Economic Co-operation and Development, *Economic Surveys, 1983–1984, Japan* (Paris, 1984), p. 58.

Chapter 7: The Political Pendulum Suddenly Swings

1 William Greider, *Secrets of the Temple* (New York, 1987), p. 144.
2 Michael G. Rukstad, *Macroeconomic Decision Making in the World Economy*, 2nd edn (Chicago, 1989), p. 143.
3 Bruce W. Kimzey, *Reaganomics* (St Paul, MN, 1983), p. 48.
4 Kenneth Jameson, 'Latin America's Burden: the Debt', in James M. Rock, ed., *Debt and the Twin Deficits Debate* (Mountain View, CA, 1991), p. 157.
5 Rukstad, *Macroeconomic Decision Making in the World Economy*, pp. 208.
6 Ibid., p. 187.

Chapter 8: The Floodtide of the Capitalist Revolution

1 Francisco L. Rivera-Batiz and Luis Rivera-Batiz, *International Finance and Open Economy Macroeconomics* (New York, 1985), p. 340.
2 World Bank, *World Development Report, 1993* (Oxford, 1993), p. 264.
3 Franklin Edwards, *The New Finance: Regulation and Financial Stability* (Washington, DC, 1996), p. 150.
4 Campbell McConnell and Stanley Brue, *Economics*, 12th edn (New York, 1993), p. 759.
5 Rivera-Batiz and Rivera-Batiz, *International Finance and Open Economy Macroeconomics*, p. 560.
6 Ibid., p. 560.
7 Rudiger Dornbusch, 'International Debt and Economic Instability', in *Debt, Financial Stability, and Public Policy*, Federal Reserve Bank of Kansas City Symposium (Kansas City, 1986), p. 77.
8 Ibid.
9 Michael Mussa and Morris Goldstein, 'The Integration of World Capital Markets: Implications for Monetary Policy', Federal Reserve Bank of Kansas

City Symposium, (Kansas City, 1993) p. 246.

10 World Bank, *World Development Report, 1989* (Oxford, 1989), p. 125.

11 Ibid., p. 131,

12 Karl Habermeier, 'India's Experience with the Liberalization of Capital Flows Since 1991', in International Monetary Fund, *Capital Controls: Country Experiences with Their Use and Liberalization, Appendix II*, IMF Occasional Paper 190 (17 May 2000), p. 81.

13 Ibid.

14 Inci Otker-Robe, 'Malaysia's Experience with the Liberalization of Capital Flows', in International Monetary Fund, *Capital Controls: Country Experiences with Their Use and Liberalization, Appendix III*, IMF Occasional Paper 190 (17 May 2000), p. 94.

15 Abbass F. Alkhafaji, *Restructuring American Corporations: Causes, Effects, Implications* (New York, 1990), p. 149.

16 John Donahue, *The Privatization Decision: Public Ends, Private Means* (New York, 1989), p. 6. .

17 Dun and Bradstreet, Inc., 'Privatization: Is it a Panacea', *D & B Reports*, XXXI/1 (January/February 1998), p. 41.

18 Alkhafaji, *Restructuring American Corporations*, p. 143.

19 Robert Hahn, *Reviving Regulatory Reform: A Global Perspective* (Washington, DC, 2001), p. 14.

20 Ibid., p. 19.

21 Christopher Adam, William Cavendish and Percy Mistry, *Adjusting Privatization: Case Studies from Developing Countries* (London, 1992), p. 171.

22 World Bank, *World Development Report, 1991* (Oxford, 1991), p. 143.

23 Ibid., p. 144.

24 World Bank, *World Development Report, 1996* (Oxford, 1996), p. 59.

25 Hahn, *Reviving Regulatory Reform*, p. 16.

26 World Bank, *World Development Report, 1999/2000* (Oxford, 2000), p. 90.

Chapter 9: The Force of Speculation Enrolled in the Cause of Globalization

1 'Will Gold Catch Speculative Fever Again?', *Business Week*, 2669 (29 December – 5 January), p. 148.

2 Robert Prechter, 'Elliot Waves See $388 Gold – Then $5,044', *Commodities*, x/3 (March 1981), p. 48.

3 'A Bursting Bubble', *Wall Street Journal* (2 June 1977), p. 1, col. 6.

4 Bruce Gardner, 'U.S. Commodity Policies and Land Prices', Department of Agricultural and Resource Economics, University of Maryland, Wp02–02 (College Park, MD, 2002), p. 8.

5 Bernice Cohen, *The Edge of Chaos: Financial Booms, Crashes, and Chaos* (New York, 1997), p. 288.

6 Ibid., p. 55.

7   Ibid.
8   Ibid., p. 257.
9   Ibid., p. 320.
10 Ibid.
11 Charles Kindleberger, *World Economic Primacy* (New York, 1996), p. 207.
12 International Monetary Fund, *Singapore-Statistical Appendix*, IMF Staff
    Country Report No. 98/52 (Washington, DC, 1998), p. 36.
13 Dow Jones & Company, *Dow Jones Guide to the World Stock Market* (Englewood
    Cliffs, NJ, 1994), p. 7.
14 Gustavo Lombo, 'World Markets in Review', *Forbes*, CLIII/ 2 (17 January 1994),
    p. 116.
15 Gustavo Lombo, 'World Markets in Review', *Forbes*, CLV/8 (10 April 1995), p. 120.
16 Ibid.
17 David DeRosa, *In Defense of Free Capital Markets* (Princeton, 2001), p. 8.
18 Gustavo Lombo, 'World Markets in Review', *Forbes*, CLVII/ 5 (11 March 1996),
    p. 186.
19 World Bank, *World Development Report, 1999/2000* (Oxford, 2000), p. 261.
20 Ibid., p. 250.
21 International Monetary Fund, *World Economic Outlook Statistical Appendix*
    (Washington, DC, 2003), p. 180.
22 World Bank, *World Development Report, 1999/2000*, p. 69.
23 Ibid., p. 7.
24 Ibid., p. 71.

Chapter 10: Global Confidence and Global Panic

1   Asian Development Bank, *Asian Development Outlook: 1998* (Manila, 1998), p. 256.
2   John Christy, ' World Market Review', *Forbes*, CLXII/13 (14 December 1998), p. 280.
3   George Soros, *Crisis of Global Capitalism* (New York, 1998), p. 136.
4   Asian Development Bank, *Asian Development Outlook: 1998*, p. 33.
5   Ibid., p. 21.
6   Soros, *The Crisis of Global Capitalism* (New York, 1998), p. 142.
7   John Christy, 'World Markets Review', *Forbes*, CLX/5 (8 September 1997), p. 222.
8   John Christy, 'World Market Review', *Forbes*, CLXII/5 (9 July 1998), p. 246.
9   John Christy, 'World Market Review', *Forbes*, CLXII/13 (14 December 1998), p. 280.
10 International Monetary Fund, *World Economic Outlook Statistical Appendix*
    (Washington, DC, 2003), p. 174.
11 Ibid., p. 185.
12 Ibid., p. 197.
13 Ibid., p. 174.
14 International Monetary Fund, *Deflation: Determinates, Risks, and Policy Options–
    Findings of an Interdepartmental Task Force* (Washington, DC, 2003), p. 8.
15 Ibid., p. 50.
16 International Monetary Fund, *World Economic Outlook Statistical Appendix*, p. 201.

Selected Further Reading

'A Bursting Bubble', *Wall Street Journal* (2 June 1977), p. 1, col. 6

Adam, Christopher, William Cavendish and Percy Mistry, *Adjusting Privatization: Case Studies from Developing Countries* (London, 1992)

Adams, T. F. M. and Iwao Hoshaii, *A Financial History of the New Japan* (Tokyo, 1972)

Alkhafaji, Abbass F., *Restructuring American Corporations: Causes, Effects, Implications* (New York, 1990)

Allen, G. C., *Japan's Economic Expansion* (Oxford, 1965)

Asian Development Bank, *Asian Development Outlook: 1998* (Manila, 1998)

Bank for International Settlements, *Eight European Central Banks* (New York, 1963)

Bernhard, Richard, 'English Law and American Law on Monopolies and Restraints of Trade', *Journal of Economics and Law*, III (1960), pp. 136–45

Blinder, Alan, *Economic Policy and the Great Stagflation* (New York, 1981)

Bronfenbrenner, Martin, 'The Appeal of Confiscation in Economic Development', *Economic Development and Cultural Change*, III/3 (1955), pp. 201–18

Bruck, W. F., *Social and Economic History of Germany* (1938, reprint New York, 1962)

Chang, Kia-Ngau, *The Inflationary Spiral: The Experience in China, 1939–1950* (Cambridge, 1958)

Christy, John, 'World Markets Review', *Forbes*, CLX/5 (8 September 1997), p. 222

—, 'World Market Review', *Forbes*, CLXII/5 (9 July 1998), p. 246

—, 'World Market Review', *Forbes*, CLXII/13 (14 December 1998), p. 280

Cohen, Bernice, *The Edge of Chaos: Financial Booms, Crashes, and Chaos* (New York, 1997)

DeRosa, David, *In Defense of Free Capital Markets* (Princeton, 2001)

Donahue, John, *The Privatization Decision: Public Ends, Private Means* (New York, 1989)

Dornbusch, Rudiger, 'International Debt and Economic Instability', in *Debt, Financial Stability, and Public Policy*, Federal Reserve Bank of Kansas City Symposium (Kansas City, 1986)

Dow Jones & Company, *Dow Jones Guide to the World Stock Market* (Englewood Cliffs, NJ, 1994)

Dun and Bradstreet, Inc., 'Privatization: Is it a Panacea', *D & B Reports*, xxxi/1 (January/February 1988), pp. 41-3

Economic Report of the President (Washington, DC, 1975)

Edwards, Franklin, *The New Finance: Regulation and Financial Stability* (Washington, DC, 1996)

Friedman, Benjamin, 'US Fiscal Policy in the 1980s, Consequences of Large Budget Deficits at Full Employment', in *Debt and the Twin Deficits Debate*, ed. James M. Rock (Mountain View, CA, 1991), pp. 149-72

Galbraith, John Kenneth, *The Affluence Society* (Boston, 1956)

—, *The New Industrial State* (Boston, 1971)

—, *Economics and the Public Purpose* (Boston, 1973)

Gardner, Bruce, 'US Commodity Policies and Land Prices', Department of Agricultural and Resource Economics, University of Maryland Working Paper 02-02 (College Park, MD, 2002)

Greider, William, *Secrets of the Temple* (New York, 1987)

Habermeier, Karl, 'India's Experience with the Liberalization of Capital Flows Since 1991', International Monetary Fund, *Capital Controls: Country Experiences with Their Use and Liberalization, Appendix II*, IMF Occasional Paper 190 (17 May 2000), pp. 80-93.

Hagan, Everett E., *The Economics of Development* (Homewood, IL, 1975)

Hahn, Robert, *Reviving Regulatory Reform: A Global Perspective* (Washington, DC, 2001)

Harbison, Mark, trans., *Japan's Post-War Economy: An Insider's View of its History and its Future* (New York, 1983)

Higgins, Benjamin, *Economic Development: Problems, Principles, and Policies* (New York, 1968)

Hirschmeir, Johannes, and Tsunehiko Yui, *The Development of Japanese Business* (Cambridge, 1975)

International Monetary Fund, *Singapore–Statistical Appendix*, IMF Staff Country Report 98/52 (Washington, DC, 1998)

—, *World Economic Outlook Statistical Appendix* (Washington, DC, 2003)

—, *Deflation: Determinates, Risks, and Policy Options–Findings of an Interdepartmental Task Force* (Washington, DC, 2003)

Johnson, Brian, *The Politics of Money* (London, 1970)

Johnson, Peter, *The Government of Money: Monetarism in Germany and the United States* (London, 1998)

Kimzey, Bruce, *Reaganomics* (St Paul, MN, 1983)

Kindleberger, Charles, *World Economic Primacy: 1500-1990* (London, 1996)

Lombo, Gustavo, 'World Markets in Review', *Forbes*, CLIII/2 (17 January 1994), p. 116

—, 'World Markets in Review', *Forbes*, CLV/8 (10 April 1995), p. 120

—, 'World Markets in Review', *Forbes*, CLVII/5 (11 March 1996), p. 186

Mankiw, N. Gregory, *Macroeconomics*, 5th edn (New York, 2003)

McCallum, Bennett, *Monetary Economics: Theory and Policy* (New York, 1989)

McConnell, Campbell, and Stanley Brue, *Economics*, 12th edn (New York, 1993)

McLean, David, 'Finance and Informal Empire before the First World War',

Economic History Review, 2nd series, XXIX (1976), pp. 291-305

MacLennan, Malcolm, Murray Forsyth and Geoffrey Denton, *Economic Planning and Policy in Britain, France, and Germany* (New York, 1968)

Morton, Katheryn, and Peter Tulloch, *Trade and Developing Countries* (New York, 1977)

Mussa, Michael, and Morris Goldstein, 'The Integration of World Capital Markets: Implications for Monetary Policy', Federal Reserve Bank of Kansas City Symposium (Kansas City, 1993), pp. 245-313

Organization for Economic Co-operation and Development, *Economic Surveys, 1983-1984, Japan* (Paris, 1984)

Otker-Robe, Inci, 'Malaysia's Experience with the Liberalization of Capital Flows', International Monetary Fund, *Capital Controls: Country Experiences with Their Use and Liberalization, Appendix III*, IMF Occasional Paper 190 (17 May 2000), pp. 94-119

Prechter, Robert, 'Elliot Waves See $388 Gold – Then $5,044', *Commodities*, x/3 (March 1981), p. 48

Rivera-Batiz, Francisco, and Luis Rivera-Batiz, *International Finance and Open Economy Macroeconomics* (New York, 1985)

Root, Franklin, *International Trade and Investment*, 4th edn (Cincinnati, 1978)

Rostow, W. W., *The World Economy: History and Prospect* (Austin, TX, 1978)

Rukstad, Michael, *Macroeconomic Decision Making in the World Economy*, 2nd edn (Chicago, 1989)

Shannon, Ian, *International Liquidity* (Chicago, 1966)

Shapiro, Edward, *Macroeconomic Analysis*, 4th edn (New York, 1978)

Soros, George, *The Crisis of Global Capitalism* (New York, 1998)

United Nations, *Economic and Social Survey of Asia and the Pacific*, 1975 (Bangkok, 1976)

—, *Economic Survey of Latin America, 1981* (New York, 1981)

—, *Economic and Social Survey of Asia and the Pacific* (Bangkok, 1981)

—, *Economic and Social Survey of Asia and the Pacific* (Bangkok, 1982)

Valdes, Juan Gabriel, *Pinochet's Economists: The Chicago School in Chile* (New York, 1995)

Waldman, Don, *The Economics of Antitrust: Cases and Analysis* (Boston, 1986)

'Will Gold Catch Speculative Fever Again?', *Business Week*, 2669 (29 December – 5 January), p. 148

World Bank, *World Development Report, 1989* (Oxford, 1989)

—, *World Development Report, 1990* (Oxford, 1990)

—, *World Development Report, 1991* (Oxford, 1991)

—, *World Development Report, 1993* (Oxford, 1993)

—, *World Development Report, 1996* (Oxford, 1996)

—, *World Development Report, 1999/2000* (Oxford, 2000)

Index

advertising, and price competition 12, 46, 57
aerospace industry 41
Africa 70–71, 148
agricultural land reform 73–7
agricultural materials, imports and prices 38, 39–40, 60
agricultural policy, of EEC 56
agricultural productivity:
    and land reform 76
    and postwar prosperity 39–40, 56, 80
agricultural reform, China 159
airline industry deregulation 109
Alcoa (Aluminum Company of America) 42–3
Algeria, land reform in 77
Alliance for Progress 75, 77
aluminium production 42–3
Anaconda Company 66
Angola 60
Anti-Monopoly Law 1947 (Japan) 43
Anti-trust legislation:
    in Japan 44, 53
    in the US 22, 42–3, 55, 62
    in West Germany 51
Argentina 27, 70, 104
Articles of Agreement (World Bank) 26
Asia:
    bank insolvencies in 147–8
    East Asian financial crisis 14, 186–92
    inflation and economic growth 70
    land reform programmes 75–6
Australia, economic policy 127
automobile industry 55

baht (Thai currency) 189–91
'banana wars' 164
Bangladesh, grain imports 104
Bank Deutscher Lander 32
Bank of England 49

Bank of France 49
bank insolvencies 147–8
Bank of Japan 118, 176, 177
Bank of Thailand 190, 191
banks/banking industry:
    borrowing and deposit insurance 147–8
    in developing countries 65
    and East Asian crisis 190–91, 192
    investment in multinationals 63
    investment in silver speculation 125–6
    Japanese 53, 118, 176, 177
    nationalization of 20, 26–7, 32, 48–9, 57
    and postwar inflation 19–20
    share ownership in West Germany 51–2
    US deregulation of 110
Barings Bank 27, 185
Belgian Congo 60
Blair, Tony 130
Bolivia 64, 74, 158
borrowing:
    and deposit insurance 147–8
    for speculative investment 170
Brazil:
    economic development and inflation 70
    expropriation in 64–5
    land reform in 74
    World War II and postwar inflation 18, 58
Bretton Woods Conference (1944) 11, 23
Bretton Woods system 11, 12, 23–7, 34, 35
    and move from gold standard 87, 89
Britain see United Kingdom
British Empire and Commonwealth 59–60
Bronfenbrenner, Martin 67
Bruck, W. F. 46–7, 88
Bryan, William Jennings 123
budget surpluses and deficits 187
buffalo 160–61
Bundesbank see Deutsche Bundesbank

Burma, land reform in 75
business tax cuts 137
Business Week (periodical) 169
businesses, and economic planning 51, 53
businessmen's associations, Japanese 54

Canada, signatory to NAFTA 162
capital flows, liberalization of 150-4, 184
capital gains taxes, cuts in 136-7
capital investment 138-9
capital mobility 133, 138-9, 150-4
capitalism:
    as cause of Great Depression 29
    in the developing countries 59-79, 151
    future of 205-6
    global 10-14
    global renaissance of 1980s 126-42, 151
    global revolution of 1990s 13-14, 143-65
    monopoly capitalism 41-2
    success of in East Asia 98-100
cartels:
    in Germany 21-2, 41-2, 44, 46-7
    in Japan 53
Carter, J. President 106, 108, 109, 110, 113, 116-17
cash holding, and deflation 201-2
Central America, expropriation in 63-4
Cerro Corporation 66
Chicago Board of Trade (CBT) 185
Chile:
    economic growth 70, 97
    expropriation policies 66, 67
    inflation rates 104
    privatization 156
    World War II and postwar inflation 18, 40
China:
    agricultural reform 159
    current growth 204
    devaluation of renminbi 189
    Hong Kong returned to 60
    World War II and postwar inflation 17-18, 39
    see also Free China; Taiwan
Chirac, Jacques 181
coffee production 69
Colm, Gerhard 31
Colombia 69
colonialism 11, 29, 59-62
Committee for European Economic Cooperation (later OEEC) 30
Commodities (periodical) 169
Common Market (European) 55-6
communication technologies 14, 152
communism 29, 30, 37
compensation, for expropriation 65, 67
Confucian philosophy 99, 187
Consumer Price Index (CPI) 83, 141-2
corporations:
    assets of 45-7

economic planning by 48, 53-4, 57
corruption 10
Cosmo Shinyo Kumiai 177
cost of living 109
credit, for speculative ventures 125-6
credit controls 113
creditors, debtors, and inflation 146-50
crude materials index 145
crude oil see oil
Cuba 64
currency flows:
    and fixed exchange rates 24-5, 107-8, 119
    and real exchange rates 189
currency reform:
    in postwar Germany 31-2
    in postwar Japan 33-5
    see also devaluation
currency speculators 181, 189, 191-2
currency values:
    during East Asian crisis 189-92
    in foreign exchange markets 107-8, 111, 138, 152, 168
    and move from gold standard 87-90
    of yen 107, 118, 119, 121

Dai Ichi Bank 53
debt:
    and inflation 15, 124
    Iran and foreign debt 113
    US postwar public debt 15-16
debtors, creditors, and inflation 146-50
deflation:
    global 200-4, 205
    and inflation 122-6
    political economy of 9-14
    postwar policy initiatives 21-3
denationalization:
    in Britain 49-50, 129-30, 154-5
    in West Germany 51
    see also nationalization; privatization
Depository Institutions Deregulation and Monetary Control Act 1980 (US) 110
depreciation:
    of East Asian currencies 189-91
    tax deductions for 137
Depression see Great Depression
deregulation 108-10, 116, 117-21
    of Japanese international financial transactions 178
    of prices, and privatization 160
Deutsche Bundesbank 20, 32, 91-2, 94
Deutsche Mark (East) 33
Deutsche Mark (West) 32, 57-8
    floating of 87, 89, 90
    value in foreign exchange markets 107, 111
devaluation:
    and debt in developing countries 149-50
    and move from gold standard 87-90

postwar European 57
and price wars 23–4, 25
of renminbi 189
of US dollar 87, 88, 89, 90
developing countries:
    annual inflation rates 104
debt burdens 148–9, 150
    economic inequality and land reform 71–7
    economic planning in 54–5
    effects of disimperialism 60–2
    exchange rate controls in 68–9
    expropriation policies 63–7
    foreign aid to 54–5, 75, 77
    foreign investment in 78–9, 96
    inflation and growth 14, 69–71, 77
    integration and speculation in 182–5
    liberalization of capital flows 151, 152–4
    multinationals in 62–3
    as oil exporters and importers 96–7
    privatization in 156, 157–8, 160
    oterms of trade against 205
    see also industrialized countries
direct foreign investment 14, 184–5
discount rates 193–4, 195, 196–7
disimperialism 59–62
disinflation 111–13
DJIA (Dow Jones Industrial Average) 166, 167,
    172, 173, 193. 194
Dodge, Joseph M. 31, 34
dollar (US):
    devaluation of 87, 88, 89, 90
    falls in crash of 1987 175
    value against the yen 174, 176
    value in foreign exchange markets 12,
    107–8, 111, 138, 168
Dow Jones Industrial Average (DJIA) 166, 167,
    172, 173, 193, 194

East Asia:
    economic growth 98–100, 183–4
    financial crisis of 2000 14, 186–92
    inflation rates in 1970s 104
East Germany, postwar currency reform 33
Eastern Bloc:
    privatization 158–9
    shuns postwar foreign aid 30
economic development, and income
    inequality 73
economic growth:
    in 1970s Japan 117–18
    as antidote to deflation 204
    in East Asia 98–100
    pre-1970s 80–83
    see also GDP growth; GNP growth; postwar
    prosperity
economic inequality, in developing countries
    71–7
economic planning 12

derailed by rising oil prices 93–4
    in developing countries 77
    postwar period 48–57
Economic Planning Agency (Japan) 54
Economic Recovery Act 1948 (US) 30
Economic Recovery Tax Act 1981 (US) 136–41
economic theory:
    locomotive theory 106–9, 134
    macroeconomics 9, 187
    monetary theory 201
    Mundell's theories 133–6
    Supply-side economics 131–6
economic trends:
    postwar 56–8
    prewar long-term 38–40
Ecuador, land reform in 74–5
Egypt:
    land reform in 75
    privatization 156
    and the Suez Canal crisis 65–6
elections, US presidential 199–201
electronics industry 41
Elimination of Excessive Economic
    Concentration, Law for (Japan) 43
Emergency Monetary Measures Ordinance
    1946 (Japan) 33
emerging countries, deflationary trends in 204
emerging markets 179–80
employment:
    and government spending 47
    oligopolies as employers 45–6
    slavery and indentured servitude 59
Employment Act 1946 (US) 19
Employment Acts 1980 and 1982 (UK) 129–30
energy supplies 144–5
England:
    sixteenth century deflation control 21
    see also United Kingdom
entrepreneurship 13, 14, 129
environmental issues 82, 160–2
Euchen, Walter 50
Europe:
    colonial powers 59–60
    postwar foreign aid to 29–30
European Atomic Energy Commission 55–6
European Coal and Steel Community 56
European Common Market 55–6
European Economic Arena 163
European Economic Community (EEC) 55, 56,
    89–90
European Recovery Program (Marshall Plan)
    29–30
European Recovery Program Fund 52
European Union 55–6, 206
exchange rate 9
    and 1970s monetary expansion 107
    controls of 68–9
    and East Asian crisis 189, 192

see also fixed exchange rates
exports:
  and Japanese postwar prosperity 37–8
  see also terms of trade
expropriation 63–7
Exxon 63

Falldin, Thorbjorn 128
Federal Reserve System 110, 111, 113, 126
  lowers discount rate 193–4, 195, 196–7
finance capitalism 22
financial derivatives 185
Finland 17
fiscal policy, US 133–9
fixed exchange rates:
  the Bretton Woods system 12, 23–4, 34, 35
  and Mundell's theories 134
  replace the gold standard 24, 27, 89, 90,
    101–2
floating exchange rate 9, 90–2, 133, 190–1
foodstuffs supplies:
  crises in 1970s 103, 104–5
  prices and demand 80, 81, 94–5, 96
  and terms of trade 61, 144–5
  see also agricultural productivity
Ford, Gerald, President 105, 113
foreign aid:
  and expropriation compensation 65, 67
  to developing countries 54–5, 75, 77
  to postwar Europe 29–30, 31–3
  to postwar Japan 29–30, 33–5
Foreign Exchange and Foreign Trade Control
    Law (Japan) 120
foreign exchange markets 181
  currency values in 107–8, 111, 138, 152, 168
  value of yen 107, 118, 119, 121
foreign exchange reserves 25
foreign investment:
  in developing countries 78–9, 96
  and liberalization of capital flows 154
  and private banking systems 27, 63
foreign portfolio investment 185
foreign trade 10–11, 58
forward markets 181
franc, devaluation of 88
France:
  annual inflation rates 102–3
  colonial empire 60
  consumer prices 84
  economic planning 48–9, 52, 57
  and postwar German monetary reform 31
  postwar prosperity 41
  privatization 155
  socialist agenda and monetary policies 141
  and World Bank 26
Fraser, Malcolm 127
Free China 17–18, 39
free markets:

deflation and inflation 10, 122–3
  future of 203–4
  policies 13, 108–10, 114–21
Free Silver Movement 123
free trade, postwar economy principles of 27–9
FTSE index 173
fuel prices:
  1970s deregulation of 108
  and postwar prosperity 40, 80
Fuji financial group 53

Galbraith, John Kenneth 46, 88
  The Great Crash 166
GATT 28–9, 35, 163
GDP growth:
  and inflation 200–1, 203
  in Japan 176, 200
  and oil price rise 95–6
  in US 95, 176, 198–201
  in world economy 182–3
General Agreement on Tariffs and Trade *see*
  GATT
Germany:
  cartelization 21–2, 41–2, 44, 46–7
  economic policies 88
  postwar foreign aid to 29–30, 31–3
  postwar prosperity 41
  pre- and postwar anti-inflation initiatives
    17, 23
  social insurance policies 21–2
  tariff policies 28, 50
  see also East Germany; West Germany
global commons 160–62
global economy:
  capitalist renaissance of 1980s 126–42
  the East Asian crisis 186–92
  effect of stock market boom 173
  future trends 204–6
  and global deflation 200–4
  inflation versus economic controls 101–20
  Japanese investment in US financial
    markets 174, 176
  and postwar prosperity 40–41
  revolution of 1990s 13–14, 143–65
  and speculation 192–7
  and US recession 197–200
  see also postwar economy; speculative
    investments
GNP deflator 102, 115
GNP growth:
  annual per capita GNP 72–3
  and monetarist policies 114, 115–16
  postwar period 41
gold, speculative dealing in 168
gold reserves ownership 82–3
gold standard 12, 16, 87–90
  as cause of deflation 123, 203
  replaced by fixed exchange rate system 24,

27, 90, 101–2
Goldsmith, Raymond 31
González, Felipe 13, 142
government employees, wage levels during
    inflation 10
government ownership 156
government spending:
    and postwar prosperity 38–9
    and the private sector 47, 57
    pro-capitalist policies 10, 13
grain:
    imports 81, 104–5
    prices 94
Great Depression:
    capitalism as cause of 29
    legacy of 11, 12, 15–16, 20–21, 23
    and markets 145–6
    prewar deflationary phases 39
Greece, postwar foreign aid to 30
Greenspan, Alan 196
growth *see* economic growth; GDP growth; GNP
    growth; postwar prosperity
Guatemala, expropriation in 63–4

Halifax summit 181
Hang Seng index 188
Holding Companies Liquidation Commission
    (Japan) 43
Holland, colonial empire of 60
Honduras, expropriation in 64
Hong Kong:
    fall of stock market 206
    Hang Seng index 188
    per capita income 98
    returned to China 60
housing:
    shortages 171
    speculation 169–70
Hungary 17
Hunt, Nelson and Herbert 125, 169
hyperinflation 10

IMF (International Monetary Fund) 24, 25
    capital flow liberalization 152, 153
    debt rescheduling agreements 150
    and East Asian crisis 191
    and floating exchange rate 90
Import Duties Act 1932 (UK) 28
imports:
    and exchange rate controls in developing
        countries 68–9
    Japanese oil imports 119–20
    prices and agricultural materials 38,
        39–40, 60, 81–82
    US fiscal and monetary policies for 139, 175
incentives 129
income inequality 71–3, 205, 206
    see also wages

indentured servitude 59
India:
    capital flows liberalized 153
    grain imports 105
    land reform in 76
    and World Bank 26
Indonesia:
    disimperialism and expropriation 60, 65
    economic growth 183
industrial production:
    action against monopolistic practices 42–5
    in Japan 118–20
    nationalization of 49–50
    and postwar prosperity 40–1
industrialized countries:
    bank insolvencies in 147
    deflationary trends in 204, 205
    economic growth and oil price rises 95–6
    see also developing countries
inflation:
    in 1950s and 1960s 58, 143
    and deflation 122–6
    in developed countries, 1970 and after 12,
        81–3, 84, 86
    global economy in 1980s 143–6
    global, versus economic controls 101–20
    and growth in developing countries
        69–71, 77
    monetarist policies for 92, 110–17, 121
    oil and food price rises 94–5
    political economy of 9–14
    World War II and postwar period 16–19,
        34–5
information technologies 14, 152
insolvencies, bank 147–8
insurance companies, nationalization of 49
interest rates:
    and deflation 201–2, 205
    deregulation in 1980s 151, 172
    inflation-adjusted 201–2
    Japanese monetary policies 118, 119, 177
    monetarist policies 111, 112, 113, 115
    and postwar inflation 19–20
    US inflation adjustments 137–8
    and US recession 197–8
International Bank of Reconstruction and
    Development *see* World Bank
International Development Association 26
International Finance Corporation 26
    global composite index 180–81
International Monetary Fund *see* IMF
International Trade Organization 28
International Whaling Commission (IWC) 161
investment *see* capital investment; foreign
    investment; government spending; port-
    folio investment; speculative investments
Iran:
    1978 revolution 110

land reform in 77
oil production 93
repudiates foreign debt 113
Iraq:
land reform in 75–6
oil production 93
Israel 93

Jamaica, privatization 157
Japan:
annual inflation rates 103
automobile industry and the US 55
deflation in 9, 201, 202
economic planning 53–4, 57
GDP growth 176, 200
investment in US financial markets 174, 176
locomotive theory 106, 107, 108
monetary policies 117–21, 140, 176
monopoly capitalism in 42, 43–4
political changes 140
postwar foreign aid to 29–30, 33–5
postwar prosperity 37–8, 39–40, 41
privatization 155
the Tokyo Bubble 175–8, 195
World War II and postwar inflation 17
jawboning 83
J. P. Morgan 22

Kahn, Alfred 109
Kennecott 66
Keynes, John Maynard 23
Kohl, Helmut 13
Korean War 11, 35, 37
aftermath, compared with 1980s 143, 154
Kyoto Agreement 162

Laffer, Arthur 131, 132
Laffer Curve 131
laissez-faire capitalism 41–5
land reform in developing countries 73–7
land speculation 170–71
Latin America:
bank insolvencies and debt crises 148, 149–50
economic growth 97
economic plan 77
expropriation in 64–5
income inequality and land reform 72, 73–5
inflation and economic growth 70
terms of trade 61, 81
World War II and postwar inflation 18
legislation:
anti-monopolistic 22, 42–5, 51
for West German economic development 52
Liberia 66–7

liquidity trap theories 201
loans, from World Bank 26
locomotive theory 106–9, 134
low and middle-income countries 183

M3, annual growth of 114–15, 116
macroeconomic theory 9, 187
Malaysia:
capital flows liberalized 153–4
and East Asian crisis 188
economic growth 183
privatization 157–8
manufactured goods:
deflated prices of 204
and postwar prosperity 40, 80
market deregulation see deregulation
market-orientated policies 13, 145–6, 150–54
markets:
created by large corporations 46–7
see also free markets
Marshall Plan 11, 29–30, 35
media, and price competition 12, 46, 57
Medium and Small Enterprises' Basic Law 1963 (Japan) 54
Mexico:
debt burdens 149–50
expropriation 64
financial crisis, 1994 179–80
income inequality and land reform 72, 73–4
as oil exporter 96–7
privatization 156
signatory to NAFTA 162
M1 growth 111–12
Middle East:
disimperialism and expropriation 61, 65–6
inflation rates in 1970s 104
military coups 64
Miller-Tydings Act 1937 (US) 22
miners' strikes (UK) 85, 86
minimum wages 109, 110
mining, Chilean interests expropriated 66
MITI (Ministry of International Trade and Industry) (Japan) 53, 54
Mitsubishi 44
Mitsubishi financial group 53
Mitsui 44
Mitsui Bank 53
Mitterrand, François 13, 141, 155
monetarism 91–2, 110–17, 121
monetary growth targets 114
monetary policy:
and Mundell's theories 133–6
in Germany 91–2
in Japan 117–21, 140, 176
in UK 114–17, 129
in US 110–13, 116–17, 134–41, 175

monetary theory 133–6, 201
money stock growth 91–2, 110–11
money supply growth 203
money supply targeting 172
monopolistic practices (price fixing) 22, 42–5
Monopoly and Restrictive Practices (Inquiry and Control) Act 1948 (uk) 44
Moody's investor service 191
Morocco 71
mortgages 112, 170
motor vehicle industry 41
Mozambique 60
multinationals 11–12, 62–7
multiple exchange rate regimes 68–9
Mundell, Robert A. 133–4, 138
mutual fund managers 179

NAFTA (North American Free Trade Association) 162–3
NASDAQ speculative bubble 14, 194–5, 196–7
National Bureau of Economic Research (NBER) 198
National Insurance Act 1946 (UK) 48
nationalization:
    of banks 20, 26–7, 32, 49–50
    in France 49–50, 57
    see also denationalization; privatization
natural gas production 82, 108
negative growth rates 96–7, 116, 203
negative real interest rates 111
Netherlands Bank 49
New Zealand, deregulation in 152, 160
Nigeria 71
Nikkei index 173, 176–7, 195
Nixon, Richard, President 83, 84, 85, 87
North American Free Trade Association (NAFTA) 162–3

OECD countries, privatization in 155–6
oil:
    prices 92–4, 96–8, 108, 110, 115, 119
    production and demand 81–2, 136, 139
    speculation in 172–3, 196
oil companies, and expropriation 64, 65, 66–7
oligopolistic corporations 12, 45–8, 55
OPEC (Organization of Petroleum Exporting Countries) 82, 93, 139
Operation Birddog 32
optimal currency area 133–4
Orange County, California 185
ownership:
    foreign, of Japanese bonds 120–21
    share ownership in West Germany 51–2
    of US gold reserves 82–3

Pakistan:
    grain imports 105
    land reform in 76

Peru, land reform in 74
peso, devaluation of 149–50, 180
petrochemical industry 41
Philippines:
    currency depreciation 189
    land reform in 76–7
political climate:
    anti-inflationary policies 127–31
    consequences of deflation and inflation 122–6
political economy 9–14
portfolio equity flows 184
portfolio investment 139
Portuguese Empire 60
positive growth rates 203
postwar economy 15–36
    Bretton Woods system 23–7
    free trade principles 27–9
    Germany and Japan 31–7
    inflation 16–19
    Marshall Plan 29–30
    policy initiatives 19–23
    see also global economy
postwar prosperity:
    economic growth up to 1970s 80–83
    in Europe 62
    the European Union 55–6
    growth and global economy 40–41
    growth trends 56–8
    Japan 37–40
    and laissez-faire capitalism 41–5
    and oligopolies 45–8
    rise of economic planning 48–55
pound sterling, monetarist policies for 114, 115, 116
presidential terms, and GDP annual growth rates 199–201
price competition:
    large corporations shunning of 12, 46–7, 57
    in West Germany 50, 51
price controls:
    and fixed exchange rates 23–4
    monetarist policies 110–17, 121
    postwar policies 21–23, 32–3
    and wages in 1970s 13, 83–7, 108–9
price fixing (monopolistic practices) 22, 42–5
price wars, and devaluation 23–4, 25
prices:
    deregulation of and privatization 160
    large corporations' monopolies of 46–7
    postwar world trends 12–13, 38–40
private capital inflows 187–8
private debt flows 184
private sector:
    foreign investment 27, 63, 79
    ownership and resource exploitation 160–61
    in West Germany 51

privatization 154–60
 of nationalized industries 129–30
 see also denationalization; nationalization
Producer Price Index (PPI) 145
product development, competition in 46, 57
property prices 177
property speculation 169–70
prosperity *see* postwar Prosperity
Puerto Rico, annual per capita GNP 72

Radcliffe Report (UK) 20
railroad industry deregulation 110
raw materials:
 in developing countries 61
 and postwar prosperity 38, 39–40, 56, 57
 rising prices and demand for 81
Reagan, Ronald, President 13, 113, 131, 141
real estate investment 13, 124, 170–71, 176
real hourly compensation growth 95–6
real interest rates 201–2
recession:
 and monetarism 112–13, 114
 and tax cuts 132
 in US 197–200
regulation *see* deregulation
Reichsmarks 31–2
renminbi, devaluation of 189
rental property, speculation in 170–71
resources, exploitation and protection of
 160–62
Restrictive Trade Practices Act 1956 (UK) 44–5
ringgits, speculative dealing in 189
Rio Declaration 162
Robinson-Patman Act 1936 (US) 22–3
Rothschilds 27
rouble, fall in value of 193
Russia:
 stock market 192, 193
 see also Soviet Union

Sanwa financial group 53
savings:
 domestic 119
 rates in East Asia 187
September 11 terrorist attacks 198
Shanghai 17–18, 39
shareholding, in West Germany 51–2
Sherman Antitrust Act 1890 (US) 22, 43
Short-term interest rates 202
shortage and surplus 11, 13
silver speculation 123, 125–6
Singapore 98, 183, 188
slavery 59
small businesses 51, 53
small farmers 165
Smoot-Hawley Act 1930 (US) 28
Smoot-Hawley Tariff 101
'the snake in the tunnel' 90

social insurance policies 21–2, 47–8
social market economy, concept of 50
socialism, capitalism replaces 142, 146, 153, 156
Soros, George 181, 189
 The Crisis of Global Capitalism 191–2
South Korea 70, 105, 183
Soviet Union 30, 31–2
 see also Russia
soybean prices 103
Spain:
 economic deregulation 141–2
 postwar economy 30
speculative investments 13, 123–6, 146, 166–71
 the 1980s 171–5
 in developing countries 182–5
 the East Asian crisis 189–92
 emerging markets in 1990s 178–82
 global 1996–2000 192–7
 Tokyo Bubble 175–8, 195
spot markets 181
stagflation 114–17
Standard Drawing Rights (paper gold) 83
Statute of Artificers 1563 (England) 21
steel industry 41
stock market:
 development and privatization 159–60
 speculation 167–8, 171–8, 181–2, 188–92,
  192–7, 206
Stockholm Conference 161
Suez Crisis (1956) 65–6
Sumitomo financial group 53
Supply-side economics 131–6
surplus and shortage 11, 13
Sweden:
 economic policy 127–8
 postwar foreign aid to 30
Switzerland 16–17

Taft-Hartley Act 1947 (US) 80
Taiwan 75, 183
 see also China; Free China
tariff policies:
 and economic planning 50
 German 28, 50
 global 163
tax credits 137
taxation:
 cuts and deregulation 13, 151–2, 172
 Japanese policies 140
 UK policies 128, 129
 US monetary and fiscal policies 131–9
terms of trade 61, 81–2, 143–4, 151, 183–4
 against developing countries 205
terrorist attacks of 9/11 198
Texas Railroad Commission 82
Thailand, and East Asian crisis 188, 189–91
Thatcher, Margaret 13, 114, 128–9, 130, 154
Tokyo Bubble 175–8, 195

trade barriers 27–9
 see also terms of trade; world trade
trade organizations 162–5
Trade Union Act 1984 (uk) 130
trade unions 80, 86, 128, 129–30
trucking industry deregulation 109–10
trusts, anti-trust legislation 22, 42–4, 51, 53
Turkey, postwar foreign aid to 30

Ullsten, Ola 128
unemployment:
 and global speculation 195–6
 and inflation 58, 81, 85
 and recession 112–13, 197
United Electricity and Mining Company 51
United Fruit Company 63–4
United Kingdom:
 annual inflation rates 102
 anti-monopolistic legislation 44–5
 anti-price fixing measures 22, 44–5
 consumer price controls 83, 84–6
 denationalization 154–5
 distribution 72
 economic controls in 1980s 128–9
 economic planning 49–50, 57
 foreign investment 78–9
 free trade, and trade barriers 28
 GDP growth 95
 monetarist policies 114–17, 129
 post-World War II economic measures 16
 postwar foreign aid to 30
 and postwar German monetary reform 31
 postwar prosperity 41
 prewar deflation 39
 sixteenth-century deflation control 21
 social insurance policies 48
 and World Bank 26
 World War II and postwar inflation 18, 20
United Nations Committee on Environment
 and Development conferences 161, 162
United Nations Monetary and Financial
 Conference *see* Bretton Woods Conference
United Shoe Machinery Corporation 43
United States:
 annual inflation rates 102
 anti-trust legislation 22, 42–3, 55, 63
 consumer price controls 83, 84–5
 effect of oil price rises 93–4, 136
 foreign aid programme 75, 77
 foreign investment 78–9
 free market policies 108–10
 GDP growth 95, 176, 198–201
 gold reserves ownership 82–3, 168
 income distribution 72
 locomotive theory 106–7, 108–9, 134
 manufacturing corporations in 45–6, 63
 monetary policies in 1980s 110–13, 116–17,
  134–41, 176

and postwar German monetary reform 31
postwar planning and prosperity 41, 57
postwar public debt 15–16
pre- and postwar anti-inflation initiatives
 11, 18–20, 22–3
prewar deflation 39
prewar tariff policies 28
privatization 155
recession 197–200
social insurance policies 47–8
speculative ventures 123, 125–6, 166–71,
 181–2
support for military coups 64
and World Bank 26
upper middle–income countries 183

value added tax 129
Venezuela, land reform in 74
Volcker, Paul 110, 112, 125, 126, 172
Volkswagen 51
voluntary wage and price controls 108–9
voodoo economics 131–6

wages:
 controls of in 1980s 128
 levels of and inflation 10, 21, 22–3, 81
 minimum 109, 110
 and price controls in 1970s 13, 83–7, 108–9
 see also income inequality
Wall Street crash 1929 166, 175
Wall Street crash 1987 173
West Germany:
 annual inflation rates 103–4
 anti-cartel legislation 44
 consumer price control 83–4, 86–7
 economic deregulation 142
 economic planning and policies 50–52, 57,
  88–9
 locomotive theory 106, 107, 108
 monetarism in 91–2
 postwar inflation policy initiatives 20
 postwar currency reform 33
 and World Bank 26
 see also Germany
World Bank, founding of 25–6
world trade 11, 37–40, 205–6
World Trade Organization (wto) 163–5, 206
World War I 15, 16
World War II, and global postwar economy
 15–36

yen:
 value against the us dollar 174, 176
 value in foreign exchange markets 107,
  118, 119, 121
Yom Kippur War 93

zaibatsu 42, 43, 44, 53